A Photographic History of

AIRBORNE WARFARE

1939-1945

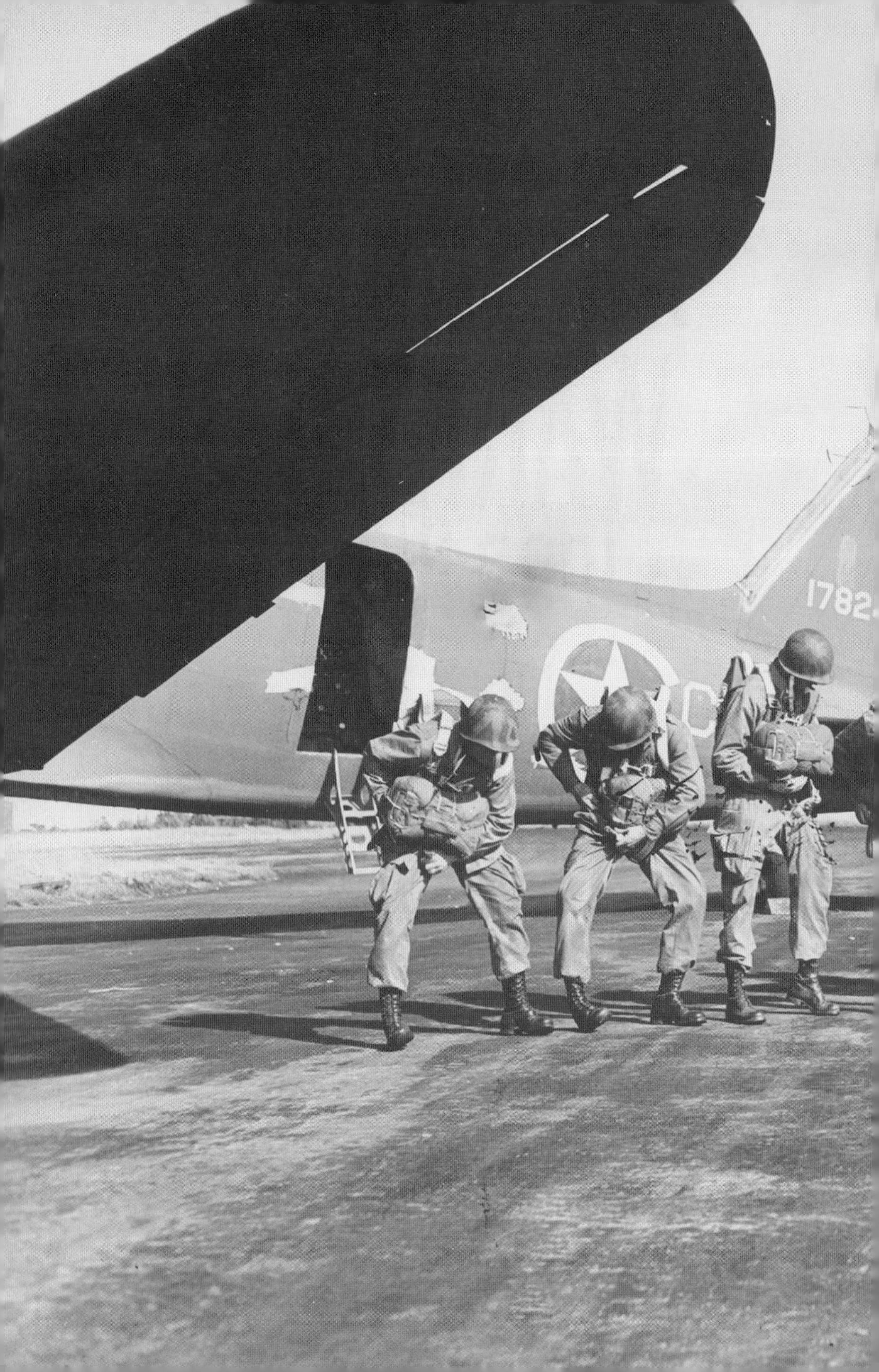

A Photographic History of
AIRBORNE WARFARE
1939-1945

SIMON & JONATHAN FORTY

Pen & Sword
MILITARY

First published in Great Britain in 2021 by
PEN & SWORD MILITARY
an imprint of
Pen & Sword Books Ltd,
47 Church Street,
Barnsley,
South Yorkshire.
S70 2AS

Copyright © Pen & Sword 2021

A CIP record for this book is available from the
British Library.

ISBN 978-1-39901-114-3

The right of Simon and Jonathan Forty to
be identified as Authors of this Work has
been asserted by him in accordance with the
Copyright, Designs and Patents Act 1988.

Printed and bound by CPI Group (UK) Ltd,
Croydon, CR0 4YY

Pen & Sword Books Ltd incorporates the Imprints
of Pen & Sword Aviation, Pen & Sword Maritime,
Pen & Sword Military, Wharncliffe Local History, Pen
& Sword Select, Pen & Sword Military Classics and
Leo Cooper.

For a complete list of Pen & Sword titles please
contact
Pen & Sword Books Limited
47 Church Street, Barnsley, South Yorkshire, S70
2AS, England
E-mail: enquiries@pen-and-sword.co.uk
Website: www.pen-and-sword.co.uk

Acknowledgements

A big thank you to Richard Charlton Taylor, who
provided material for the appendices, significant
numbers of illustrations and a lot of information.
The text includes a number of directly quoted or
edited excerpts from a number of works which
are identified in the text and covered in the
Bibliography. Many of these came via the excellent
online resources of the Ike Skelton Combined Arms
Research Library (CARL) Digital Library. Please note
that some of these excerpts are contemporary and
produced based on intelligence available at the time:
there will be some, understandable, inaccuracies.

There are a number of websites that proved
invaluable for help with captions and information. In
particular we'd like to reference the US Center of
Military History for high quality histories and access
to technical manuals.

Finally, thanks to Rupert Harding of Pen & Sword
for being such an understanding editor and for
pointing out a number of inaccuracies.

Previous page: Men of the
509th PIR conduct final checks
before a training jump.

This page: Jeep and Polsten 20mm AA gun
off-loading from a Horsa glider.

Contents

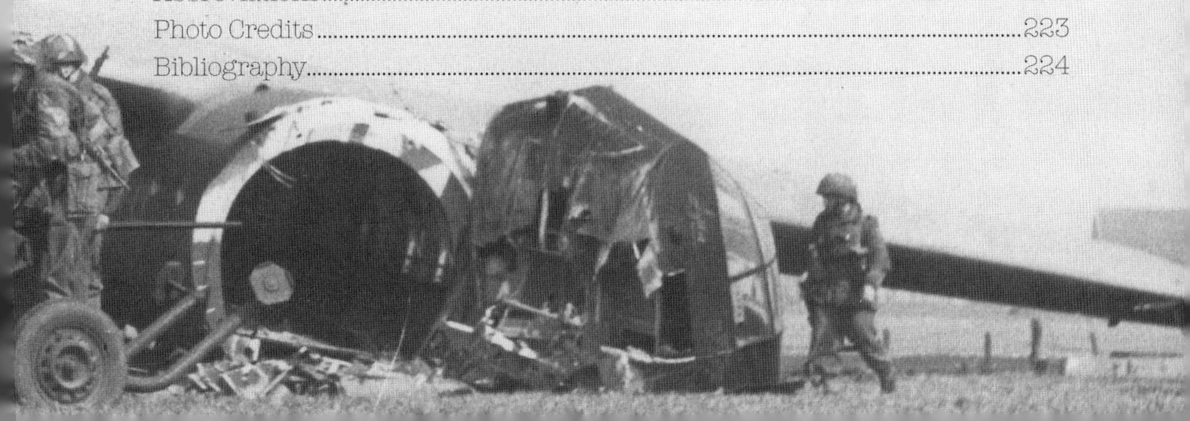

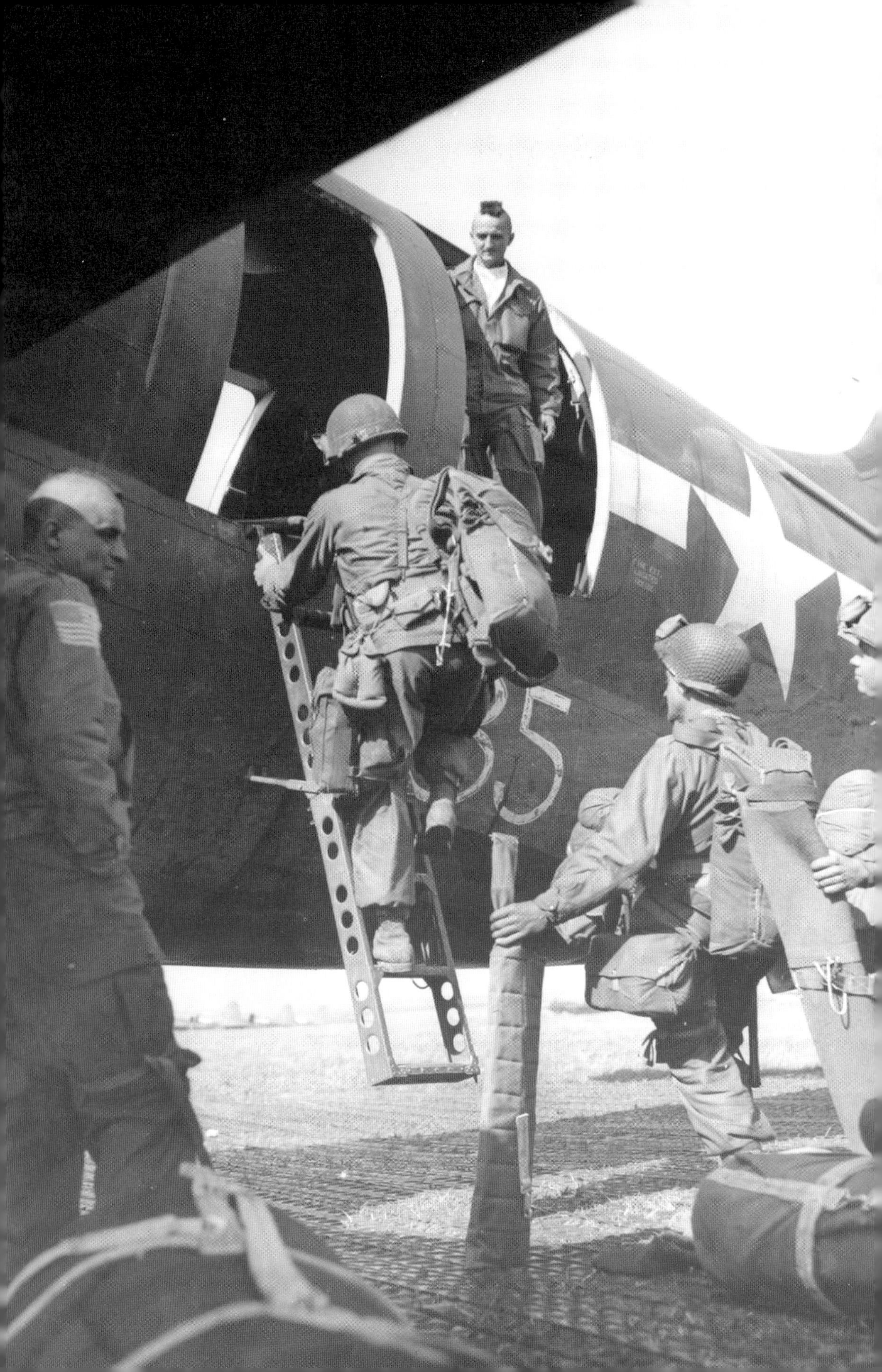

Introduction

Air warfare dominated World War 2. At sea the aircraft carrier became the indispensable capital ship and long-range aircraft helped destroy the U-boat menace. Over land, strategic bombing devastated industries and cities. Tactically, ground-attack aircraft spearheaded Blitzkrieg. Later, in the North African desert and after the invasion of France, Allied air supremacy ensured that every German troop movement was fraught with danger; every counter-attack a target for medium and fighter-bombers.

There was a cost: huge numbers of Allied airmen died during the strategic bombing campaign. The proliferation of Flak emplacements, development of the proximity fuse and improvements to radar and other technologies meant that air forces paid a high price, and nowhere was that more true than with airborne forces.

Before parachutes were commonplace their military use had been theorised. In the 1920s and 1930s those theories became fact, as first the Russians and then the Germans developed the airborne concept. In 1940 it was put into practice with devastating results: at Eben Emael in Belgium, a seemingly impregnable fortress fell to a small glider-borne force; important bridges were taken and held for the Panzer spearheads; in Denmark and Norway *Fallschirmjäger* (German paratroops) played a significant role in the surprise attacks; at the Corinth Canal in Greece another coup de main operation proved successful.

The problems came when commanders extrapolated the successes of small, highly trained teams into larger operations. Crete was the first of these. The Germans' success in taking the island could not hide the appalling casualties suffered by the attacking airborne troops. Hitler was unnerved by this and never allowed his airborne commander, General Student, to revisit such an attack. The Fallschirmjäger would henceforth acquit themselves brilliantly as infantry but their attacks from the air would be limited to very minor operations.

The Allies, however, took another view: that Crete showed the potential for the vertical envelopment of a target. Quickly, they developed the equipment and trained the men and, from late 1942 onwards, used them in increasing numbers: North Africa, Sicily, Italy,

Heavily laden US paratroops board the aircraft that will take them behind enemy lines. Bulky parachutes mean that they can carry little equipment, most of which – including the unit's heavy weapons – will have to be retrieved from containers dropped at the same time, a difficult proposition in the dark particularly in the bocage or when the Germans have flooded the area.

Normandy, northwest Europe – huge aerial fleets were involved and an Allied Airborne Army was developed and played an important role in the final stages of the war.

Was it worth it? Did these airborne forces contribute significantly to Allied victory?

The answers to those questions depends, of course, on careful assessment, the balancing of the shock value of the arrival of troops behind enemy lines with the undoubted costs to men and materiel involved in getting them there and supporting them. In Sicily and Normandy, for example, large numbers of the airborne troops were dropped in the wrong place – in Sicily that often meant into the sea and almost certain death. Had the amphibious landings at Utah Beach been better opposed and less successful, the small bands of 82nd and 101st Division troops would have had an even more difficult job. The brilliant success of the British at Pegasus Bridge hides the fact that the British 6th Airborne Division achieved only limited objectives. Operation Market Garden was a bold concept that made big use of airborne troops. Delivery was excellent, but the operation failed, and many died or were made captive. The resupply operations at Arnhem led to heavy aircraft

Australian paras practise. The Aussie 1st Parachute Battalion was raised in 1943 and disbanded in 1946 without having dropped in anger. The aircraft are ex-civil DC-2s of which ten were supplied to Australia in 1940–41 and some were used by the Parachute Training Unit. This photograph shows well the process (see also p173) whereby the static line pulls out the chute which then deploys.

casualties. The final major set-piece operation of the war, Varsity, saw a successful outcome to which airborne troops contributed – but the delivery of British airlanding troops by glider was inconvenienced by smoke and AA fire.

In the end, the most effective use of the airborne forces was probably as elite infantry: Van der Heydte's Fallschirmjäger performed heroically in the Netherlands and were a major reason for Allied failure; the US 82nd and 101st Airborne Divisions, then Eisenhower's strategic reserve, were trucked into Bastogne and ahead of Peiper's Leibstandarte spearhead and blunted the German surprise attack in the Ardennes.

This book examines the use of airborne forces in every theatre – including their limited use on the Eastern Front and in the Indian and the Pacific campaigns – quoting from contemporary documents to show the evolution of the concept and the analysis of its effectiveness. It doesn't cover the clandestine operations by such organisations as SOE or the OSS. Extensive appendices examine airborne troops' kit and training.

The Russians may have developed the concept of airborne troops but they didn't make great use of them during the war other than as infantry. This memorial in Cybinka, Poland, remembers Soviet paratroopers.

1 Conception

From the cauldron of WWI many new methods of warfare emerged, one of the most radical being that which used the very air itself. The machines in which to conduct this form of combat began their speedy arc of development, from passive observer and spotter aircraft to active fighters and bombers, with the parachute eventually developed as a potential life-saving aid and means of safe escape. Using a static line design to activate, it was attached to the pilot with a harness and packed into a bag on which he sat, which was also anchored by a length of line to the aircraft, triggering the canopy to launch when taut. Only towards the war's end was the possibility entertained that the parachute could be used aggressively to drop troops behind enemy lines, but no practical idea was developed to actually achieve it. Postwar the more settled victorious states turned primarily to the civil applications of air transport and the continued development towards a workable safety parachute system with which to leave a moving plane. Small advances occurred internationally and sometimes simultaneously through both inspired amateurs and emerging professionals of this new technology, and by the mid-1920s parachutes had evolved considerably. They were now worn with a main vented canopy folded into a soft pack which was fitted by a harness to the pilot's back, with a smaller drogue chute packed on top that launched first to draw out the larger chute. They could be either static-line linked or free and unconnected to the aircraft with the wearer using a ripcord for manual deployment.

Beyond some research and experimentation, it was left mainly to the most troubled and totalitarian states of the time to explore the parachute's military potential. Russia and Germany, having recently undergone military defeat and internal revolution, were fragile enough to be looking closely at any new military technology to empower and reassure their new regimes, and this eventually lead them to collaborate against the prevailing status quo of the western nations.

It was the Soviets who first conducted the most eclectic exploration of the airborne concept with their vision of 'vertical envelopment', part of their 'deep battle' theory emphasising manoeuvre warfare to attack the enemy from any or all directions simultaneously. Airborne forces were potentially perfect for this role as they could be transported long distances to deploy rapidly and take the enemy by surprise in his flanks or rear. To this end regular Soviet airborne troops – *Vozdushno-desantnye voyska* or VDV – were established at the beginning of the 1930s, along with the development of gliders and the

The French Farman Goliath was designed to be a bomber in 1919 but the end of the war came before it saw action. It was sold as an airliner and bomber (here an F.68 in the Polish Air Force). The Poles also trained paratroopers from it. *NAC*

modification of existing aircraft in which to transport and drop them. This was enabled in no small part thanks to Gleb Kotelnikov, an inventor fixated with parachute design whose ideas resonated with the growing popularity of parachuting as a sport and its potential application in other fields. In the mid-1920s Gelb came up with a working system that was soon adopted by the Soviet military and in the early 1930s he invented the brake or drag chute to slow aircraft as they touched down, enabling much smaller area landings. In the fervour and excitement of a growing industrial and revolutionary setting the Soviets began an intense phase of experimentation to work out their air-war ideas, using a variety of modified aircraft and gliders to deliver parachutists, heavy machine guns, artillery, T27 tankettes and an assortment of light vehicles.

They began to evolve two main types of operation: the airdrop into enemy-held territory using parachute or glider and the airbridge, which required a captured air-field for continuous resupply of more conventional troops by air. The airdrop required the true daredevil air warrior – someone tough, resourceful and confident enough to fight behind enemy lines and crazy enough to jump out of aeroplanes in the first place. (All the paratroop units of the different nations began with completely volun-tary recruitment appealing to this kind of fighter.) The airbridge required the develop-ment of an airborne landing detachment consisting of a rifle company, sapper, com-munications and light vehicle platoons, a heavy bomber squadron and a corps aviation detachment. By the mid-1930s the Soviets had a substantial and dynamically evolv-ing airborne force of almost 10,000 men and this led to a showcase demonstration of future warfare that stunned foreign military observers, when in 1935, the first live airborne airdrop witnessed two full battalions of paratroopers with light field guns landing in under ten minutes to seize their objective. Exciting though this was to military theorists its aggressive implications ensured that it did not long survive an initial burst of

Above: A group jump of paratroopers from a height of 400m at Mokotów airport, Warsaw in 1933. *NAC*

Left: Using Farman Goliaths or Tupolev TB-3 aircraft, the Russian VDV was established in 1932. The Russians developed the theories and practice of airborne operations but were unable to put their plans to good use during World War II following first Stalin's purges and second, thr withering intensity of Unternehmen Barbarossa.

interest, for the western states were tired of war and really only interested in defence.

The British thought such an airborne attack force was at odds with the defensive requirements of empire, the lack of heavy equipment limiting it to the role of mere saboteurs. The French experimentation consisted of two parachute companies created in 1937 who would form the basis of their later airborne effort post-1943. Fascist Italy conducted early experiments in the late 1920s, culminating in the 1941 formation of a 5,000-man parachute division designated the 185th Parachute Division Folgore, whose destiny was to end up serving as ground troops. But for the Nazi regime in Germany, secretly rebuilding its armed forces and searching for new methods of warfare, the Soviet airborne demonstration was an epiphany and they immediately set about forming their own paratroop forces. Unfortunately for the VDV the demonstrations of 1935 and 1936 were a premature high watermark, for in a paranoid fit Stalin began a series of political and military purges against everyone he felt threatened by. The effect on the Soviet military was as devastating as any Blitzkrieg and would hamstring the Red Army for some years as those with any vision and ability were swiftly eliminated. The airborne forces were not disbanded, but more fast moving events were soon to skew their intended role.

Just as Heinz Guderian, the father of the Panzerwaffe, followed closely all armour developments worldwide to synthesise his new combat formula, so too did the soon-to-be father of the Fallschirmjäger, Kurt Student, with all matters aeronautical. Student was a veteran WWI pilot assigned to military research who had spent time in the USSR observing both glider and parachute development. After

Above left and Left: Practice techniques soon evolved to include towers – the US built one in New Jersey in 1935. The Poles used this one at the Polish Army Stadium Marshal Józef Piłsudski in Warsaw 1937. The parachute tower in Katowice, built in 1937, is still extant.

Opposite: The German Fallschirmjäger performed with great daring and skill in the early war years. They jumped from the Junkers Ju52 with a parachute they couldn't control and their weapons in a separate container. Note the knee pads.

witnessing the Soviet demonstration in 1935 he returned to Germany to join the secretly reestablished Luftwaffe and play a key role in developing Germany's glider and parachute capability. In 1938 he assumed command of all airborne and airlanding troops and became commanding general of Germany's first paratroop division, a role he would continue for the war's duration. In conjunction with the Luftwaffe's development of the Fallschirmjäger and their delivery systems, the Germans began creating supporting formations that could reinforce them once an aerial bridgehead had been established. These other elements were transported primarily by Junkers Ju52s, but also used gliders. With fierce enthusiasm and efficiency that made the process fast, the Nazis created effective airborne forces with both airdrop and airlanding capability. In 1939 on the eve of war, only the USSR and Germany possessed such airborne troops.

It seems puzzling in retrospect that Britain and the United States had little real interest in developing their own airborne forces. This was a decision they were just about to deeply regret, for they would soon be frantically trying to catch up, starting virtually from scratch and actually during hostilities.

Two brand new military formations the Panzerwaffe and the Fallschirmjäger were about hit the world stage and blaze their brief trail across history.

An illustration from *Ganze Männer* – the life and experience of the German paratroopers. It shows well the position required by the Fallschirmjäger in exiting the Junkers Ju52. Note the static line – the German parachutes were *Rückfallschirm, Zwangablösung* or 'Backpack Parachute, Static Line Deployment.'

2 Blitzkrieg

The new German doctrine of manoeuvre warfare manifesting in an all-arms Blitzkrieg was now unveiled to the world in a series of lightning strikes across Europe. As well as the awesome panzers and the fanatical SS, there were also the air warrior Fallschirmjäger. Commanded by Generalmajor Kurt Student, under the aegis of Herman Göring, they, too, were mainly specially selected volunteers from the Hitler Youth who underwent constant training and indoctrination to foster a gung-ho esprit de corps and an aggressive self-confidence. Combat-ready on 1 September 1938 as 7. Flieger-Division, it's perhaps ironic that this formation's first fighting took place a year later serving as motorised infantry in the German invasion of Poland.

Denmark and Norway

The first use of German airborne forces actually parachuted into combat occurred during Unternehmen Weserübung, the spring invasion of Denmark and Norway. The first three Fallschirmjäger drops took place on 9 April 1940. The first two virtually simultaneously yet 400km apart when one company of I./FJR1 dropped to seize the important airfields of East and West Aaborg, while another two took the fortress bridge linking the Danish islands of Falster and Fyn. In both cases surprise was complete and the assaults against unprepared defences were almost over before they began.

A second operation began a little later that same day with another two companies of I./FJR1 targeting the critical Oslo-Fornebu airfield. As the first wave of Ju52s carrying the Fallschirmjäger neared the Norwegian coast they encountered thick fog down to ground level which eventually led to two of the first wave of aircraft colliding and one crashing into the sea. The remainder then aborted the mission and flew instead to Aalborg. The following second wave also turned back except for the operation commander and pilot Hauptmann Wagner who continued, believing that the mission abort was an

Kurt Student was CG of the Fallschirmjäger and Luftlandetruppen (paras and airlanding troops). This is Wolfgang Willrich's 1941 portrait of the General der Flieger.

enemy trick. He was soon disabused of this notion when he was killed by AA fire from below, his co-pilot managing to rescue control and limp back to Aalborg. Now eight Bf110s, along with more Ju52 transports containing two airlanding infantry battalions of 22. Luftlande-Division and an engineer company detailed to support the operation, presuming the airfield already taken by the preceding Fallschirmjäger, tried to land only to come under attack from fighter and ground fire. Not having enough fuel to return to base they had no choice but to try again and having strafed the defenders did so, resulting in two aircraft destroyed and five severely damaged in addition to a further five shot down in dogfights with Norwegian Gloster Gladiators based at the airfield. Backed up with their rear gunners poised for a shoot out, they were surprised their bravado had succeeded in making the Norwegians abandon their positions – the airfield had fallen and the Fallschirmjäger then returned from Aalborg to hold it until relieved.

The final air assault that took place on 9 April was at Sola near Stavanger, Norway's largest and most modern airfield at the time. After a preliminary softening up by eight Ju88s, over 100 paratroopers from I./FJR1's third company parachuted directly onto the airfield defended by two companies of Norwegian infantry. Pinned down by machine-gun fire from a bunker and unable to reach their weapon canisters, the Fallschirmjäger suffered casualties before they could finally secure the airfield and create an airbridge for the landing of over 200 aircraft and two infantry battalions over the course of the day.

On April 17 another company of I./FJR1 dropped on a road and rail junction high in

THE "TEN COMMANDMENTS"

Here is a translation of a document captured from a German parachute trooper who was taken prisoner in Greece. Its title is "The Parachutist's Ten Commandments."

1. You are the elite of the German Army. For you, combat shall be fulfilment. You shall seek it out and train yourself to stand any test.
2. Cultivate true comradeship, for together with your comrades you will triumph or die.
3. Be shy of speech and incorruptible. Men act, women chatter; chatter will bring you to the grave.
4. Calm and caution, vigour and determination, valour and a fanatical offensive spirit will make you superior in attack.
5. In facing the foe, ammunition is the most precious thing. He who shoots uselessly, merely to reassure himself, is a man without guts. He is a weakling and does not deserve the title of parachutist.
6. Never surrender. Your honour lies in Victory or Death.
7. Only with good weapons can you have success. So look after them on the principle— First my weapons, then myself.
8. You must grasp the full meaning of an operation so that, should your leader fall by the way, you can carry it out with coolness and caution.
9. Fight chivalrously against an honest foe; armed irregulars deserve no quarter.
10. With your eyes open, keyed up to top pitch, agile as a greyhound, tough as leather, hard as Krupp steel, you will be the embodiment of a German warrior.

the mountains of the Gudbrandsdal valley near Dombas in the Norwegian rear, with the aim of blocking Allied movement and defending the German hold on Trondheim until they could link up with land forces approaching from the south. Launched in haste without proper reconnaissance, the insufficiently equipped forces ran into problems almost immediately, when one of the 15 Ju52 transports carrying the company of 160 men to the drop zone was shot down. In failing light and deep cloud the Fallschirmjäger were then scattered over a wide area with many of their critical weapons canisters lost, to be captured or killed in sporadic firefights with enemy soldiers. An attempted resupply drop also proved disastrous as the canisters were dropped without chutes and mainly lost or destroyed. A surviving group of some 65 men managed to survive for four days permanently on the move and relentlessly pursued, until they ran out of ammunition and the last 34 surrendered.

The final drop of 'Weserübung' was made to reinforce the German troops holding out in the Narvik area and occurred without any major mishaps. The whole battalion of I./FJR1 was deployed as well as mountain troops who had been given some basic parachute training. Despite the addition of these men, had the Allies not broken off their

Above: The German invasions of Norway and Denmark involved a number of Fallschirmjäger operations. Here they are at the Masnedoe Fort, Denmark, 9 April 1940.

Below: Fallschirmjäger at Bjørnfjell. Typical of all German troops, they are clutching ammo boxes for their MG34s. Notably absent is the usual metal container for the gasmask which was carred in a canvas bag.

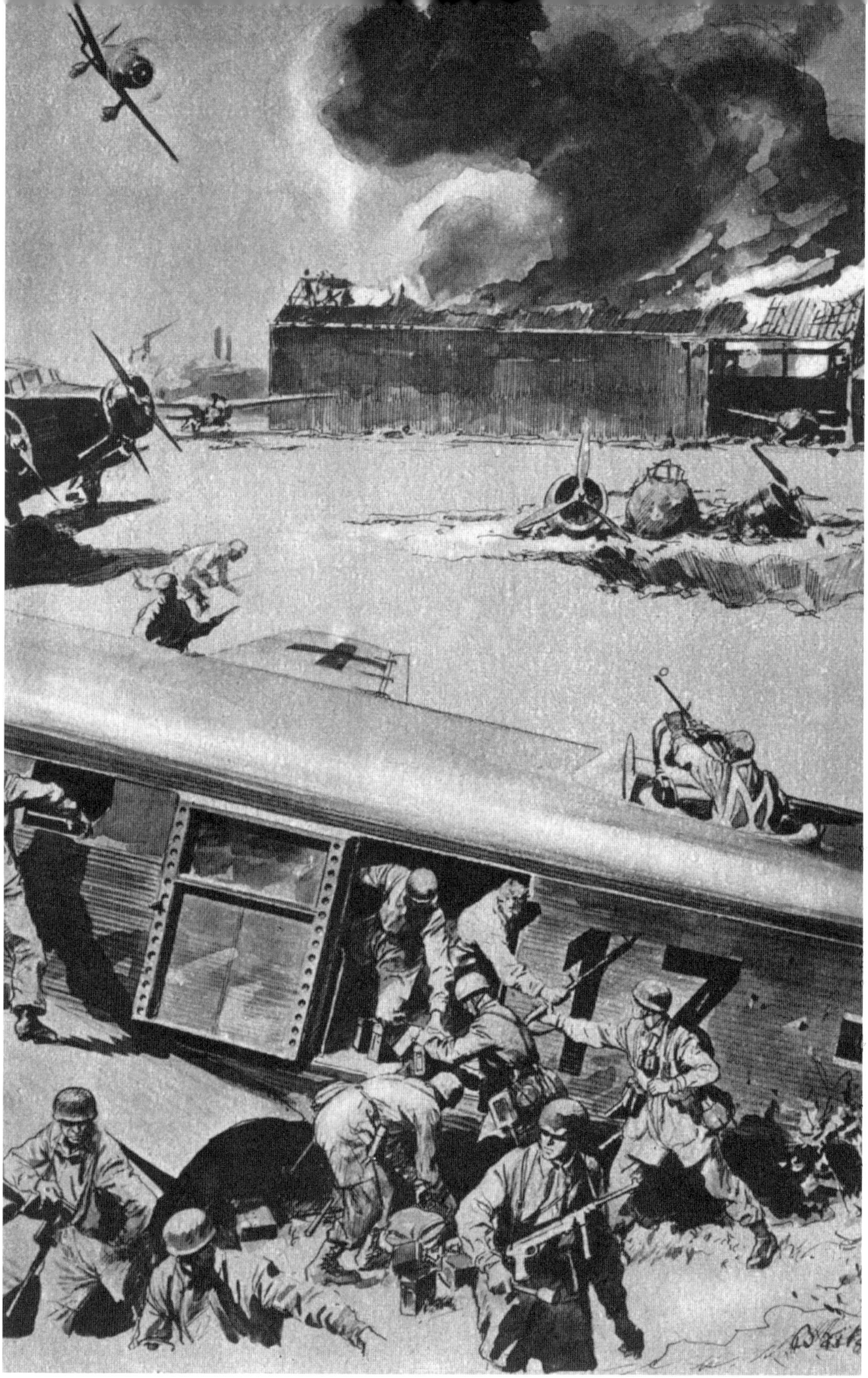

Opposite: Another illustration from *Ganze Männer*, this one showing airlanding troops disembarking from their Ju52s.

Right: Fallschirmjäger graves at Narvik. They weren't intended to be used at Narvik, but the 3. Gebirgs-Division became isolated and needed help. First, 200 Gebirgsjäger who received a basic modicum of parachute training were dropped. They were followed up by I./FJR1 – in total around 600 men.

attacks to concentrate on unfolding events in France, the Germans would have been unable to hold Narvik.

The short Norwegian campaign provided in microcosm examples of the potential and problems of airborne operations and emphasised their inherently precarious nature. Extraordinarily successful when conducted with surprise and support at the correct target or to resupply and reinforce cut-off friendly forces, they were potentially disastrous against defended DZs without fire support or when the weather caused chaos.

There were other problems specific to the Fallschirmjäger. The design of their parachute system precluded the ability to carry their larger weapons beyond pistols and grenades. Heavier weapons were dropped in canisters – often with completely calamitous results. Another was Student's choice of small-scale converging 'oil drops' tactics – to split the attacking force over a wider area (to be able to attack from all sides) rather than concentrate it. Both these crucial concerns remained and would come back bite them.

Belgium and the Netherlands

The next German airborne campaign in May 1940 was their largest to date. Part of the Fall Gelb feint towards the Low Countries, it included the entire airborne force – 2,000 troops of 7. Flieger-Division and 12,000 troops of the 22. Luftlande-Division. As ever surprise was completely vital for the high risk involved and would bring some spectacular successes, albeit overshadowed somewhat by the armoured Blitzkrieg bursting out of the Ardennes just a few days later. Fall Gelb's success depended on convincing the Allies that Belgium was where the main German thrust would occur and the spectacular capture of the state-of-the-art fortification of Eben Emael and two out of three of the Albert Canal Bridges intact did just that.

There was an astonishingly modern level of special forces preparation and equipment for the Fallschirmjäger attacks. The assault force of approximately 500 volunteers from 7. Flieger-Division's I./FJR1 and an engineer platoon was created and named Sturmabteilung Koch with the overall operation codenamed Granit. It was divided

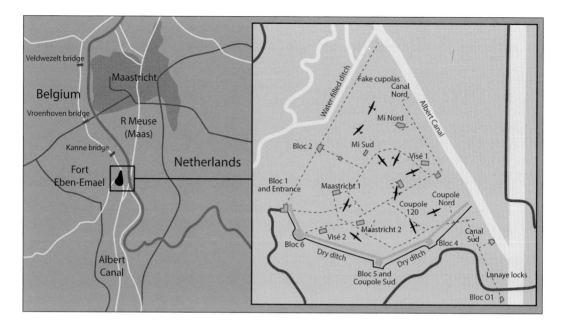

Above: The spectacular success of Group Granit at Eben Emael on 10 May 1940 has overshadowed the equally daring coup de main operations to take strategic bridges. Those at Veldwezelt and Vroenhoven were successful, but the armoured column reached Kanne early enough to give the game away and the Fallschirmjäger landed on a knocked-out bridge.

1 Aerial view of Fort Eben Emael. **2** The pockmarked entrance to the fort after the battle. **3** One of the cupolas that was attacked by the Germans' secret weapon – shaped charges.

Above: Oberleutnant Rudolf Witzig led the Sturmabteilung Koch in the Eben-Emael attack. If you could see his Waffefarben they'd be canary yellow.

Above right: Hitler presenting awards to the Fallschirmjäger. To his immediate left, Lt Joachim Meissner who led the attack on Kanne bridge.

Below: The German jumping technique saw them leap headfirst from the Ju52 transports.

into four teams for the four codenamed targets – *Granit* (Granite – the fort Eben Emael), *Stahl* (Steel – Veldwezelt Bridge), *Beton* (Concrete – Vroenhoven Bridge) and *Eisen* (Iron – Kanne Bridge), each assigned 9–11 gliders carrying 8–9 men and their weapons. They were then completely isolated for intense specialist training of more than six months in every aspect of the operation, including practising specific tasks using scaled and full-size models, accurate grouped night glider landings,

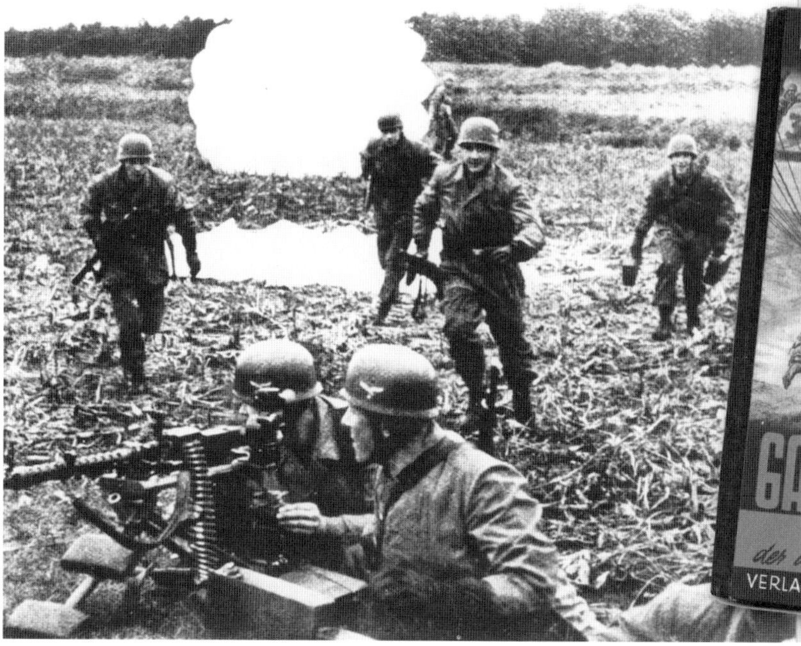

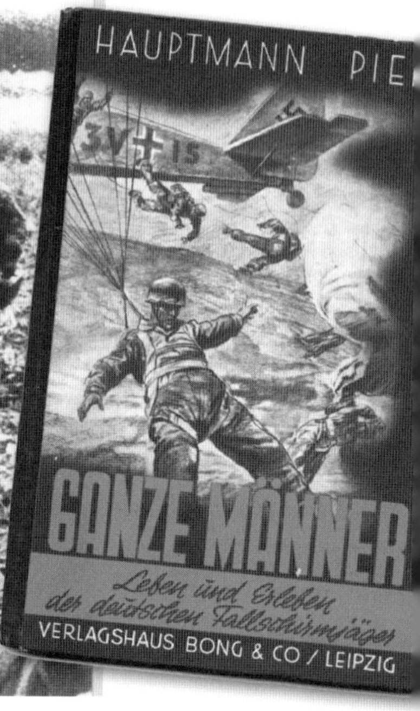
HAUPTMANN PIE
3V 15
GANZE MÄNNER
Leben und Erleben der deutschen Fallschirmjäger
VERLAGSHAUS BONG & CO / LEIPZIG

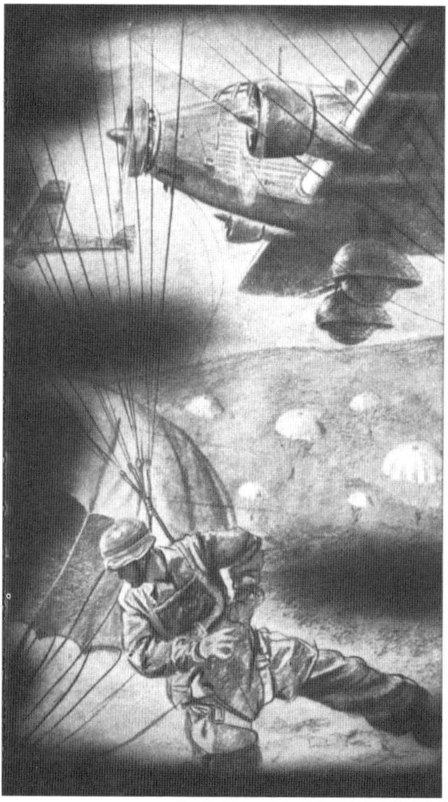

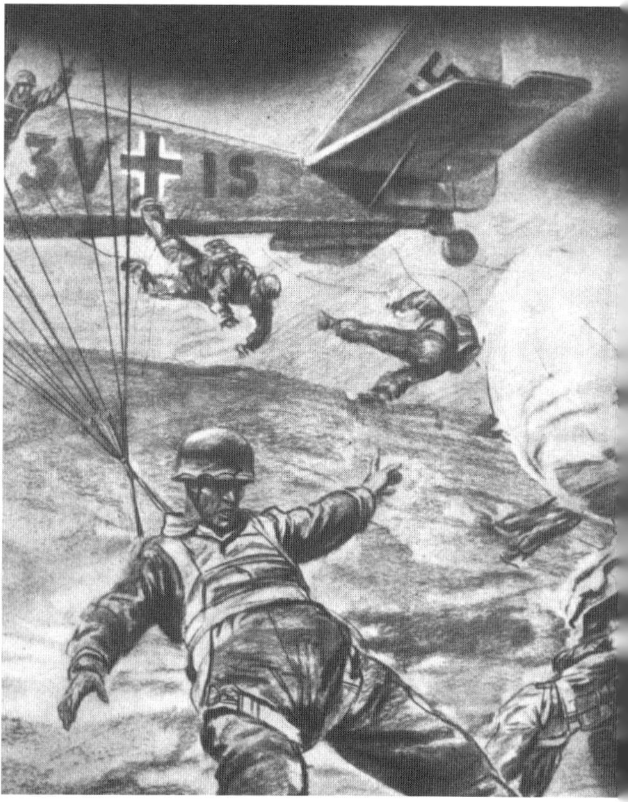
3V 15

Opposite: Hauptmann Piehl's *Ganze Männer* was published in 1943 when the exploits of the Fallschirmjäger were still fresh in the minds of an adoring public.

Above right and Below: German paratroopers land in the Netherlands on 10 May 1940. They landed as shown on the map below and around The Hague (right and see next page).

Centre and Below right: The Moerdijk bridges cross Hollandsch Diep between Dordrecht and North Brabant (**A** below). On 10 May, at 04:00, the German attack began with Stukas attacking the local AA defences. At 04:45 the Fallschirmjäger arrived. After a hard fight they secured the bridges and held them for four days.

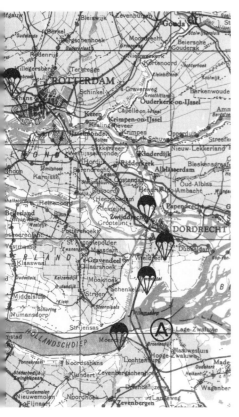

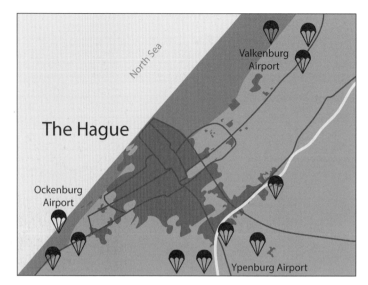

The parachute landings around The Hague concentrated on the airfields. They were contained by brave Dutch defence. Up to 400 Fallschirmjäger were killed and 1,745 were captured. The loss of these men and many Ju52s weakened the German airborne forces considerably.

explosives, demolition of casements and cupolas and assuming another section's mission if necessary. The superfit, super-confident, super-trained volunteers were encouraged to take individual initiative to ensure the mission's success. Germany led the world in military glider development with its DFS230, already in operational use by 7. Flieger-Division. For Unternehmen Granit all emblems and identifying marks were removed and, to stop swiftly on the fort's roof and on canal banks, they were modified with a handbrake and their skids wrapped in barbed wire. A Luftwaffe forward air controller and communications officer was also assigned to the team to call in airstrikes against counterattacks and coordinate resupply drops.

On 10 May 1940, 42 Junkers Ju52 transport aircraft each towing a DFS230 assault glider released their tows before they left German airspace, letting them complete their journey in silence. Each glider section had a complement of weapons including a machine gun, flamethrower and numerous explosives including the new top secret *Hohlladungwaffe* (hollow-charge weapon). Beginning with the fort itself, the engineer platoon succeeded in destroying the rooftop gun emplacements and cupolas, bottling up the garrison inside. The operation was a remarkable coup. In its detail not everything went exactly to plan, but the adaptability and confidence of the Fallschirmjäger ensured its success. Surprise was almost complete – one bridge was blown before it could be captured because the gliders landed too far away, but the overall effect of this operation upon the Allies was truly striking.

However, the attacks into Fortress Holland did not fare so well. The Germans critically underestimated the Dutch and the resistance they would display, until their ruthless heavy bomber attack on Rotterdam almost obliterated its historic centre and forced their capitulation.

The battle plan had been to hold bridges and airfields for the advancing German

This photo: The landings at Ockenburg.

Below: Victory parade at the Inner Court of The Hague. Note the plain smocks with short, tailored step-in legs and the Kar98k ammo bandoleers tucked under their belts. These had 12 pockets, each taking 10 rounds. Later, a similar bandoleer for the FG42 took eight 20-round magazines.

9.Panzer-Division and in a separate attack to aim for the heart of The Hague and seize both the king and the government. The boldness and innovation of Student's Fallschirmjäger and his use of 22. Luftlande-Division provided some extraordinary initial feats of arms. The Willems Bridge over the Maas River was captured with a daring seaplane landing. Other bridges and the Ypenburg, Ockenburg and Valkenburg airfields were also taken. But the attack stalled. The Dutch airfields were too small to land many troops simultaneously, their AA fire proved much stronger than anticipated with many aircraft lost and their counterattacks grew increasingly ferocious. The inner citadel of The Hague was never taken and the airfields recaptured with many Germans taken prisoner. Also at some point during the fighting the division commander Kurt Student was accidentally shot in the head, almost certainly by friendly fire. The 9. Panzer-Division suffered considerable losses in a failed assault on the centre of Dordrecht. A repeat of the Dombas debacle was avoided when on 14 May the centre of Rotterdam was carpet-bombed and the Dutch surrendered.

This and a number of the photographs in this chapter are taken from the 1942 propaganda book *Kreta, Sieg der Kühnsten* (Crete, Victory of the Boldest). Unternehmen Merkur (Mercury) would be the last major airborne operation of the Fallschirmjäger whose casualties were severe. Their victory owed much to the mistakes of the Allies as well as the dogged bravery of the paratroops. Additionally, the loss of so many transport aircraft would be a big problem for the Luftwaffe.

3 Crete: The Turning Point

Having proved such a success in 1940, it's unsurprising that the Germans turned to the Fallschirmjäger in 1941 when they invaded Greece. The coup de main operation on the Corinth Canal showed exactly what German airborne troops were there for. However, drawn into the fighting by Mussolini's stalled 1940 invasion, there's no doubt that Hitler's subsequent Balkan and Mediterranean campaign didn't receive the attention that it needed. Strategic mistakes – not taking Malta – were compounded by the ill-considered attack on Crete that may have ended in victory, but saw severe losses to both the airborne troops and, perhaps more importantly, the Ju52 transports. As production of these vital aircraft lagged, so German resupply operations were affected. The position of the German-Italian forces in North Africa (in early 1941 the Germans had to come to Mussolini's help in the desert after the massive British victory, Operation Compass) saw the Mediterranean take on a big significance and the decision to concentrate on the east rather than on the supply routes for Africa meant that Malta would be a thorn in the Axis side for the rest of the war. Crete turned out to be a turning point for what remained of the Fallschirmjäger – never used again en masse – and for the Allies who realised the potential of vertical envelopment and started pushing for an airborne component to their arsenal.

EXCERPTS FROM DIRECTIVE NO. 28 UNTERNEHMEN MERKUR

1. As a base for air warfare against Great Britain in the Eastern Mediterranean we must prepare to occupy the island of Crete For the purpose of planning, it will be assumed that the whole Greek mainland including the Peloponnese is in the hands of the Axis Powers.
2. Command of this operation is entrusted to Commander-in-Chief Air Force who will employ for the purpose, primarily, the airborne forces and the air forces stationed in the Mediterranean area.

   The Army, in co-operation with Commander-in-Chief Air Force, will make available in Greece suitable reinforcements for the airborne troops, including a mixed armoured detachment, which can be moved to Crete by sea.
3. All means will be employed to move the airborne troops and 22nd Division, which is under the command of Commander-in-Chief Air Force, to the assembly area which he will designate. The necessary space for freight lorries will be put at the disposal of the Chief of Armed Forces Transport by the High Commands of the Army and Air Force. These transport movements must not entail any delay in the mounting of 'Barbarossa'.
4. For anti-aircraft protection in Greece and Crete, Commander-in-Chief Air Force may bring up anti-aircraft units of 12th Army. Commander-in-Chief Air Force and Commander-in-Chief Army will make the necessary arrangements for their relief and replacement.
5. After the occupation of the island, all or part of the airborne forces must be made ready for new tasks. Arrangements will therefore be made for their replacement by Army units.

Unternehmen Hannibal

The last thing that Hitler wanted while preparing for the invasion of Russia, the Nazis were drawn into the side issues of the Balkans and North Africa through Mussolini's various military disasters. The Fallschirmjäger saw action during the German invasion of Greece when they were first tasked with the capture of the Corinth Canal bridge. 'Hannibal' was a mixed parachute and glider assault north and south of the canal and at either end of the bridge itself. The bulk of the regiment (FJR2) was dropped by parachute while the bridge assault force, consisting mainly of 50 or so combat engineers, landed either side in gliders. The attack began early on 26 April 1941 with high-altitude bombing of the general area followed by low-level Stuka dive-bombers and Bf110 fighters to eliminate AA defences and prohibit movement on the Corinth road. Despite knocking out most of the AA positions there were still two emplacements functioning at

Below: Aerial view of the Isthmia end of the canal. This bridge had already been destroyed.

Below right: The German parachute and glider drop on 26 April 1941. Six gliders (•) took on the BEF's defensive positions (■). The flag shows the HQ of 4th Hussars. Other units were: **1** 10 Pl. B Coy, 19 Bn; **2** 11 and 12 Pl. B Coy, 19 Bn; **3** Coy, 2/6 (Aus) Bn; **4** 4 guns 16 Hy AA Bty; **5** C Sqn (NZ) Div Cav Regt; **6** HQ 6 (NZ) Fd Coy, 1 and 3 Sect; **7** Coy, 2/6 (Aus) Bn.

Opposite, Above: The Corinth Canal is a narrow four-mile long fissure created in 1881–93 along a path originally worked by the Emperor Nero in 67AD.

Opposite, Below: German reconnaissance photo of the canal. The bridge is at **A**.

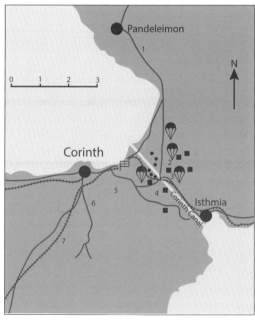

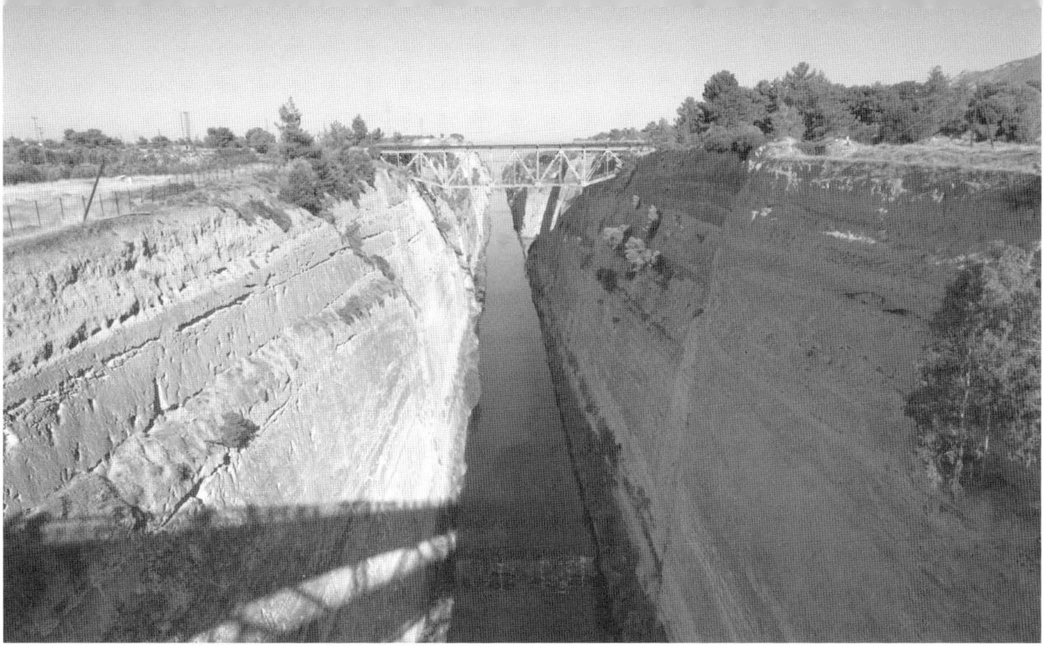

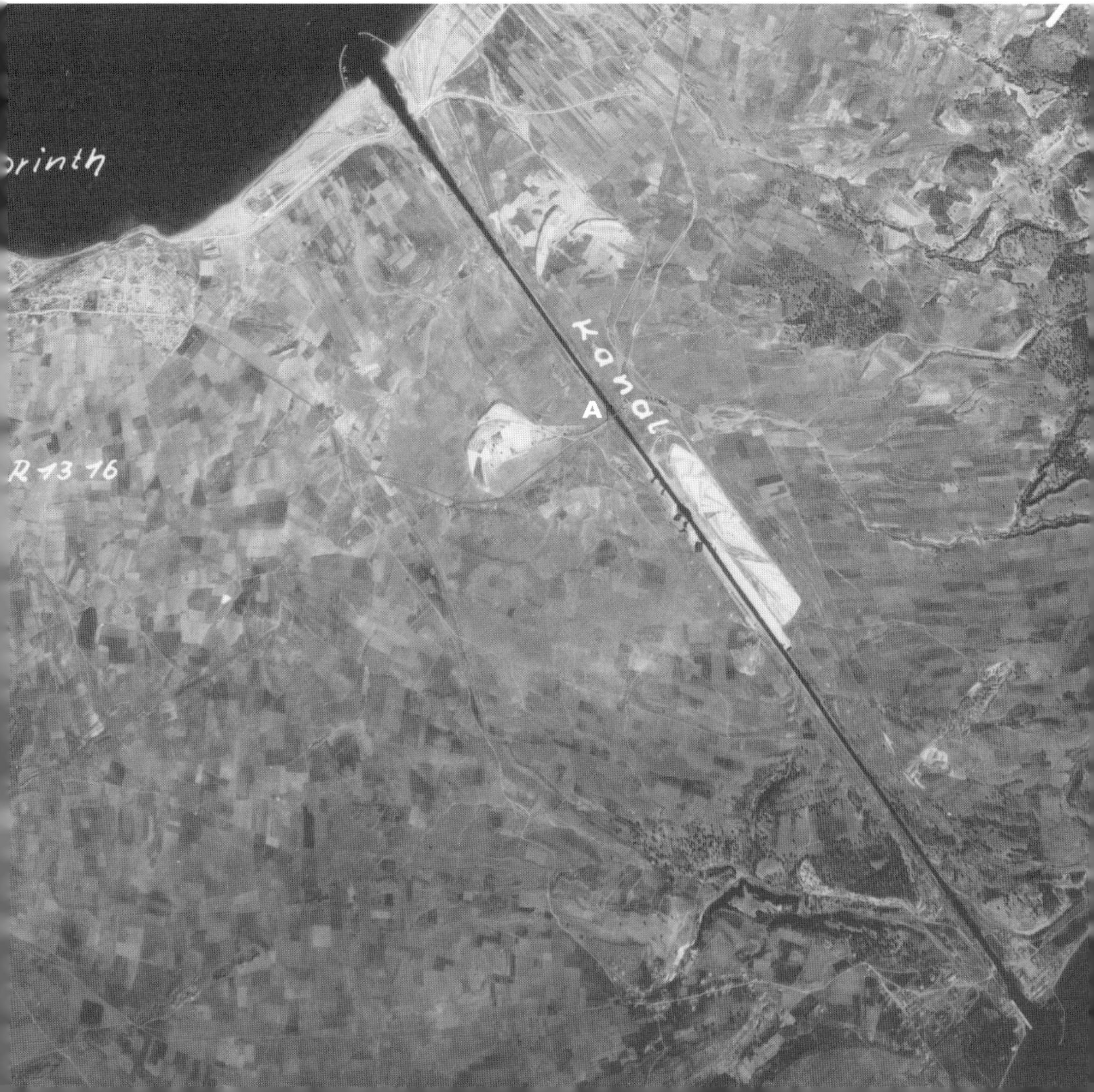

orinth
Kanal
A
R 13 16

Left and Centre left: The Fallschirmjäger captured Greek soldiers and men of the British Expeditionary Force – mainly of 6th (Aus) and 2nd (NZ) Infantry Divisions along with those of British 4th Hussars and the NZ 2nd Div's cavalry regiment. In total, some 1,000 men were taken. It could have been more if the bridge hadn't been destroyed.

Below left: The Fallschirmjäger take part in a victory parade in Athens. They had played an important role in the speedy capture of Greece – Unternehmen Marita. Nearly 15,000 Commonwealth troops entered captivity, but the Allies were able to evacuate 40,000 men to Crete and Africa. The battle for Crete was to follow as the Axis tightened its grip on the Eastern Mediterranean.

Opposite: By 20 May some 15,000 German troops had airlanded on the island.

the southern end of the bridge as the gliders came in to land, and one of them took out a glider. After a brief firefight the bridge was stormed and the remaining enemy guns silenced, the engineers began to unfasten the explosive charges, piling them up for removal. It is at this point, when the battle seemed over, that either random or deliberate fire hit some of the charges, setting them off and destroying the bridge and any Germans on it. Despite this shock, the Fallschirmjäger continued to advance aggressively and attack the local towns on both sides of the canal, forcing the surrender of all Allied and Greek troops before linking up with approaching German ground forces. A temporary structure was built across the canal by the morning of 28 April, but the blowing of the bridge had delayed pursuit and aided the evacuation of Allied forces from the Peloponnese.

Unternehmen Merkur (Mercury)

Hitler decided to defend his Balkan flank and the Romanian oilfields by selecting Crete over Malta as the next target. 'Merkur' was organised hurriedly in not much more than a fortnight, yet was the largest airborne operation in the world up to that date and unique in that it would depend almost exclusively upon airlanded troops for resupply. Some 11,000 glidermen and paratroops and 5,000 airlifted mountain troops were

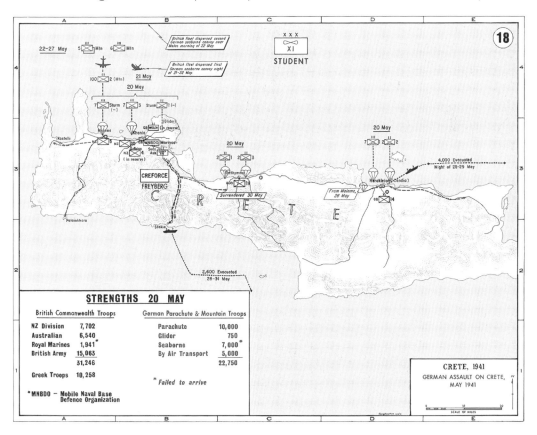

STRENGTHS 20 MAY			
British Commonwealth Troops		German Parachute & Mountain Troops	
NZ Division	7,702	Parachute	10,000
Australian	6,540	Glider	750
Royal Marines	1,941*	Seaborne	7,000*
British Army	15,063	By Air Transport	5,000
	31,246		22,750
Greek Troops	10,258		

*Failed to arrive

*MNBDO – Mobile Naval Base Defence Organization

CRETE, 1941
GERMAN ASSAULT ON CRETE, MAY 1941

SCALE OF MILES

Left: Preparations for the jump over Crete. Parachutes and life jackets (**A**) make difficult companions. The Luftwaffe kapok-filled jacket could keep a man afloat up to 24 hours (they were better than the inflatable versions) but was bulky to use – too bulky for those in single-seat fighters or dive-bombers. Its only down side was its high collar that could roll the wearer face forward in the water. Note the knee protectors (**B**), helmets (**C** they had a larger harness to keep them firmly positioned; inside, the para helmets had extra padding), camouflaged smocks and the Oberfeldwebel (**D**) carrying an MP40. Around a quarter of the Fallschirmjäger carried machine-pistols. The rest had to make do with pistols and grenades until their heavy weapons arrived by container. The attacking force of 10,000 paratroops were delivered by the trusty 'Tante Ju' Ju52 transport aircraft, whose corrugated fuselage matches the ribs of the life jackets. The flight to Crete took 2–3 hours.

allocated to the invasion – FJR 1, 2, 3 and the Luftlande-Sturm-Regiment 1 to be delivered as far as possible at low level – divided into three battlegroups codenamed Comet (West), Mars (Centre) and Orion (East). Targets were the port facility of Canea and the three vital Cretan airfields of Rethymnon, Maleme and Heraklion respectively, so that reinforcements – 5. Gebirgs-Division which had never air-dropped before but was chosen because 22. Luftlande-Division was involved in Russia – could be flown in immediately to expand the airheads.

However, German reconnaissance and intelligence had been appallingly minimal – they estimated the garrison at 5,000 when there were, in fact, some 40,000 British, Commonwealth and Greek soldiers on the island! A lack of transport aircraft meant the assault would have to be staggered in two waves with a return trip to southern Greece to refuel and reload. Enigma decryptions meant the British also knew they were coming. The morning targets were the airfield at Maleme and the port facility of Canea; the afternoon's Rethymnon and Heraklion.

Despite the intelligence, the British still presumed and prepared for a primarily seaborne assault and hoped their naval superiority and numbers would suffice, for most of their troops had recently retreated down the Greek mainland and been evacuated to Crete without heavy weapons. Crucially, the last few RAF aircraft had been withdrawn to North Africa, ceding the skies to the Luftwaffe. The cautious Allied commander, Maj Gen Bernard Freyberg, divided the island into four defence boxes, spreading his forces mainly along the northern and western coasts to oppose potential Axis landings. The rocky terrain suited concealment and defence, but the battle would hinge on German air supremacy and the taking of Maleme airfield.

Paratroopers exiting from a Ju52 over Suda Bay during the German assault. Another Ju52 is burning and trailing smoke, having being hit by Allied ground fire. During the 10-day campaign, the Ju52s airlifted over 22,000 soldiers, 711 motorcycles, 353 light artillery pieces, 5,358 supply drop containers and 2,403,435lb of supplies to Crete. On their return, they evacuated 3,173 wounded.

The German attack unfolded as an almost complete disaster as the failure of Student's piecemeal 'oil-drop' tactics – a widespread drop in small numbers rather than an overwhelming concentration – was laid bare. On 20 May the parachute and glider assaults launched after the usual preliminary bombing and strafing, but the clumsy low-flying Ju52 transports and their gliders were easy targets – more than a dozen were destroyed in flight. Hundreds of paratroopers were then released directly over Allied positions and killed in the air, while others were scattered far from their objectives and picked off. Hundreds more were killed immediately upon landing before they could access their canisters, many of which were lost or destroyed. At Maleme airfield Luftlande-Sturm -Regiment I ended with fewer than 600 men isolated in two pockets about a mile apart, almost out of ammunition. FJR3 was similarly pinned down outside Canea. The afternoon wave fared no better – FJR2 became isolated on a hilltop at Rethymnon and most of FJR1 dropped onto a full British regiment in Heraklion. By the end of the day the Fallschirmjäger had endured close to a 50% casualty rate with over 3,000 men dead and more wounded, the rest cut off and surrounded by superior forces. The attacks had been shattered and, to make matters worse, the Royal Navy had intercepted and destroyed the first wave of Axis seaborne support forces, so the second wave had been postponed.

But at Maleme the remnants of Luftlande-Sturm-Regiment I now had a stroke of luck. A loss of communications between the forward companies of the defenders (22nd (NZ) Inf Bn) prompted their confused withdrawal from Hill 107, the high ground overlooking the airfield, allowing the Germans to seize it and consolidate a temporary local control. Into this small window of opportunity Student desperately threw his last reserves of paratroops, followed by units of 5. Gebirgs-Division. With ferocious determination the Germans maintained their airbridge, and the surge of troops tipped the balance of the battle for the airfield and the island. Allied counterattacks were repulsed with vital air support despite heavy Luftwaffe losses. Using air and artillery bombardments they then pushed the Allies ever eastwards, linking up with a successful seaborne landing.

After a week of bitter fighting the British evacuated 18,000 troops between 28 May and 1 June, leaving 4,000 dead and over 11,000 PoW. But the Fallschirmjäger had been badly savaged, and the Luftwaffe had lost vital aircraft that would have been very useful in Russia. Crete changed Hitler's mind: for him, the day of the paratrooper was done.

> **XI Fliegerkorps casualties**
> **Unternehmen Merkur**
> - 5,415 casualties of the nearly 22,000 men engaged on Crete (25%)
> - 7. Flieger-Division 1,653 dead, 1,441 missing (presumed killed), and 2,046 wounded of its c. 11,000 troops engaged (47%).
> - 5. Gebirgs-Division, airlifted as reinforcements, 262 dead, 318 missing and 458 wounded of c. 9,000 troops engaged (12%)
> - Ju52 squadrons lost 151 aircraft (143 destroyed, 8 missing presumed lost), 120 damaged (repairable); airlift fleet had 271 aircraft casualties of the 502 Ju52s (54%).

1 Fallschirmjäger dropping. If dropped at above 500ft the defenders had a good chance of hitting the men in the air; 2 Fallschirmjäger march into Canea on 27 May; 3 A break in the fighting – time for this machine gunner to have a smoke. Note the goggles; 4 Fallschirmjäger had little organic transport and many local donkeys were impressed into service. This one's carrying 3.7cm PaK ammo; 5 Para officers in their baggy smocks; 6 Medal ceremony at Maleme – Oberst Ramcke presents awards to men of Luftlande-Sturm-Regiment 1 which suffered heavy losses in the battle (a 67% casualty rate).

Left: Maleme airfield. Defended by NZ 22nd Battalion whose men were dug in on the heights at Hill 107. Unsupported during the German attack, they withdrew and the Germans were able to take the crucial high ground. They held it and the airfield against counterattacks thus paving the way for reinforcements and, ultimately, victory.

Left and Below: A well-known sequence of photos shows the lightly armed Fallschirmjäger fighting among the terraces and olive trees.

Right: Mortar crew – note rangefinder (man at left) and the boxes of 81mm rounds.

THE LESSONS OF CRETE
(as identified by British HQ MEC 6 June 1941)

(a) Aerodromes being enemy main objectives must be organized for all-round defence ...

(b) All ranks of all arms must be armed with rifles and bayonets and a high proportion of Tommy guns to protect themselves, and in the case of Artillery, their guns.

(c) By day it should be easy to deal with parachutists, but ... [they] may land at night and secure an aerodrome. ... There must be mobile reserves, centrally placed, preferably with tanks.

(d) Defence must be offensive. ... good system of intercommunication is vital. Delay may allow enemy air to prevent movement.

(e) During bombing phase, AA and LMGs should remain silent unless required to protect own aircraft on the ground.

(f) AA layout should include dummy AA guns and alternative positions. Positions of AA guns should be continually changed.

(g) Arrangements must be made quickly to render aerodromes liable to attack temporarily unfit for landing.

(h) Equally important to quick action of mobile reserve is position of fighter aircraft support, the existence of which might prevent any airborne landing from succeeding ...

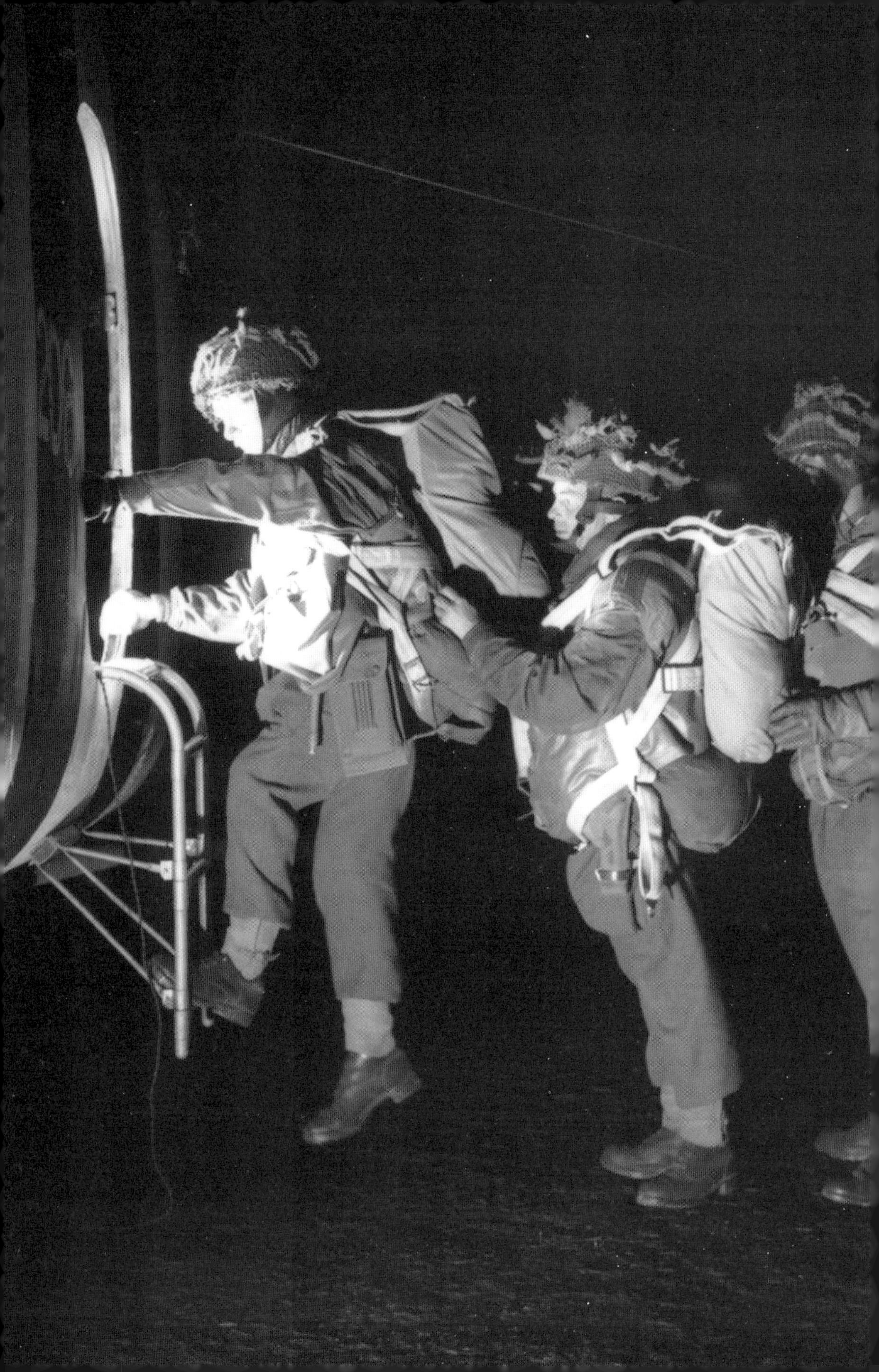

4 The Allies

The Allies had toyed with airborne forces during the 1930s, aware of the opportunities they offered but not prepared to invest in them. The consequence was that, after the German successes in 1940, they had to play catch up. Winston Churchill got the ball rolling for the British in June 1940, by writing to General 'Pug' Ismay, his chief military assistant: 'We ought to have a corps of at least 5,000 parachute troops, including a proportion of Australians, New Zealanders and Canadians, together with some trustworthy people from Norway and France.'

The letter led to the creation of the Parachute Training School at Manchester's Ringway Airport and, in August 1942, to the creation of the Parachute Regiment. By that time the first operations had been performed – the first, Colossus on 10 February 1941 (see p42). This – and the successful Operation Biting – was but a raid, performed by special forces, and showed that small operations were feasible. In America, a small paratroop establishment was also formed.

The turning point was the battle for Crete (end of May 1941). Galvanised by the concept of aerial attack by large numbers of troops, both the British and American military establishments sat up. On 22 May 1941, the US War Department published a new version of *FM 100-5, Operations* that mentioned airborne forces. By 20 May 1942 the US Army had produced *FM 31-30*, the basic field manual that outlined the tactics and techniques of airborne troops, including principles for their use (see box p45). *FM 100-5* noted:

'Suitable missions for troops transported by air include:
a) Seizing and holding, or otherwise exploiting, important tactical localities or installations, in conjunction with or pending the arrival of other military or naval forces. Such missions include seizure and clearance of landing fields, beachheads, strong points, and ports; seizure of essential observation or other critical terrain; severing hostile lines of

Continued on p45.

Paras of 12th Parachute Bn board a Stirling on 5 June 1944: next stop Normandy! Operation Tonga would see 8,500 men of the division land by parachute and glider in Normandy. Its casualties by 7 June were 800, but it had to a large extent accomplished its mission and continued to fight until withdrawal on 27 August 1944 following its advance to the Seine.

Operation Colossus

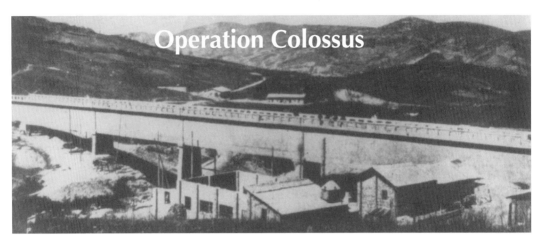

The first airborne operations of the war were raids. Operation Colossus was an attack on an aqueduct near Tragino (**Above**), Italy by X Troop – men of 11th SAS Battalion. who had trained assiduously (**Left** – note the rubber training helmets). At 17:40 on Monday, 10 February 1941, the first of eight Whitley bombers, six of which had been converted to carry paratroops, left Malta (**Below left** – note high para boots). Nearly four hours later, at 21:40, the first men were dropped. A total of 35 men landed in Italy, but not everything went according to plan. As with so many airborne operations, getting all the men and all their munitions together in one place at the same proved impossible. While the aqueduct was blown up, it wasn't destroyed and the Italians were able to repair the damage without major problems. However, the raid did prove a morale-booster to Britain's nascent airborne forces and taught a number of lessons. 34 men survived and became PoWs. The Italian interpreter, Fortunato Picchi, was tortured and executed.

Operation Biting

Operation Biting is perhaps better known for the location it raided – the German radar station at Bruneval on the north coast of France – and its commander, Major J.D. Frost who would gain everlasting fame at Arnhem. Frost's C Company of 2nd Parachute Battalion dropped on the night of 27/28 February 1942. This photograph (**Left**), taken in December 1941, shows the Würzburg radar that was the object of the exercise and the reason that an RAF technician, Flt Sgt C.W.H. Cox, who had never jumped before, was on the team. The mission went pretty much perfectly and the men were extracted by sea along with the Würzburg components and two prisoners (one of whom was a Würzburg operator) they had taken. Casualties were light: two dead and six missing. The modern memorial (**Below**) was erected in 2012. Another airborne raid, Operation Freshman in November 1942, targeted the German heavy water plant in Telemark. It was unsuccessful with all the men either killed in transit or murdered after interrogation. The objective was later destroyed in February 1943 by Operation Gunnerside.

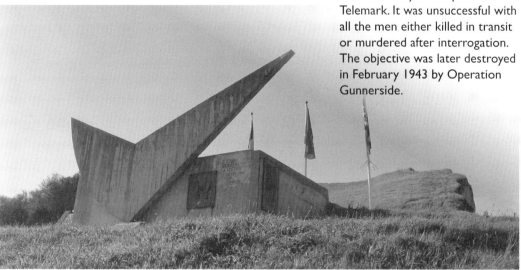

Operation Torch

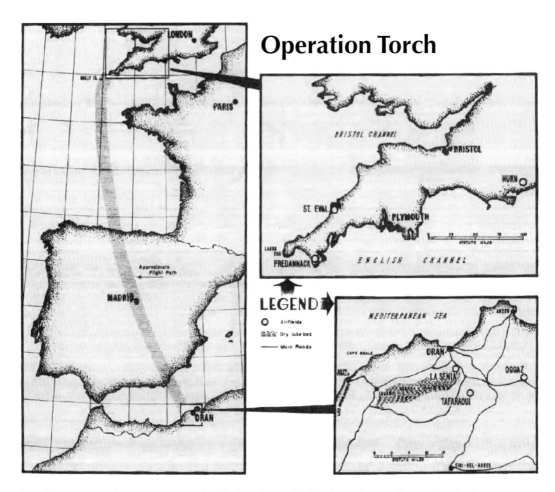

The first major airborne operation by the US Army, the landings during Operation Torch, saw 2/509th PIR fly from the UK. The operation went awry but the paratroops marched to their objective (the airfields of Tafaraoui and La Senia). On 15 November 1942, 300 men of the battalion dropped on and secured Youks-les-Bains airfield, which they found to be in French hands.

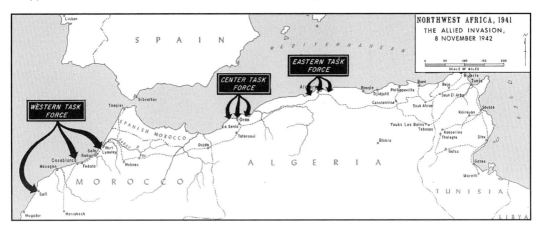

43. Principles of Employment

The following considerations govern employment of parachute troops:

a. The element of surprise must be present.

b. Parachute troops should not be used for missions that can be performed by other troops.

c. Decision to use parachute troops should be made well in advance of the scheduled date of the operation.

d. A comprehensive knowledge of the terrain involved in the operation is essential.

e. A long-range forecast of meteorological conditions should be carefully considered during the planning phase.

f. Because of technical requirements, all parachute troop missions should start from a base which affords the required facilities for packing of parachutes and for making minor repairs. From this base, parachute units may be flown directly to their objective or transported by any available means to a designated airfield, to be picked up by their transport airplanes.

g. Terrain objectives to be seized and held should lie in the path of the contemplated advance of friendly forces.

h. Local air superiority must exist.

i. Combat aviation is essential for the protection of parachute troops while in flight and during landing, and for supporting fires before, during, and after landing.

j. Parachute troops should be relieved and withdrawn to their base as soon as practicable after arrival of supporting ground forces.

k. All principles of offensive and defensive action applying to infantry combat are equally applicable to parachute troops

communication and supply; the destruction of bridges, locks, public utility enterprises, and other designated demolitions; seizure of river crossings, defiles, and other bottle-necks; blocking a hostile counterattack; interrupting the movements of hostile reserves; cooperating in the pursuit or breakthrough by ground forces by operating against enemy reserves and lines of communication, and blocking hostile avenues of retreat; and preventing the enemy from destroying essential installations, supplies, and matériel which might be of use in our own subsequent operations.

b) Executing an envelopment from the air linked with an attack by ground forces.

c) Execution of surprise attacks as a diversion or feint in connection with other air-landing or ground operations, or to create confusion and disorder among the hostile military and civilian personnel.

d) Execution of an attack against an isolated enemy position, impossible or impracticable of attack by ground forces.'

Operation Torch

The first significant operation was remarkable for its vision, even though the result was not what was hoped for. On 7–8 November 1942 556 men of 2/509th PIR, 82nd Airborne Division in 39 C-47s from 60th Group, of 51st TCW, USAAF left St Eval and Predaneck airfields in England for North Africa as part of Operation Torch – a non-stop formation flight of 1,250 miles. Operationally, they should have refuelled in Gibraltar if they were going to go into combat, but when they left they believed they

What the well-dressed US paratrooper was wearing on 9 July 1943 when Operation Husky took place. These troopers are from 2/509th PIR, at that time attached to 82nd Airborne Division. They would sit out the Sicilian campaign when the battalion was designated division reserve. This well-known colour photograph shows: **1** The 'dome' (pot)-shaped M1 was the standard Army and Marine Corps helmet during WW2. It was modified for the airborne with alterations to the 'hard hat' composite liner by extending the inner nape/rear strap to the sides terminating as 'A' straps to which the leather chin-cup was attached. This in turn was attached to the shell 'dome' by male/female press-studs (snaps) on webbing slotted through 'D'-shaped bales welded to it. These were prone to breaking and were replaced by swivel versions in 1943. All the helmet support webbing was within the liner. The helmet was camouflaged the British way and rarely painted; **2** 'Mae West' life jacket; **3** first-aid pack; **4** reserve chute; **5** holstered M1911A1 Colt; **6** the bulky gas mask in its canvas cover; **7** the obtrusive M1910 pattern T-handled entrenching tool; **8** long, laced paratrooper boots.

were going to land at La Senia airfield near Oran. On top of this, confused signal orders led to the guide boat (HMS *Alynbank*) broadcasting on the wrong frequency. Three aircraft did land at Gibraltar. Three, low on fuel, landed in Spanish Morocco. One set of paras jumped and also landed in Spanish territory. Paratroops from 12 aircraft jumped near Lourmel and then walked to Tafaraoui. 28 aircraft landed at Sebkra Dioran, a salt lake south of Oran. Subsequently some went on to Tafaraoui.

The British side of the mission – 450 paras in 34 aircraft from 64th TCG – staged through Gibraltar and landed at Maison Blanche on 11 November hoping to link up with British First Army. The immediate German response was to reinforce the area by aircraft – 1,200 Ju52 landings were

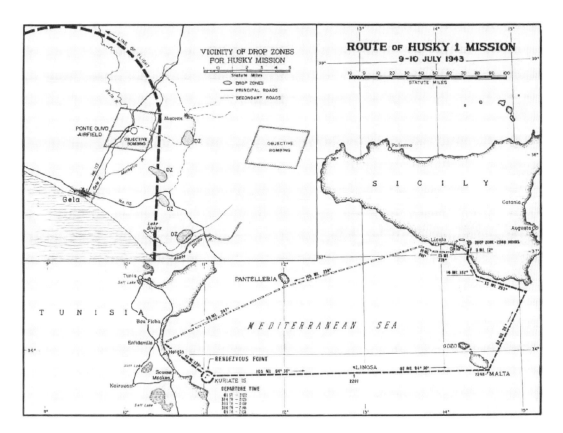

Operation Husky 1 flight routing and dropping zones. Note proximity to the island of Pantelleria which was successfully invaded and taken in Operation Corkscrew on 11 June.

said to have taken place at Bizerte and over 20,000 troops landed. Gliders were used for resupply including the huge Me321s (see p183).

On 12 November 26 transports carrying 312 paras, covered by an escort, left Maison Blanche for Bone. The airfield was seized and held in spite of bombing and attacks by the Germans, as was Souk-el-Arba airfield on 16 November by 384 paras who then took Gafsa airfield. These successes led to an ambitious plan to take three more airfields around Tunis. Some 530 British Paras of 2nd Para Bn, under the command of the then Lt-Col John Frost (of Arnhem Bridge fame), were dropped on the 29th. But the tide had turned and the German reinforcements stopped a link up with First Army. The British paras exfiltrated but 16 officers and 250 men were killed or captured.

Operation Husky

The next major operation for the Allied airborne troops was as part of Operation Husky – the invasion of Sicily. This involved heavy use of gliders – painstakingly shipped to Africa in kit form and constructed in situ. Training for the mission proved less than

Continued on p52.

With equipment so bulky, checking harnesses, equipment and fastenings was extremely important. *FM31–30* advised that before emplaning, the 'officer or noncommissioned officer designated as jumpmaster then inspects the parachute of each man.' (**Above and Below left**) Men of the 505th RCT – made up of the 505th PIR and 3/504th PIR – commanded by Col James M. Gavin, ready themselves before boarding (**Below right and Opposite, Above**) Douglas C-47-DL Skytrains. They would drop around Gela – 226 C-47 Skytrains of 52nd Troop Carrier Wing were planned to drop 3,405 paratroopers – including two batteries of 75mm pack howitzers, a company of engineers and various other small detachments – in Operation Husky 1. The 52nd TCW was based around Kairouan, with three squadrons (316th Group) near Enfidaville.

FROM *FM31–30* BASIC FIELD MANUAL:
TACTICS AND TECHNIQUES OF AIR-BORNE
TROOPS MAY 20, 1942

JUMPMASTER'S CHECK LIST

(A) PrIor to enplaning [sic].
1. Snug harness properly adjusted.
2. Fasteners snapped.
3. Shoulder adapters properly adjusted.
4. Back strap adapters properly adjusted.
5. Static line:
    (a) Snap fastener and locking pln.
    (b) Retaining loop.
    (c) Over shoulder.
6. Reserve parachute:
    (a) Riser snaps secured.
    (b) Rip cord pins.
    (c) Elastics and pack tabs.
7. Body strap secure.
8. Static line loops on back pack.
9. Junction of static line and pack cover.
10. Pack cover lacing.
11. Riser tacking
12. Feel over entire pack.

(B) Prior to jump.
1. Before the command HOOK UP:
    (a) All harness fittings secure.
    (b) Reserve pack secure.
    (c) Static line over shoulder.
2. After the commands HOOK UP and
    IN DOOR
    (a) Snap fastener on cable with pin
    inserted.
    (b) Static line over shoulder.
    (c) Static line away from head.
    (d) Position of Jumper In door.

Left: Lt Col Charles Wilmarth Kouns
commanded 3/504th PIR. His stick dropped
near Niscemi and engaged elements of the
Panzer Division Hermann Göring. Surrounded,
Kouns surrendered. He spent the rest of the
war as a PoW, ending up in Oflag 64 in Landkreis
Altburgund, German-occupied Poland. And
all for jump pay of $100 for officers ($50 for
enlisted men)!

Above: The second 82nd Division lift was due to follow the first, but was delayed until D+1 (11 July). It carried 504th PIR (less 3rd Battalion), the 376th PFAB and the 307th Airborne Engineer Bn. It was subjected to one of the worst friendly fire incidents of the war as Allied vessels fired on the 166 aircraft carrying them. Some 23 aircraft were shot down, the 504th losing 81 killed, 16 missing and 132 wounded and the 52nd Wing 7 killed, 53 missing and 30 wounded. These men of the 504th are seen before their flight. A third lift – to carry Div HQ – was delayed to 16 July (D+6) when they were flown to Olivio aerodrome.

Below: Men of the 504th PIR after the fighting in Sicily had finished. After the first phase, the three days after dropping that saw fighting at the coast, 82nd Airborne buried their dead, and prepared for the advance west. Ten days later, on 23 July, they had taken Trapani and numerous prisoners – the division was credited with over 20,000 – at a cost of 7 dead and 16 wounded.

Above: Operation Husky landings proved a mixed success. The airborne troops were widely spread but fought bravely and at Biazza Ridge affected the course of the German armoured counterattack. The 82nd's casualties were sizeable (see table on next page).

Below: These men of the 505th PIR were dropped so far from their target in the American sector that they met up with British troops as they came ashore.

Below right: Wounded paratrooper evacuated out of Sicily by ship. Note the 82nd Airborne patch on the left arm and national markings on the right.

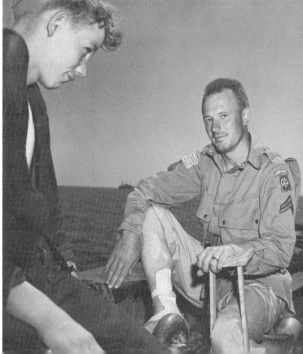

82nd AIRBORNE CASUALTIES SICILY 1943			
	Officers	*Men*	*Total*
Killed in action	25	165	190
Died of wounds		6	6
Prisoners of war	8	164	172
Missing in action	5	43	48
Missing in action/returned to duty	2	71	73
Wounded	16	121	137
Wounded/returned to duty	24	314	438
Totals	80	884	964
Div HQ	1		1
504th PIR	33	355	388
505th PIR	33	391	424
507th AEB	5	34	39
376th PFAB	2	55	57
456th PFAB	6	49	55

Opposite: The first British airborne operation in Sicily was codenamed 'Ladbroke' and was a disaster. A glider-borne attack by 1st Airlanding Brigade, 65 gliders were released early or too low and crashed into the sea. 252 men died as a result. Only 12 of the 144 gliders and 87 of the 2,075 men reached their objective: Ponte Grande Bridge near Syracuse.

satisfactory, and while the US para drop – although widespread and inaccurate – saw men of 82nd Airborne play an important part in the battles around Gela, in particular stopping a linkup between 15. Panzer-Division and the Panzer-Division Hermann Göring, the US side of the operation would be plagued by friendly fire incidents that caused a number of deaths. This was not the case on the first drop: 226 transports flew 2,781 men – mainly the 505th RCT – and 891 parapacks. The drop was scattered, but the men of 82nd Airborne performed effectively on the ground. The second US drop, however, was more problematic. It saw 144 transports deliver 2,008 paras – the 504th PIR – and 770 parapacks. They were fired upon from ships and land. Over 300 men died.

The British glider missions were also disasters. There were two: Operation Ladbroke on 9–10 July designed to take Ponte Grande outside Syracuse; the second, Operation Fustian on 13–14 July, was to take Primosole Bridge, key to Catania. Problems for 'Ladbroke' started immediately. RAF Albemarles had difficulties with US CG-4A gliders and three were lost on take off. Around 1,690 men of 1st Para Division left six different fields within a 20-mile radius in the El Djem area. Flak, cloud, a head wind and inexperience saw many gliders loosed at too low an altitude. Nearly 70 of the 133 went into the sea short of dry land. Those that did land found the terrain rougher than expected. The paras took the bridge, but hadn't enough men to hold it. They removed the demolition charges, and half an hour later, when the infantry from the beaches reached the bridge, they were able to retake it quickly. 'Fustian' also had friendly fire problems. Of over 100 aircraft carrying 1,856 men of 1st Para Bde towards Primosole bridge, 37 were shot down and only 4 gliders landed intact.

As far as the airmen were concerned, the Sicilian campaign saw serious casualties: 49 transports destroyed or write offs, 68 repairable, 227 KIA or MIA and 48 WIA.

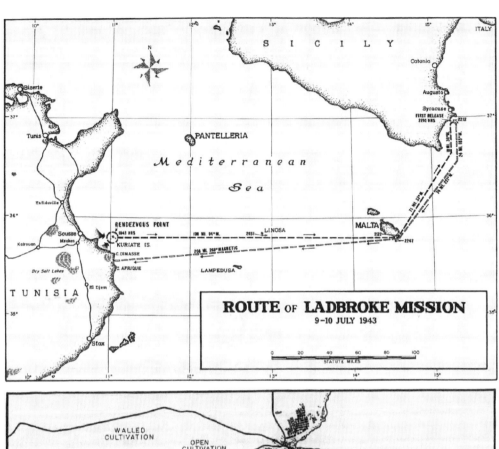

ROUTE OF LADBROKE MISSION
9–10 JULY 1943

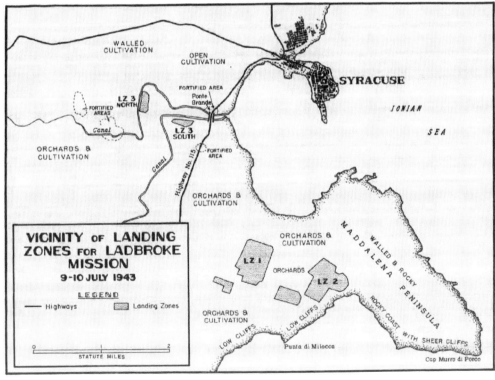

VICINITY OF LANDING ZONES FOR LADBROKE MISSION
9–10 JULY 1943

LEGEND

— Highways

▢ Landing Zones

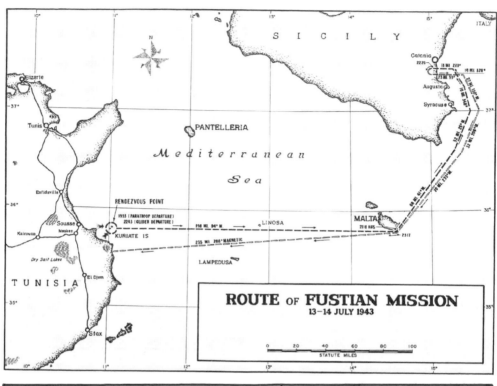

ROUTE OF **FUSTIAN MISSION**
13–14 JULY 1943

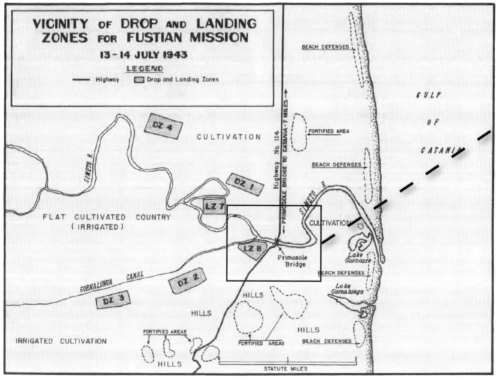

VICINITY OF DROP AND LANDING ZONES FOR FUSTIAN MISSION
13–14 JULY 1943

LEGEND
—— Highway   ▦ Drop and Landing Zones

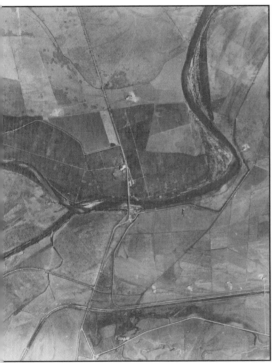

Four days after 'Ladbroke', Operation Fustian was the second British airborne operation over Sicily – another mission, Operation Glutton, was cancelled. 'Fustian' targeted the Primosole Bridge across the Simeto River, an important choke point on the way to Catania. As with 'Ladbroke', the bravery of the troops couldn't hide the faults of the operation. 1,856 men took off in over 100 Dakotas and gliders: friendly fire, enemy AA guns, poor navigation and inexperienced pilots saw few of the paras land in the correct place – only 39 of the aircraft dropped their men within half a mile of the target zones. Of the glider mission, only four landed intact. The bridge was taken by 295 men of 1st Para Brigade and held until the evening when the enemy – mainly German Fallschirmjäger – pushed them off. It was retaken two days later. 1st Para Brigade suffered over 300 casualties including at least 140 dead. This brought the total 1st Airborne Division losses in the Sicilian campaign to over 450 dead and 342 missing/wounded. The photos show one of the CG-4As before the operation and the Primosole Bridge.

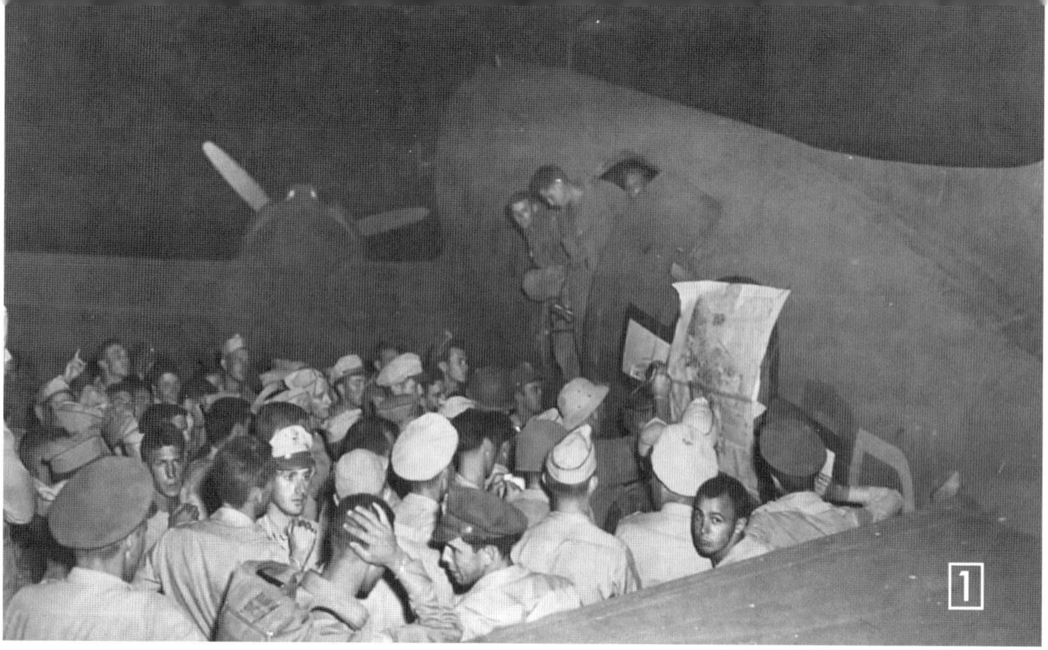

1

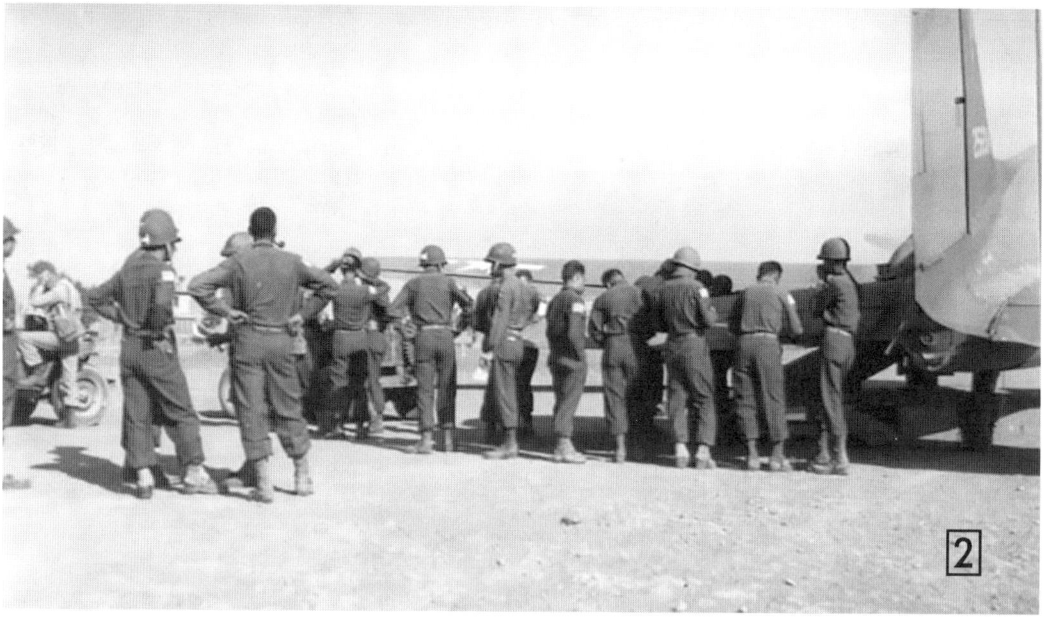

2

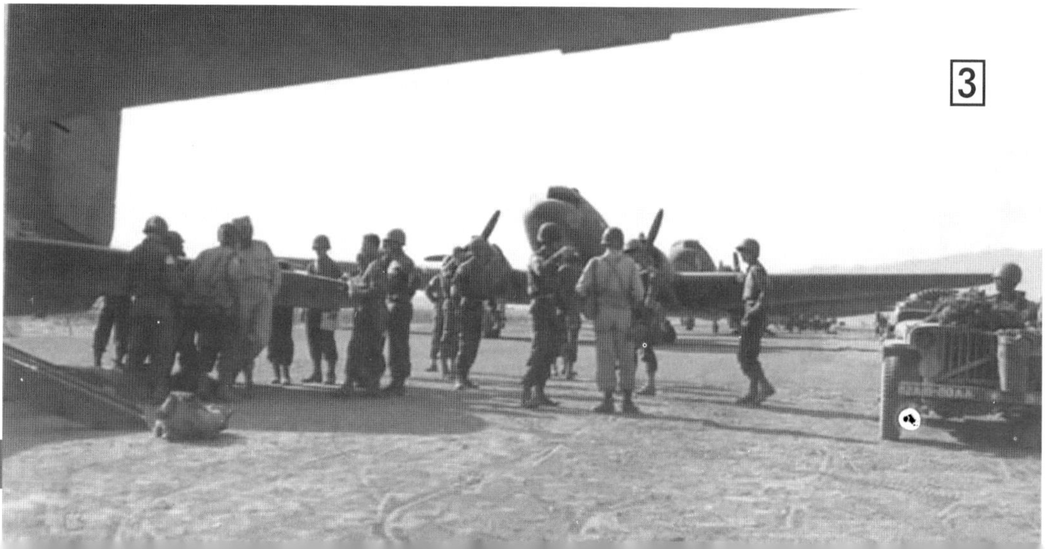

3

The response to the poor airborne missions of Operation Husky was extremely negative. Lt Gen Lesley J. McNair, CG of the US Army Ground Forces (and later killed in Normandy by misdropped bombs) wrote: 'I had become convinced of the impracticality of handling large airborne units. I was prepared to recommend to the War Department that airborne divisions be abandoned ... and that the airborne effort be restricted to parachute units of battalion size or less.' Importantly, Generals Ridgway and Williams didn't agree and Italy saw further use of the airborne troops. After a number of planned missions on Rome to link into the Italian surrender were cancelled, the next major operation for 82nd Airborne would be a drop to support the beleaguered ground forces at Salerno – some of the gliderborne elements having arrived by sea. These photos show paratroopers and glidermen of the division preparing for their operations in Italy. They flew from Sicilian airfields, having recently transitioned from Africa. Note the final briefing before the Salerno operation (**1**), men filling in their flight forms (**2 and 3**) and men attaching a tow rope to a CG-4A (**4**). Flight forms recorded the identities of the men in each aircraft/glider.

4

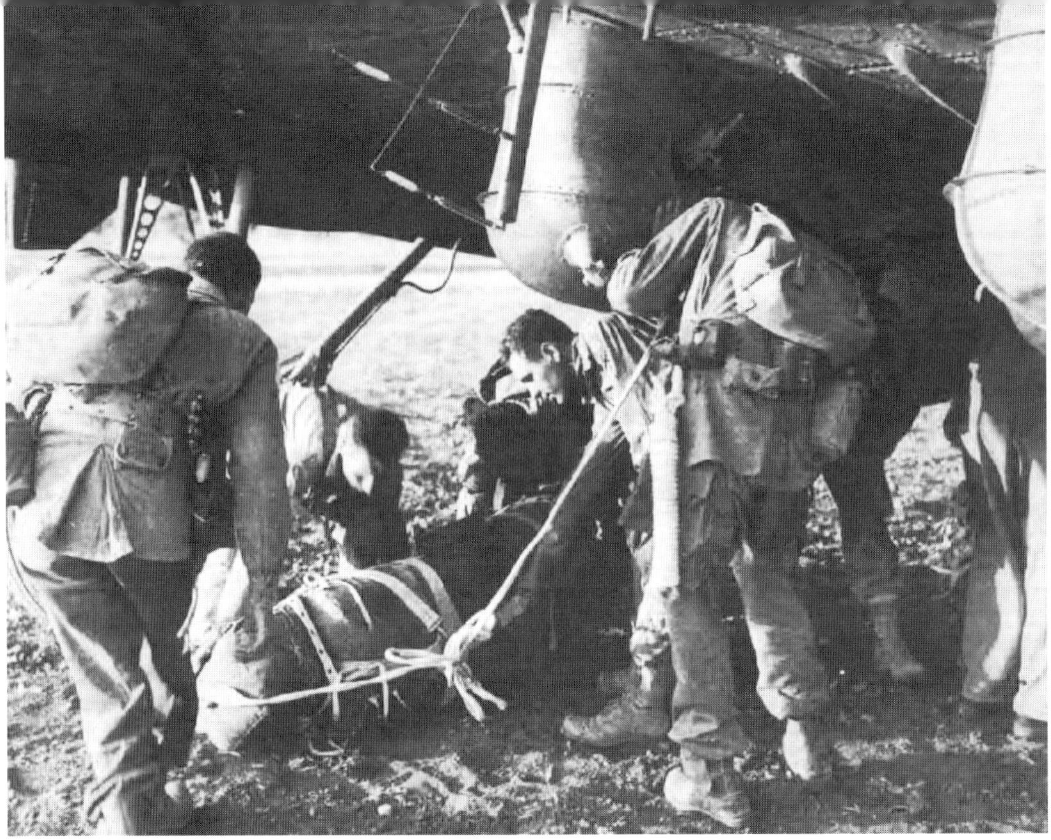

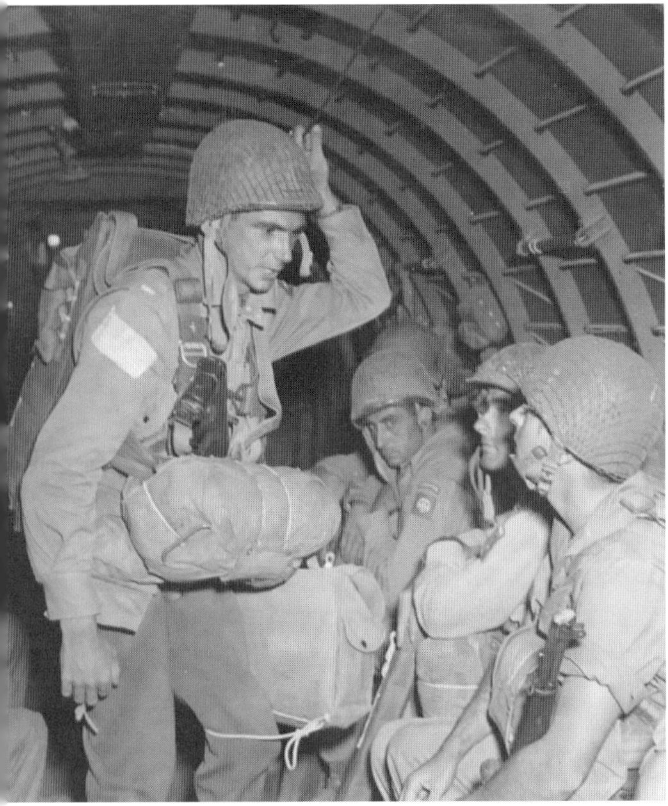

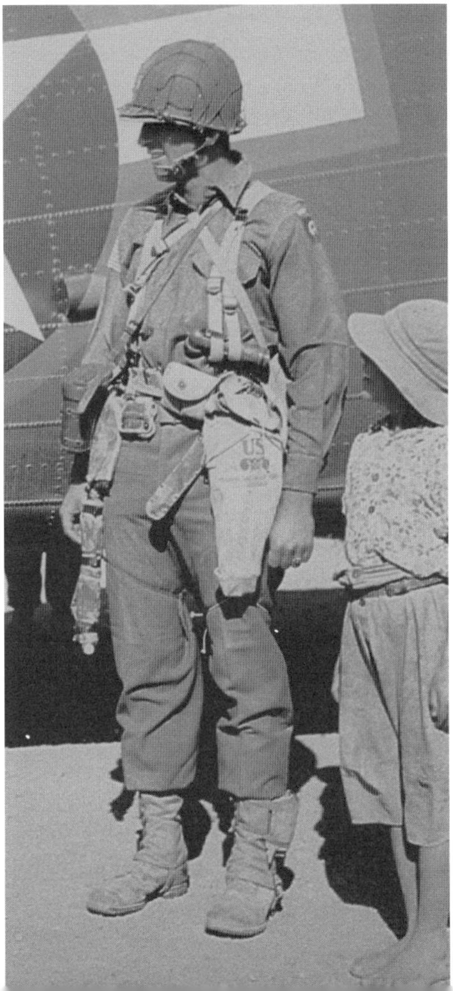
US

Opposite: Heavier weapons, ammunition, rations etc were loaded into parapacks for separate dropping. These are being attached to an aircraft for the the Salerno drop.

Opposite, Below left: En route to Salerno – note the folding stock M1A1 paratroop carbine stuffed behind the reserve chute.

Opposite, Below right: This gliderman is wearing infantry trousers, boots and gaiters, has a torch and field glasses, and there's a field dressing attached to his ankle.

Right: Readying himself for the flight to Avellino, a corporal of the 2/509th PIR attached to the 82nd, prepares for the jump. Note the early pattern gas mask container (**A**) later substituted by a black rubberised version (see p77, photo 2E).

Below: On 9 September men of the Parachute Scout Coy, 2/509th PIR took part in the capture of the island of Ventotene in a task force alongside Douglas Fairbanks, Jnr's BJU-1 – the 'Beach Jumpers'.

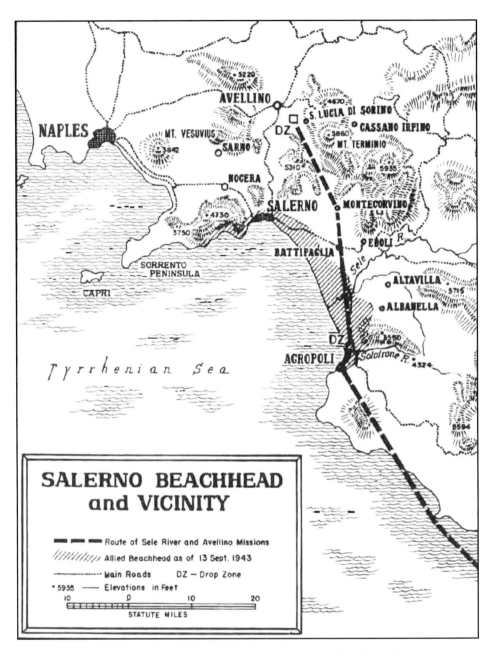

SALERNO BEACHHEAD and VICINITY

━━ ▬▬ ▬▬ Route of Sele River and Avellino Missions

////////// Allied Beachhead as of 13 Sept. 1943

·········· Main Roads   DZ — Drop Zone

• 5935 ──── Elevations in Feet

10   0   10   20

STATUTE MILES

After various operations linked to the Italian surrender were cancelled, 82nd Airborne's next combat jump took place over Italy on the night of 13–14 September 1943 when General Mark Clark called on his old friend, General Matthew Ridgway, to help him out at an hour of great need – the Allied lines were in danger of collapsing in front of a German armoured counterattack. Eight hours after the request reached him, 504th PIR jumped into action. The next night the 505th dropped at Paestum and the 2/509th, plus some of 307th Airborne Engineers, dropped on Avellino in the enemy's rear. 510 of the 640 who dropped at Avellino would reach friendly lines after three weeks of fighting.

Above: On 14 September 325th GIR and 3/504th PIR arrived at the Salerno bridgehead by sea (they had been heading for a possible operation north of Naples). Most of the 325nd's 2nd Battalion was then sent by LCI to reinforce the Rangers north of Maiori — they did, so arriving at dawn on the 18th, then fighting and holding Mount St Angelo. On the 14th, British 7th Armoured Division started unloading: they would spearhead the coastal advance to Naples. The thrust that developed would take Fifth Army to the Volturno and capture Naples, but it would need help from the 504th PIR, seen here boarding LCIs to be taken north to Maiori on 26 September.

Below: Mark Clark talks to men of the 325th GIR at Salerno. Clark, understandably, rated the 82nd very highly and specifically asked for elements to remain in Italy while the rest of the division returned to Ireland to prepare to drop into Normandy. Those who stayed in Italy — the 504th PIR, 376th Field Artillery Bn and elements of 307th Airborne Engineers — finally left in March 1944.

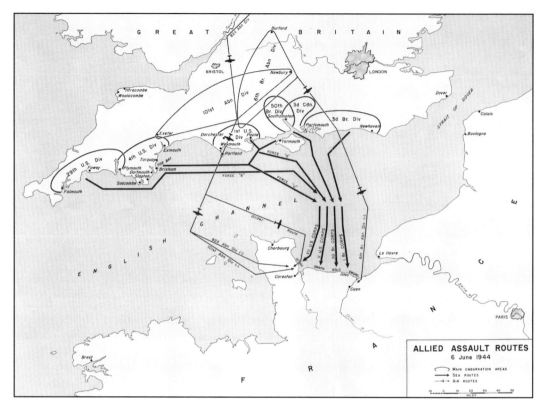

ALLIED ASSAULT ROUTES
6 June 1944

MAIN EMBARKATION AREAS
SEA ROUTES
AIR ROUTES

Operation Overlord – D-Day

Of all the airborne operations during World War II, none was as important or, ultimately, as successful as that on 5–6 June 1944 on both sides of the Allied invasion. The airborne forces had specific tasks – such as holding key bridges – as well as the general require-ment to seal off the flanks of the invasion for such time as required before they could be reinforced from the beachheads. This was accomplished in spite of the problems both the American and British transport carriers encountered – cloud, AA fire and communica-tion problems – things that seem very foreign to a modern generation brought up with satellite GPS and mobile phones.

On the British flank, the 6th Airborne Division achieved all its D-Day objectives. The distribution of the paras, however, meant that at least one of those missions – the de-struction of the battery at Merville – was only temporary. It was a remarkable achieve-ment with less than a third of the force and few of the explosives available for the assault. Operation Deadstick saw a group from the 2nd Ox&Bucks take and hold the bridges over the Orne and Canal de Caen in a coup de main operation of pinpoint accuracy. Operation Tonga, the para drop, wasn't as accurate but the landing areas were less enclosed than the bocage of the Cotentin peninsula and the British paras were able to set up a coordinated perimeter that withstood counterattacks. The supporting forces

Continued on p68.

BRITISH AIRBORNE OPERATIONS 6 JUNE 1944

Code	Planned time	Unit	Gliders or A/C	Troops	LZ/DZ
Deadstick	00:50	D/2nd Ox&Bucks	6 H	180	X and Y
Tonga	00:50	Pathfinders	27 A/C	-	
	00:50	Para advance parties			N (5 Para), V (3 Para)
					K (8 Para Bn)
		Parachute drops	255 arrived of 264	4,310	
	02:00	5 Para Bde	116 A/C	+ 611 by glider	N (5 Para)
	02:00	Adv party 6th AB HQ	A/C		N
	02:00	3 Para Bde less 8 Para Bn	71 A/C, 11 H		N
	02:00	8 Para Bn, 1st CAN Bn			V
	03:20	6th AB HQ, A/Tk Btys	68 H, 4 Hc		N
	04:30	Det 9 Para	3 H	600	Merville Bty
Mallard		6th Airlanding	226 H, 30 Hc		
	21:00	HQ, 1RUR, 6th AB ARR			N
	21:00	2nd Ox&Bucks, A/12 Devons,			
		6th AB Sp elements			W

H = Horsa, Hc = Hamilcar, A/C = aircraft

The immediate missions of 6th Airborne were to take the LZs and secure them for the gliders due that evening. Merville Battery had to be silenced and five bridges over the River Dives and Divette needed to be blown. A separate coup de main operation was to take the River Orne and Canal de Caen at Bénouville. Finally, they had to take the high ground that runs from Ranville to Le Plain and hold against the inevitable German counterattacks.

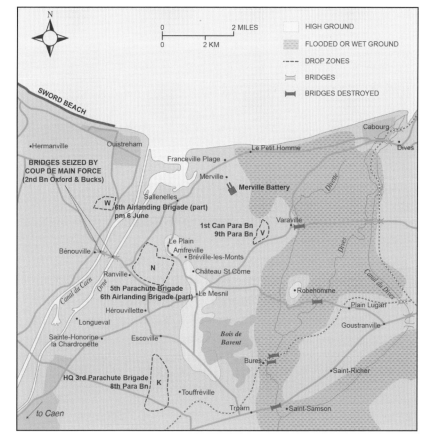

THE CHANNEL STOPPE[D]
YOU, BUT NOT US

Remember
Coventry
Plymouth
Bristol
London

Now its OUR TURN

You've had your time you GERMAN'S
WINHOUNDS

1

2

3

1 These men of 6th Airlanding Brigade prior to take-off. They were destined for DZ-W (see next page) as part of the second drop on the night of 6 June 1944. Note the distinctive RAF axes (**detail**) carried by two of the men. With insulated handles, the blades could cut through the fuselage and the pick through perspex.

2 1st Canadian Parachute Bn in a transit camp staging area prior to D-Day, early June 1944. The Canadians knocked out bridges at Robehomme and Varaville.

3 Camouflage application, essential for night landings.

4 Note Red Cross armbands on both men – at left a medic with his haversack slung to the front. The cap badge of the man at right identifies him as a Catholic chaplain attached to the unit.

5 Resupply is essential for airborne troops. Here, Stirlings drop supplies on DZ-N on 7 June. Note the upright posts – 'Rommel's asparagus' to curtail glider landings. While many were cleared by the Royal Engineers, they still constituted a major hazard to gliders.

6 Pathfinders of 22nd Independent Parachute Company synchronise watches in front of an Armstrong Whitworth Albemarle of No 38 Group, RAF at RAF Harwell.

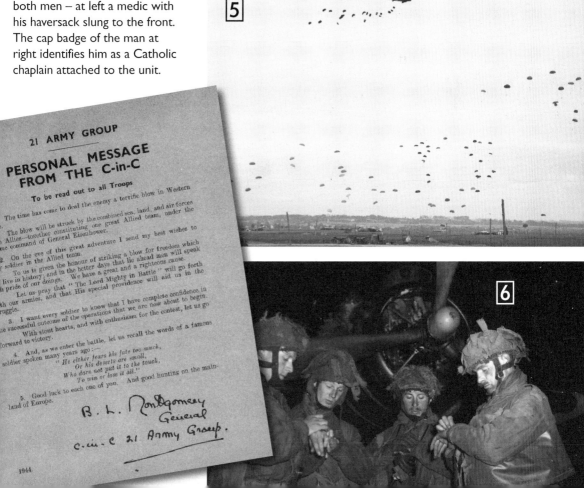

DZ–W

AUBIN
D'ARQUENAY

CANAL DE CAEN

LE
PORT

BENOUVILLE

Scale
0   100   200   300   400

Main photo: landing zones on either side of the River Orne.

Above: The Canal de Caen bridge at Bénouville – codenamed Ham – and three of the Operation Deadstick gliders.

The cemetery at Ranville, today run by the CWGC.

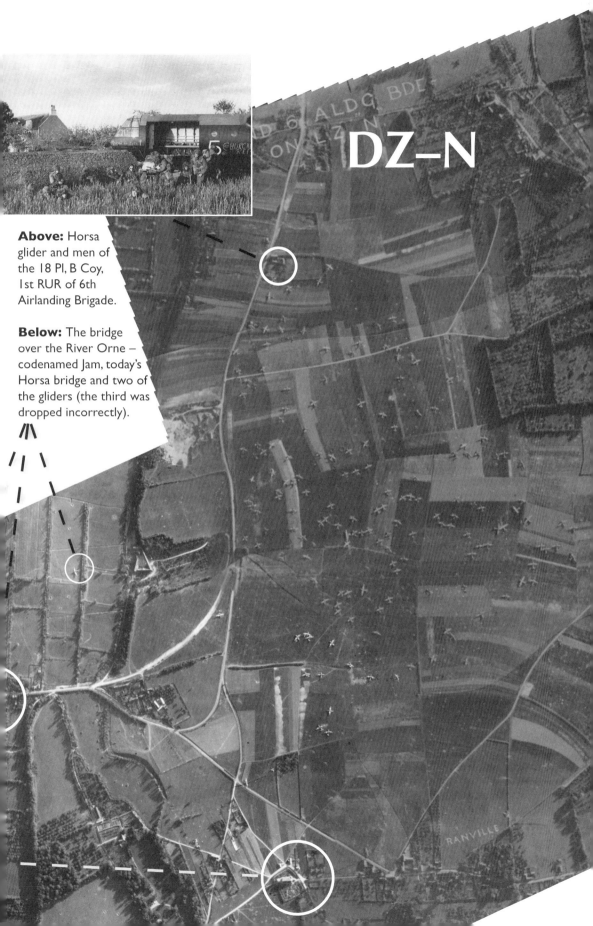

Above: Horsa glider and men of the 18 Pl, B Coy, 1st RUR of 6th Airlanding Brigade.

Below: The bridge over the River Orne – codenamed Jam, today's Horsa bridge and two of the gliders (the third was dropped incorrectly).

RANVILLE

from Sword Beach arrived in timely fashion and the glider landings of Operation Mallard in the evening of 6 June were the most accurate of all, the LZs having been partially cleared by the work of 591st (Antrim) Parachute Squadron, RE. In Mid-May the Germans moved 91st Airlanding Division to the area around St Saveur-le-Vicomte exactly where 82nd Airborne were due to land. As a result, the 82nd's drop zones were moved some 10 miles east. This meant that much of the preparatory work had to be reoriented in the week before the division moved to its airfields. The German unit was composed of two Grenadier regiments (1057th and 1058th), artillery, anti-tank, engineer, signals and AA units and had attached Panzer-Ersatz-und-Ausbildungs-Abteilung 100 with some French tanks. The troops were good but weren't of the highest standard save for the attached Fallschirmjäger Regiment 6 – the lions of Carentan, commanded by the impressively named Major Dr. Friedrich August Freiherr von der Heydte (1907–94). His name will come up a number of times in future sections.

The drop of the 82nd and 101st was haphazard but as John C. Warren pithly summed up: 'the low quality and morale of the enemy and the advance of Allied forces from UTAH Beach saved the day.' He went on to evaluate the drop: 'The troop carriers had undertaken to bring 13,348 paratroops to Normandy. Of these, about 90 were brought back for one reason or another and 18 were in a plane ditched before reaching the Continent. About 100 in ALBANY [see p72] and perhaps 30 or 40 in BOSTON were killed when the planes carrying them were shot down. The rest jumped. Of the jumpers over 10% landed on their drop zones, between 25 and 30% landed within a mile of their zone or pathfinder beacon, and between 15 and 20% were from 1 to 2 miles away. At least 55% of the pilots made drops within 2 miles of their goals. About 25%of the troops came down between 2 and 5 miles away from their zones or beacons.'

The spread of the drop was caused by four factors: clouds, enemy action, aircrew errors and the limitations of the navigational aids. However, the Americans were lucky. Warren: 'The whole history of war shows that a good fighting team can usually beat the best individual fighters, and the effective mopping up of several hundred outlying paratroops in Normandy by quite small German units bears this out. The 101st Division reported that it could not have held out in its scattered state for much more than 24 hours without support from the beaches, and it seems doubtful whether even the veteran 82d Division could have lasted 48 hours without such help.' But they did get help, and the bravery and aggression of the US airborne troops contributed to the success of the operation.

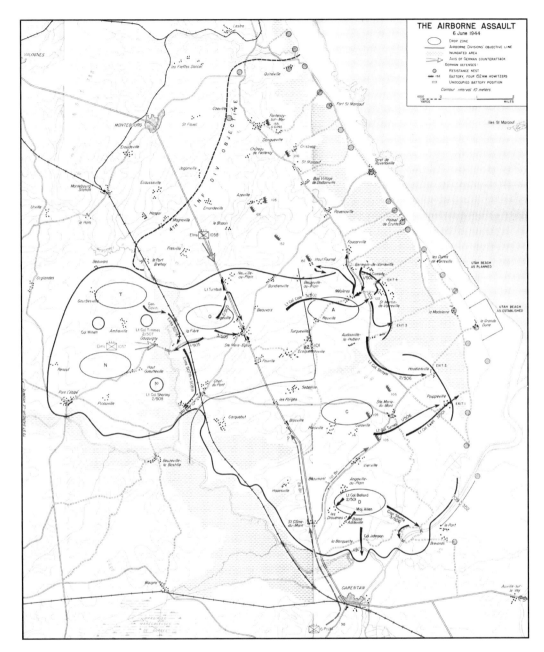

The plan saw the 82nd and 101st Airborne dropped to west and east respectively. The 82nd were to secure Ste-Mère-Église and the bridges over the Merderet river and stop reinforcements assisting the coastal defenders. The 101st was to secure the beach exits for the amphibious landing and, subsequently, take Carentan. In fact, the drop was so haphazard that the two divisions were intermingled and it took some time for order to be restored. Luckily, the defences of Utah Beach were less problematic than elsewhere and the airborne troops were able to confront the enemy alongside regular army units. The sketch (**Opposite**) is by Raymond Creekmore (1905–84).

Soldiers, Sailors and Airmen of the Allied Expeditionary Force!

You are about to embark upon the Great Crusade, toward which we have striven these many months. The eyes of the world are upon you. The hopes and prayers of liberty-loving people everywhere march with you. In company with our brave Allies and brothers-in-arms on other Fronts, you will bring about the destruction of the German war machine, the elimination of Nazi tyranny over the oppressed peoples of Europe, and security for ourselves in a free world.

Your task will not be an easy one. Your enemy is well trained, well equipped and battle-hardened. He will fight savagely.

But this is the year 1944! Much has happened since the Nazi triumphs of 1940-41. The United Nations have inflicted upon the Germans great defeats, in open battle, man-to-man. Our air offensive has seriously reduced their strength in the air and their capacity to wage war on the ground. Our Home Fronts have given us an overwhelming superiority in weapons and munitions of war, and placed at our disposal great reserves of trained fighting men. The tide has turned! The free men of the world are marching together to Victory!

I have full confidence in your courage, devotion to duty and skill in battle. We will accept nothing less than full Victory!

Good Luck! And let us all beseech the blessing of Almighty God upon this great and noble undertaking.

Dwight D. Eisenhower

Left and Below left: General Eisenhower, as supreme commander, issued an exhortation to all those involved in the D-Day landings. Here, copies of the letter are handed to members of the 508th PIR. Typical of the 82nd's regiments, on 5 June the 508th left for Normandy from Folkingham and Saltby airfields (USAAF Stations 484 and 538 respectively). Part of IX Troop Carrier Command's 52nd Troop Carrier Wing, the 313rd TCG carried 1st Bn and 3rd Bn from Folkingham; the 314th TCG took 2nd Bn and Regimental HQ from Saltby. Altogether 117 C-47s and C-53s carried just over 2,000 men as part of Mission Boston to DZ-N. Three aircraft were shot down and a number of men were hit by fire while in the aircraft and in the air. When they hit the ground, it wasn't always land. The Germans had flooded much of the hinterland and at least 36 of the 82nd drowned on arrival in France. The others – spread far and wide (one group landed some 9 miles short of Cherbourg) – were able to form up into four groups and begin to fight. They would continue doing so until leaving for England on 12–15 July. They lost 321 KIA, 660 WIA and 98 MIA.

Opposite, Above: Men of the 508th PIR, 82nd Airborne, check their gear on 5 June at RAF Saltby, a USAAF air station at the time. These men haven't clipped their reserve chutes to their harnesses yet.

Opposite, Below: Another attractive Creekmore drawing showing paratroopers and CG-4A gliders.

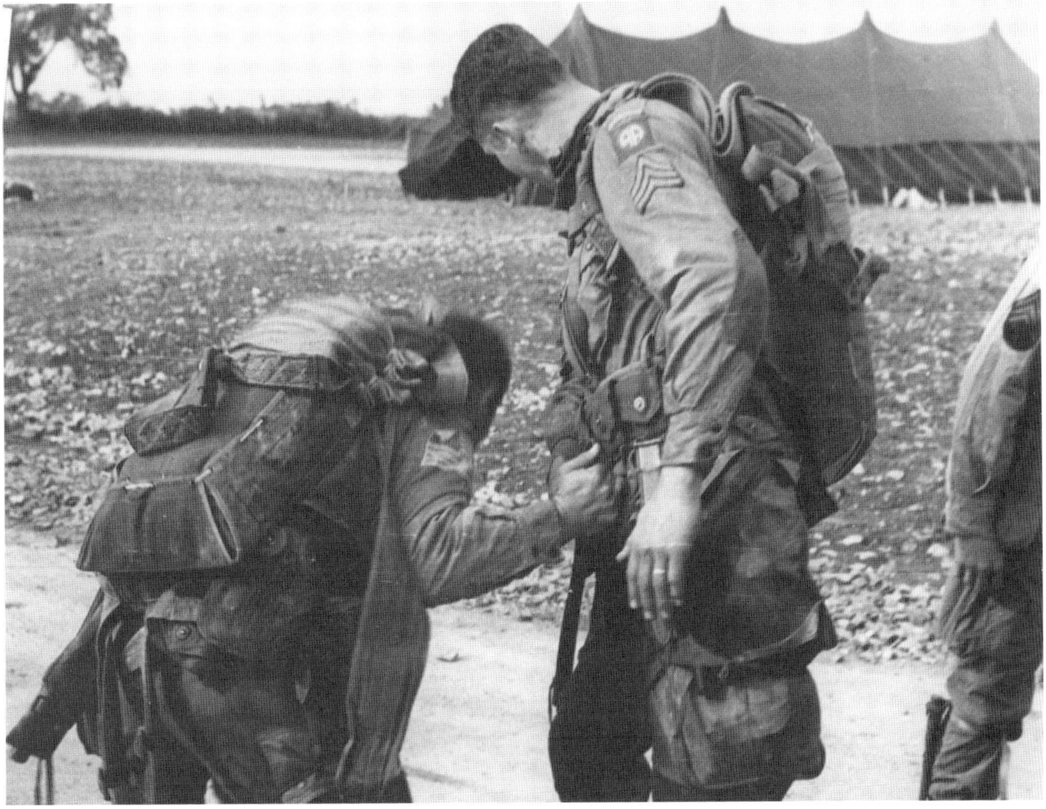

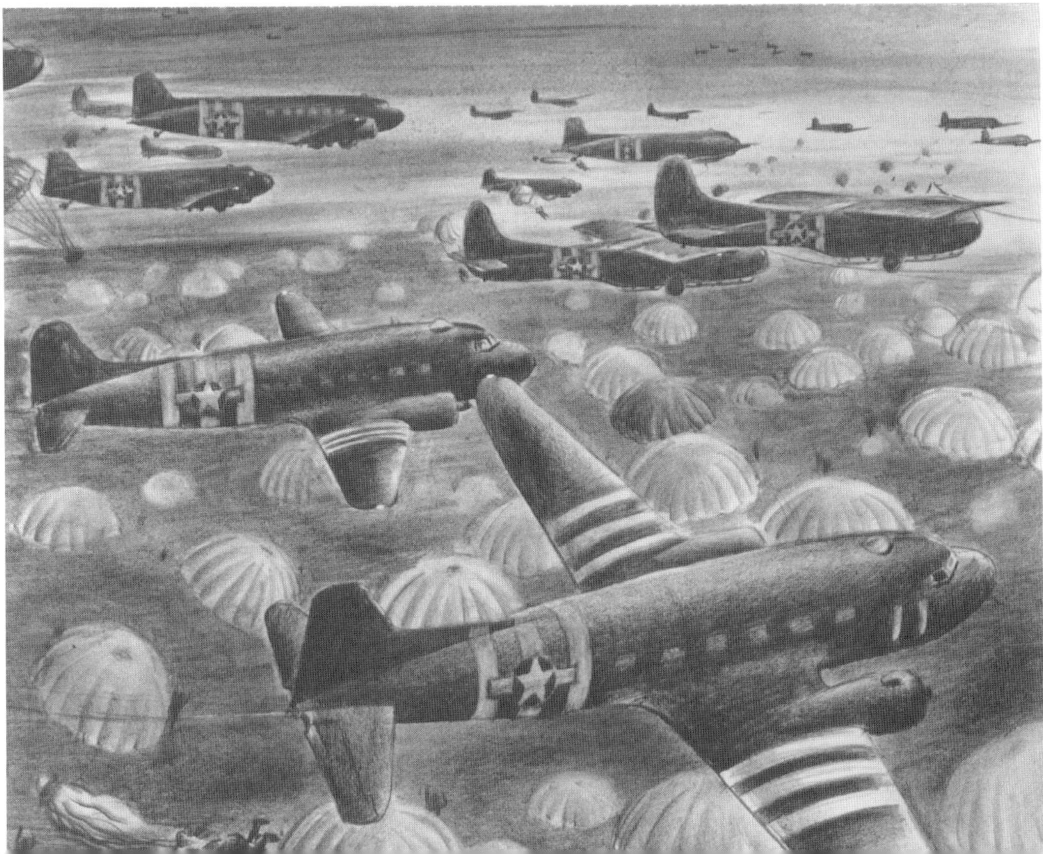

US TROOPING MISSIONS

Codename	Date	Div	A/C sent (lost)	Gliders	Troops	Casualties
Albany	D-Day	101st	436 (13)	-	6,750	A 48 K/MIA, 4 WIA
Boston	D-Day	82nd	377 (8)	-	6,350	A 17 K/MIA, 11 WIA
Chicago	D-Day	101st	51 (1)	52 W	103 landed	4 A, 14 GP, 27T
Detroit	D-Day	82nd	52 (1)	53 W	209 landed	4 A, 14 GP, 30T
Keokuk	D-Day	101st	32	32 H	157 landed	44T
Elmira	D-Day	82nd	175 (5)	36 W, 140 H	1,160 landed	1 A, 26 GP, 15 W, 142 H
Galveston	D+1	82nd	100	84 W, 24 H	927 landed	35 W, 80 H
Hackensack	D+1	82nd	101	70 W, 30 H	1,331 landed	3 GP, 16 W, 34 H

W = Waco, H = Horsa, A = aircrew, GP = glider pilots. Glider casualty numbers identified by glider type.

Above: 325th glidermen prepare to be lifted to Normandy by the 439th TCG from Upottery. They are about to board a Horsa that has been hastily painted with invasion bars and a USAAF star over the British roundel. Note the bazooka team at left, the Mae West lifejackets, M1 rifles and circular 82nd Division patches on their shoulders.

Opposite, Below left: Gliders above LZ-W south of Ste Mère-Église.

Opposite, Below right: Men of the 325th GIR wait to board their gliders. The T/5 nearest the camera is carrying bazooka rockets. He has removed his Mae West and carries it in a leg bag.

Below: The worst Horsa crash was near Holdy on DZ-C that resulted in 18 dead and 14 badly injured. Americans didn't like the Horsa – as John C. Warren put it 'American experience in Normandy indicated that the Waco was easier to fly, much easier to land, and very much more durable than the Horsa. Such a conclusion was not entirely warranted, since the unfamiliarity of their American pilots, the low release altitudes of the American missions, and the use of fields of minimum size for landings had combined to show the Horsas in an unfavourable light. In Normandy and in other operations later the British got good results with the big gliders.' The key points here are the height at which the gliders were released and the size of landing area: in the US drops the big Horsas were dropped too low and expected to land in small congested fields. This led to many accidents – and the American antipathy to the type. The skill of the pilots may also have had something to do with it. The US Army wanted quantity and was less worried about quality. Whereas only 1 in 25 trainees won RAF glider pilots wings, in the USA 18 locations taught glider pilots and many of the teachers were civilian contractors. Unlike the RAF pilots, the US pilots had no infantry skills' training with the result that they could only perform very basic duties after their flight was over – such as carry ammunition to the nearest battalion CP. On the down side, the British casualty figures among its glider pilots also reflected this belief.

PHYSICAL OBJECTIVES AND ACHIEVEMENTS – NEPTUNE[1]

Planned assault objective	Planned time allowed	Actual time required
101st Airborne Assist assault landing of 4th Inf Div by seizing the western margin of the inundated area back of Utah Beach between St. Martin-de-Varreville and Poupeville, both inclusive. (This included exits to the four causeways and a gun battery and garrison at St. Martin-de-Varreville which dominated exits 3 and 4.)	About 5 hrs. total	Exit 1 – 7 hrs Exit 2 – 13 hrs. Exit 3 & 4 – 6 hrs 20 min. Battery and garrison – 16 hrs 50 min
Seize crossings of the Jourdan and Groult rivers and of the Canal du Port de Carentan for exploitation in a southward drive to Carentan.	During D-Day (22 hrs 30 min)	Bridges – 5hrs 30min La Barquette Lock – 5 hrs 30 min Bridges at 3886 [map ref] – D+2
Seize Carentan as soon as tactical situation permits and establish firm contact between VII and V Corps beachheads.	Probably not later than D+3.	Carentan taken D+7 (Attack began D+3)
82nd Airborne Seize, clear and secure general area and establish regimental defense line through Neuville-au-Plain and Bandienville.	D-Day	4 days (Parts of this area were secured from D-Day onward and the enemy was not in full control of most of it.)
Capture Ste-Mère-Église	D-Day	7 hrs
Seize and secure crossings of the Merderet River (near la Fière and Chef-du-Pont) and a bridgehead covering them.	D-Day	4 days (La Fière bridge taken in 11 hrs 15 min but lost within one hr.)
Seize and destroy crossings of Douve River D-Day at Beuzeville-la-Bastille and Étienville (also sometimes called Pont l'Abbé).	D-Day	4 days
Protect NW flank of VII Corps within Div. Zone	D-Day onward	Neuville au Plain – 1 hr 45 min; Ste-Mère-Église – 7 hrs.
Be prepared to advance west to the line of the Douve River north of its junction with Prairies Marecageuses.	On corps order	In time required.

[1] Edited excerpts from WSEG Staff Study No. 3 *Historical Study of Some World War II Airborne Operations*

Objectives dealt with at planned time?	Objective held at time of link-up[2]	Planned assault objective
None	All	Although none of these were seized in the planned time, exits 1 and 3 were taken soon enough to assist the landings in the expected manner. Exit 4, the battery dominating this and exit 3 and the western end of exit 2 were also either under attack or dominated in time to be of assistance to the landings. A northern defense arc through Foucarville was firmly held.
2 of 2	2 of 2	This group of objectives was precariously held, the bridgeheads had been abandoned on D-Day.
1 of 1	1 of 1	Held precariously by small force on D-Day short of ammunition.
No	No	
No	No	Enemy was strong and mobile in this sector until end of battle on D+7.
No	Yes	
Yes	Yes	Enemy forces were stopped here from interfering with Allied activities.
No	Yes	Failure to secure these objectives prevented the 4th Inf Div from achieving its D-Day objectives and also delayed the amphibious forces reaching high ground for the planned northward advance in this region.
No	No	No enemy reinforcements penetrated the 82nd Div zone to influence the landings.
In part	Yes	Although this defense arc was not fully established, no enemy reinforcements ever penetrated toward the beaches.
Yes	Yes	[2] Link-up refers to the link up of airborne forces with their own sea tails containing heavy attachments and equipment. From this point onward the airborne units are considered to be fighting a standard ground engagement. This point was reached on D+2 for the 101st and on D+3 for the 82nd.

US airborne troops used both CG-4As (L and C) and Horsas on 6 June.

FORCES BROUGHT TO COTENTIN PENINSULA ON D-DAY

101st AIRBORNE

Unit	Paras	Gliders	Men landed
Div HQ & HQ Co	7	8	106
Div Arty HQ	3	3	33
Div Sig Co	2	14	70
Div Recon Pl		15	34
326th AB Med Co		6	54
326th AB Engr Bn	16		252
377th PFA Bn	12		78
501st PIR	129	8	1,967
502nd PIR	135	8	2,101
506th PIR	132	8	2,190
Totals	436	70	6,885

82nd AIRBORNE

Unit	Paras	Gliders	Men landed
Div HQ & HQ Co	7	12	155
Div Arty HQ	3	3	33
Div Sig Co	2	14	70
Div Recon Pl		15	34
80th ATk Bn (Bty A)		22	79
307th AB Engr Bn	27		388
376th PFA Bn	48		564
504th PIR	137		2,016
505th PIR	126		2,151
508th PIR	130		1,922
325th GIR	2		40
Totals	482	50	7,477

CASUALTIES

101st AIRBORNE AREA

Day	101st Division Jump/Landing	Battle	Enemy casualties	PoW
D-Day	188	35[1]	197	133
D+1	–	91	337	755
D+2[2]	–	2	73	–
D+3[3]	–	–	–	–
AB phase	188	128	607	868
Totals	316[1]		1,475	
	981[4]			
Link up	3,520[5]			
Grand total	3,836[5]			

82nd AIRBORNE AREA

Day	82nd Division Jump/Landing	Battle	Enemy casualties	PoW
D-Day	313	140	122	40
D+1	342	73	76	739
D+2[2]	–	70	41	469
D+3[3]		75	7	101
AB phase	655	358	246	1,349
Totals	1,013		1,595	
	1,853[4]			
Link up	1,990[6]			
Grand total	3,003[6]			

[1] Does not include 1,500 estimated at the time to have been captured as a result of scattered drop; many returned to unit after A/B phase.
[2] 101st A/B phase ended this day.
[3] 82nd A/B phase ended this day.
[4] Includes missing and captured, probably in the A/B phase.
[5] Includes 665 missing or captured, probably in A/B phase.
[6] Includes 840 missing or captured, probably in A/B phase.

Men of 3/506th PIR walk out to the aircraft on 5 June 1944. They are carrying their rifles in carrying cases. The C-47 is lead ship of 440th TCG, 98th Squadron.

1 Publicity shot of a 101st Airborne paratrooper in the doorway of a C-47. Note his reserve chute (**A**) – he would have had to unclip this before he could inflate his Mae West (**B**). He wouldn't have jumped with his Thompson SMG unslung.

2 Poignant photo of Lt-Col Bob Wolverton, OC 3/506th PIR, helping 1/Lt. Alex Bobuck at Exeter airfield, June 1944. Wolverton was killed shortly after landing on the 6th. Note the 506th's spade symbol on both men's helmets (**C**); general-purpose ammo bag (**D**); the black rubber bag containing the gas mask (**E**); and the M3 knife with leather M6 scabbard (**F**).

3 Pvt Joseph Ross (left) of D/2/502nd PIR at Greenham Common helping a buddy into his T5 parachute harness. They would drop into Normandy at 00:48 on the 6th. Note the gas brassard (**G**) which wasn't universally worn; water bottle (**H**); USAAF type ammo pouch (**I**) stuffed with rifle clips (his buddy's holds hand grenades); M1936 musette bag (**J**); and his buddy's goggles (**K**).

4 Two more from 101st: note the M43 entrenching tool (**L**); coil of rope (**M**); M1A1 paratrooper's carbine in carrying case (**N**). The folding stock reduced its length to around 26in; raincoat (**O**) stuffed into top of musette bag which hangs in its usual place under where reserve chute will be attached.

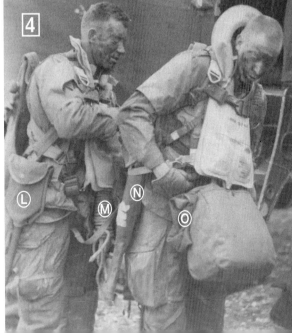

Left: Men of the 506th PIR board their C-47. Note the roughly painted invasion stripes—an attempt at IFF to reduce the number of friendly fire incidents. Certainly, unlike Sicily, the Normandy drop isn't remembered for this. They are being helped into the aircraft because they are weighed down by more kit and clobber than any soldier can carry on the battlefield—the main and reserve parachutes contributing to the bulk.

Below left: One of the hideous consequences of the overloading can be seen here. This 82nd Airborne paratrooper has drowned on arrival. The Germans had flooded the low-lying areas and allowed rivers and canals to break their banks. Their kit, their ammunition and weapons, the weight of water taken up by their clothing, the cumbersome bulk of parachutes and harness—even the carton of cigarettes or field rations shoved into a tunic at the last moment: all contributed. The number of paratroopers on western and eastern flanks of the invasion who died like this was significant but nowhere near the disaster of Operation Ladbroke.

Opposite, Above: Classic image of bazookaman Bob Noody of F/506th PIR, weighed down with his bazooka, a leg bag and – he estimated aged 90 in 2014 – 300lb of equipment. He was, he remembered, 'scared stiff'.

Opposite, Centre: Another photograph of the same unit (note Noody's bazooka at right), their faces camouflaged.

Opposite, Below: The 101st took Carentan on 12 June but had to withstand a major counterattack—which it did with the help of 2nd Armored. Here, a scene southwest of the town. The antitank gun is a British 6pdr and the StuG IV belonged to 1./SS-Pz-Abt 17.

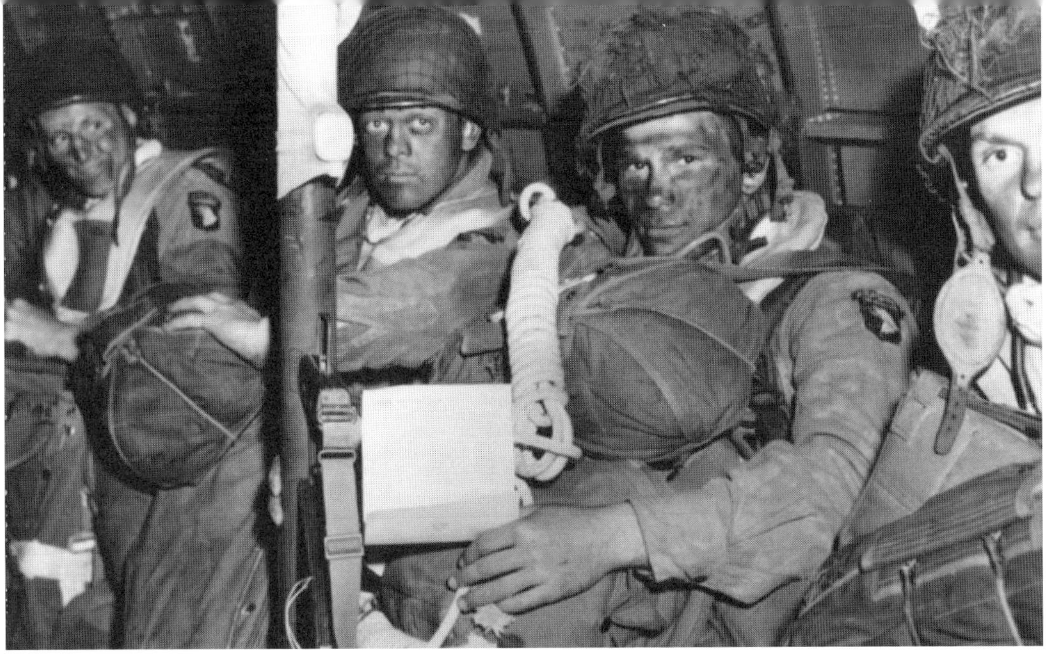

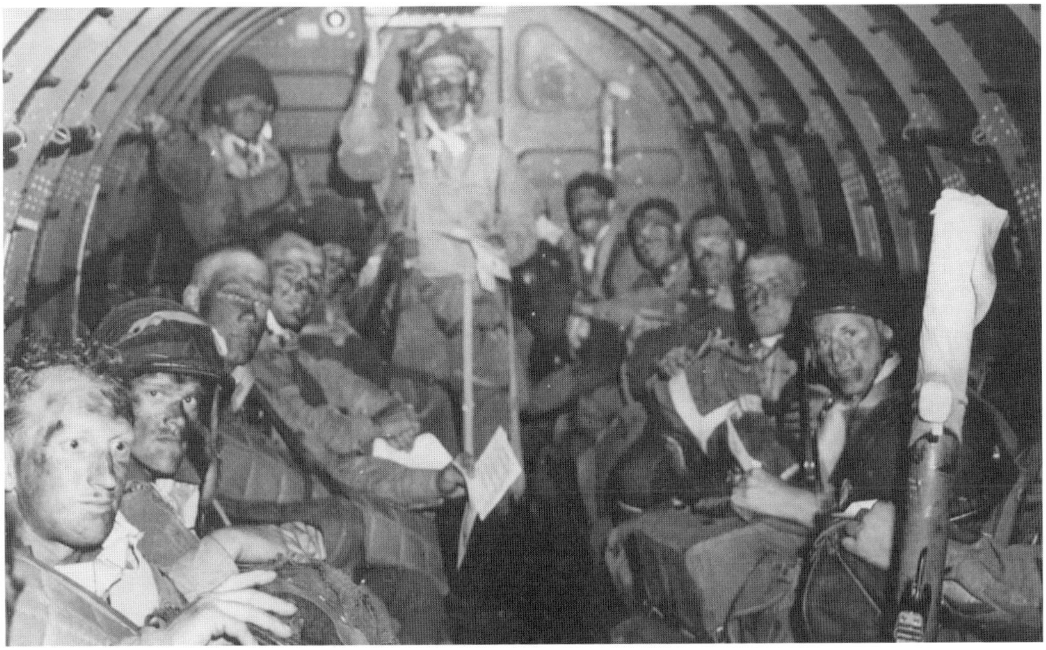

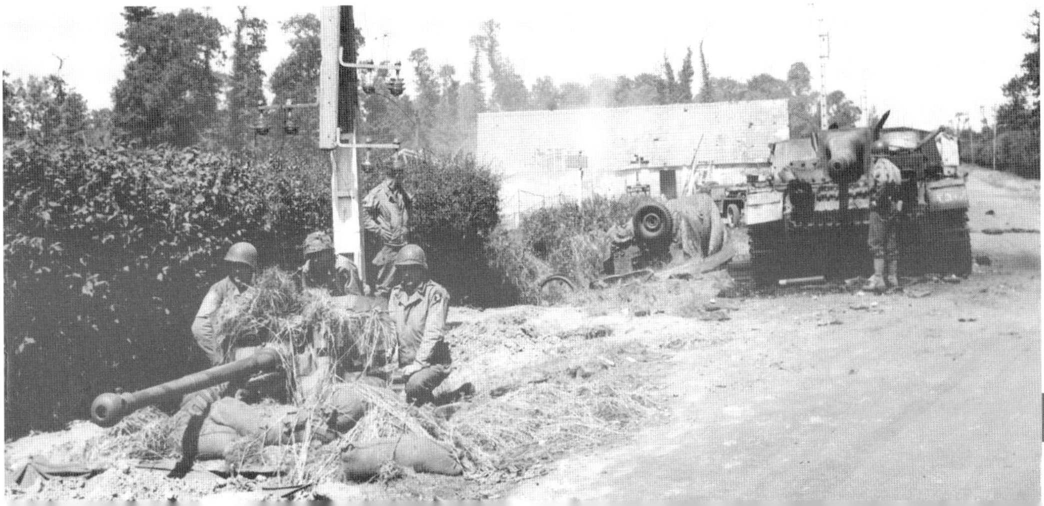

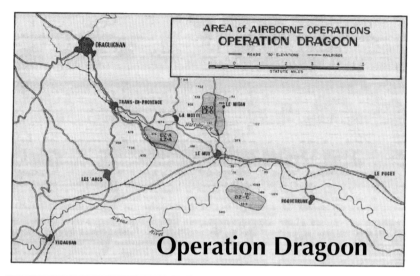

Operation Dragoon

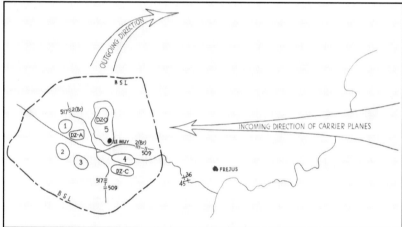

Left and Below left: After Normandy, the next major Allied airborne operation was on 15 August 1944 as part of Operation Dragoon. The plan involved dropping the 509th Battalion Combat Team on DZ-C, after which it would take area 4; the 517th RCT on DZ-A, after which it would take areas 1, 2, 3; and British 4th, 5th and 6th Para Bns on DZ-O to take area 5 and Le Muy. The latter would be supported by a glider drop with heavy weapons and the Task Force HQ. Later that day, around 18:00, additional troops would arrive: 1/551st PIR, 550th GIB, plus additional artillery etc.

Left: The Pathfinder para drops were hit by fog so the beacons weren't lit and the drop was confused. Nevertheless, helped by the FFI, all the missions were completed by D+1.

Above: On 14 August men of 1st Platoon, A/517th PIR at Canino airfield in Italy prepare for the flight to southern France. It jumped over DZ-A at 04:32 on the 15th.

Below: Men of the 517th RCT before the invasion. Having seen action at Anzio in June 1944, they were pulled out for Operation Dragoon—at that time called Operation Anvil, joining the First Airborne Task Force, led by Gen Robert T. Frederick, with 60th PFAB, 596th AEC, the Anti-tank Company of the 442nd RCT and D/83rd Chemical Mortar Bn under command. As in Normandy, the para drop was inaccurate: less than 20% of the 17th RCT landed within two miles of their intended objective. It didn't matter. By D+3 the opposition had been overcome. The 17th's casualties amounted to 19 killed, 126 wounded and 137 injured.

LA MOTTE

6 PARA BN RV.

(A)

(B)

2 PARA BDE GP. I

CLASTRON.

(C)

(D)

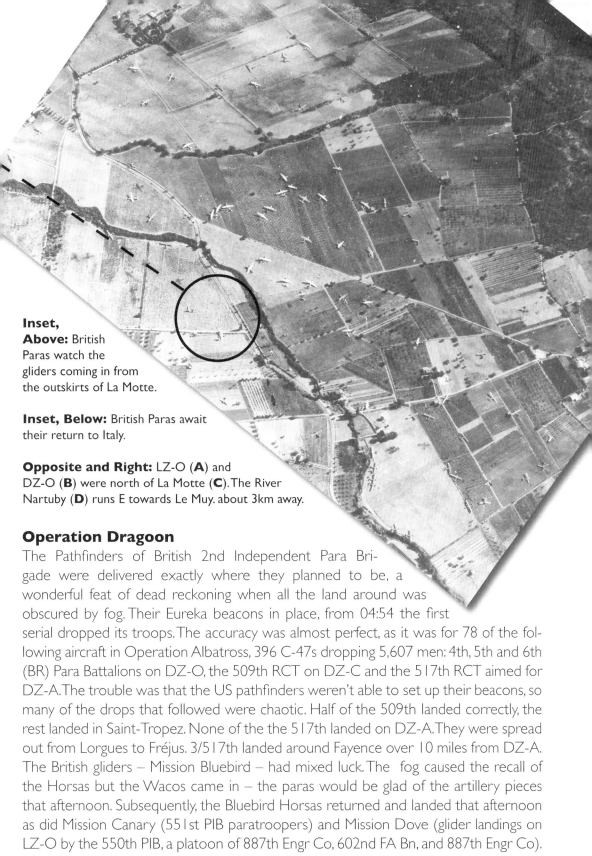

Inset, Above: British Paras watch the gliders coming in from the outskirts of La Motte.

Inset, Below: British Paras await their return to Italy.

Opposite and Right: LZ-O (**A**) and DZ-O (**B**) were north of La Motte (**C**). The River Nartuby (**D**) runs E towards Le Muy. about 3km away.

Operation Dragoon

The Pathfinders of British 2nd Independent Para Brigade were delivered exactly where they planned to be, a wonderful feat of dead reckoning when all the land around was obscured by fog. Their Eureka beacons in place, from 04:54 the first serial dropped its troops. The accuracy was almost perfect, as it was for 78 of the following aircraft in Operation Albatross, 396 C-47s dropping 5,607 men: 4th, 5th and 6th (BR) Para Battalions on DZ-O, the 509th RCT on DZ-C and the 517th RCT aimed for DZ-A. The trouble was that the US pathfinders weren't able to set up their beacons, so many of the drops that followed were chaotic. Half of the 509th landed correctly, the rest landed in Saint-Tropez. None of the the 517th landed on DZ-A. They were spread out from Lorgues to Fréjus. 3/517th landed around Fayence over 10 miles from DZ-A. The British gliders – Mission Bluebird – had mixed luck. The fog caused the recall of the Horsas but the Wacos came in – the paras would be glad of the artillery pieces that afternoon. Subsequently, the Bluebird Horsas returned and landed that afternoon as did Mission Canary (551st PIB paratroopers) and Mission Dove (glider landings on LZ-O by the 550th PIB, a platoon of 887th Engr Co, 602nd FA Bn, and 887th Engr Co).

The confusion left 17 dead and 158 wounded. Nevertheless, once on the ground the paras showed what good troops they were. By evening the British brigade had accomplished all its missions save the taking of Le Muy – due to be assaulted by 5th (Scottish) Battalion which had landed miles away. It fell to an American attack the next day. On D+1 the British forces pushed north and east of Le Muy. They were relieved on the morning of the 18th by US 36th Infantry Division, who had fought up from the coast, and sailed for Naples on 28 August. The brigade was put on alert for Operation Manna in Greece.

Meanwhile, the American units – aided by the FFI and the fact that 11. Panzer Division was west of the Rhône – did what they had done in Normandy: create confusion and fight anyone who made the mistake of showing their head. Their success led to their next mission: the Task Force and First Special Service Force were to liberate the Riviera (accomplished by 7 September).

Top: The landings at the north end of LZ-O on 15 August.

Above left: Battle-weary men of B/509th PIB on the D47 north of Le Muy.

Above: Around 10,000 men from the 1st Allied Airborne Task Force were delivered to France. Some 450 were killed, and 300 were wounded. This is the aid station at La Motte.

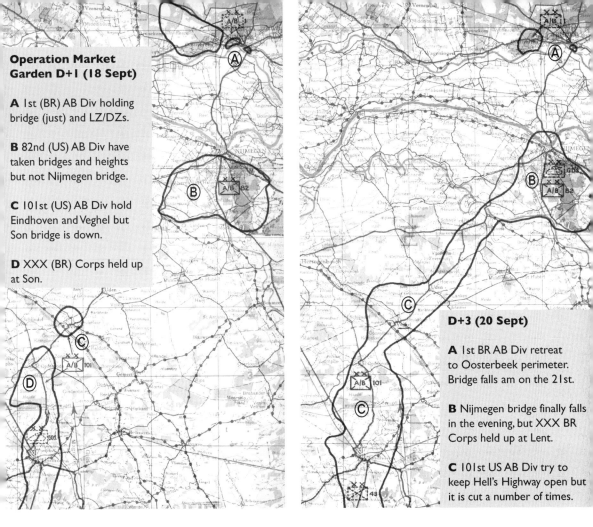

Operation Market Garden D+1 (18 Sept)

A 1st (BR) AB Div holding bridge (just) and LZ/DZs.

B 82nd (US) AB Div have taken bridges and heights but not Nijmegen bridge.

C 101st (US) AB Div hold Eindhoven and Veghel but Son bridge is down.

D XXX (BR) Corps held up at Son.

D+3 (20 Sept)

A 1st BR AB Div retreat to Oosterbeek perimeter. Bridge falls am on the 21st.

B Nijmegen bridge finally falls in the evening, but XXX BR Corps held up at Lent.

C 101st US AB Div try to keep Hell's Highway open but it is cut a number of times.

Operation Market Garden

The operation offered the Allies a chance to use top troops – the First Allied Airborne Army – to help bounce the Rhine, bypass the Westwall and strike into north Germany. Over-optimistic after the huge victory in Normandy, the plan didn't consider carefully enough the thickening defence assisted by the retreat of Fifteenth Army over the Scheldt, the ease of reinforcement by rail) and the number of enemy troops in the area. The bravery of the paras could not overcome the tactical nous of the German veterans.

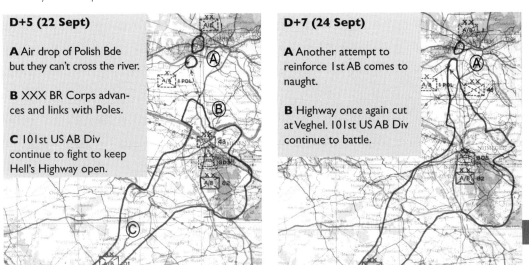

D+5 (22 Sept)

A Air drop of Polish Bde but they can't cross the river.

B XXX BR Corps advances and links with Poles.

C 101st US AB Div continue to fight to keep Hell's Highway open.

D+7 (24 Sept)

A Another attempt to reinforce 1st AB comes to naught.

B Highway once again cut at Veghel. 101st US AB Div continue to battle.

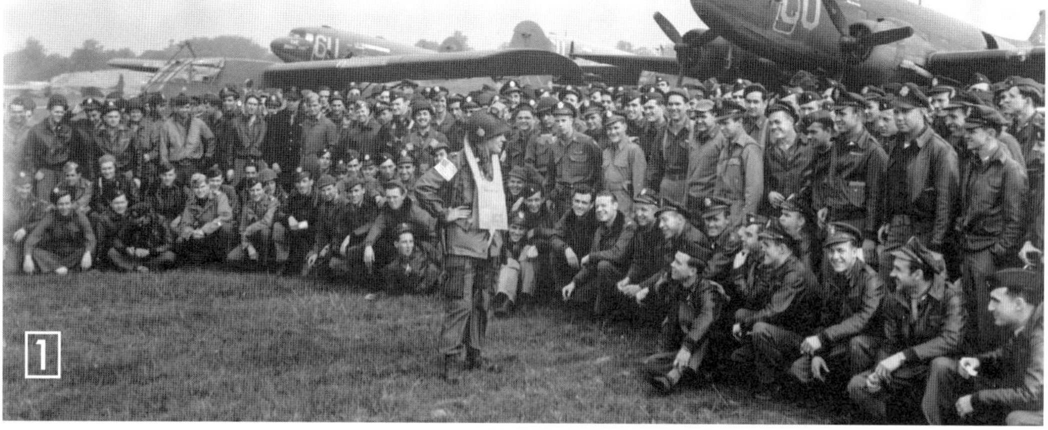
1
6U

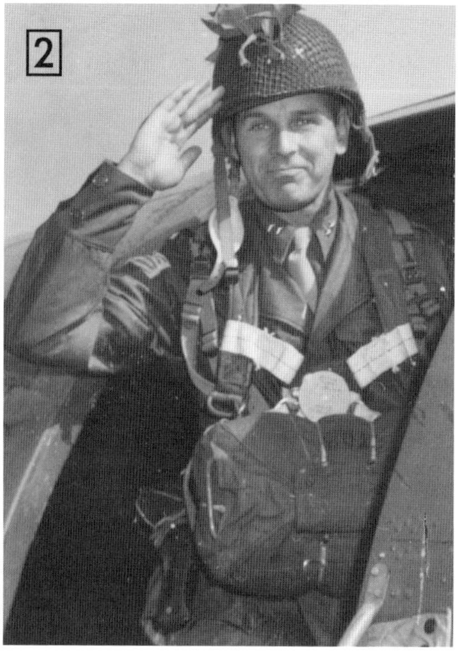
2

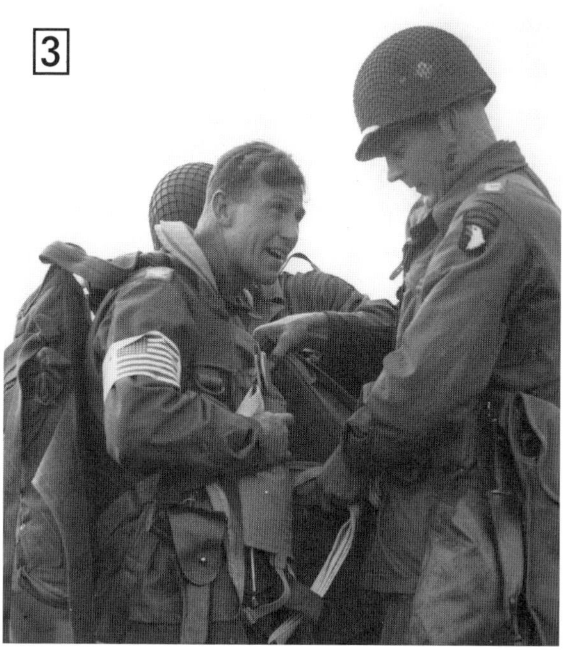
3

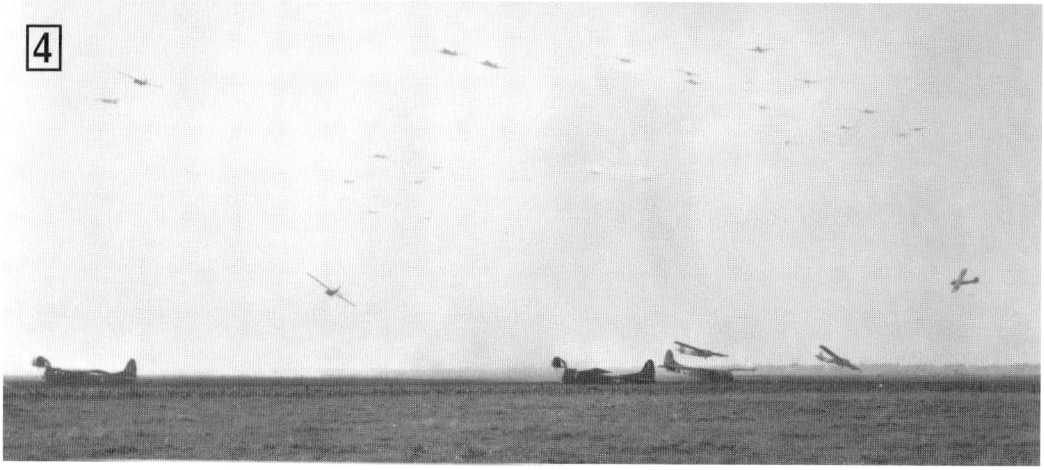
4

The 101st Airborne's para drop on D-Day was by 53rd Wing landing on DZ-A/B and – as here – 506th PIR on DZ-C. *US Army Signal Corps via Peter Hendrikx*

Operation Market – the XXX Corps advance was Operation Garden – saw the largest number of airborne troops in action in the war, some 34,600, of which 20,000 were paratroopers. Gliders delivered around 14,600 men along with 1,736 vehicles and 263 artillery pieces.

Continued on p93.

1 Gen McAuliffe of the 101st Airborne gives the second-wave crews and pilots a motivational speech. Commander of the divisional artillery, McAuliffe became assistant division commander when Don Pratt died on 6 June 1944. The 101st were tasked with capturing bridges at Son and Veghel and taking Eindhoven. Thereafter, they would fight to keep the corridor open for XXX Corps.

2 Gen Maxwell Taylor, the 101st AB Division's CO, flew from Welford with 1/502nd PIR. Taylor decided to drop without his artillery, reasoning that this would be soon provided by XXX Corps. He was correct in that assumption and having extra infantry on the ground helped in the defence of his section of Hell's Highway. The anti-tank artillery arrived on 19 September just in time to see off the 107. Panzer Brigade's attack on Son.

3 Col. Howard R. Johnson, CO of the 501st PIR, is helped by his adjutant, Capt Elvy Roberts, at RAF Ramsbury. The 501st PIR jumped over DZ-A near Veghel.

4 The 101st Airborne's glider drop – these are CG-4As – on D+1 by 50th and 53rd Wings saw most successfully arriving at LZ-W. The drops were significantly better than those on 6 June.

5 Troops of 3/506th PIR, 101st Airborne move off the LZ. The jeep was brought in by glider – supplying mobility was an important role of the gliders.

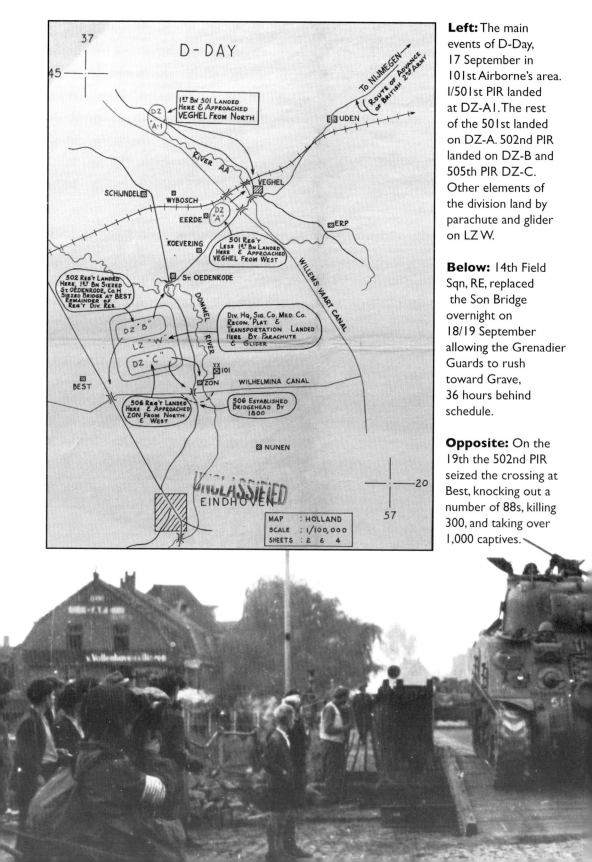

Left: The main events of D-Day, 17 September in 101st Airborne's area. I/501st PIR landed at DZ-A1. The rest of the 501st landed on DZ-A. 502nd PIR landed on DZ-B and 505th PIR DZ-C. Other elements of the division land by parachute and glider on LZ W.

Below: 14th Field Sqn, RE, replaced the Son Bridge overnight on 18/19 September allowing the Grenadier Guards to rush toward Grave, 36 hours behind schedule.

Opposite: On the 19th the 502nd PIR seized the crossing at Best, knocking out a number of 88s, killing 300, and taking over 1,000 captives.

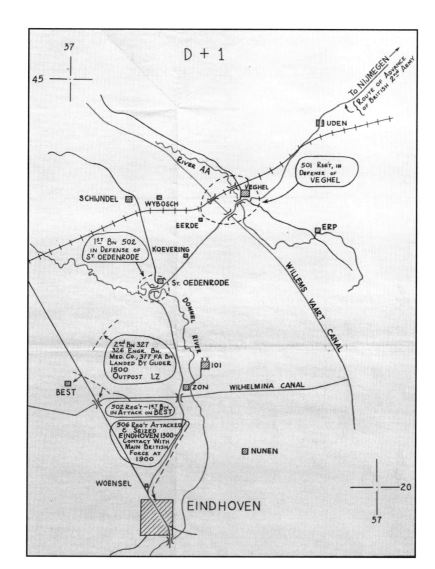

D + 1

To NIJMEGEN →
(ROUTE OF ADVANCE
of BRITISH 2nd ARMY

UDEN

RIVER AA

501 REG'T, IN
DEFENSE OF
VEGHEL

SCHIJNDEL   WYBOSCH   VEGHEL

EERDE   ERP

1st BN 502
IN DEFENSE OF
ST. OEDENRODE   KOEVERING

WILLEMS VAART CANAL

ST. OEDENRODE

DOMMEL RIVER

2nd BN 327
326 ENGR. BN.
MED. CO., 377 FA BN.
LANDED BY GLIDER
1500
OUTPOST LZ

XX
101

BEST   ZON   WILHELMINA CANAL

502 REG'T—1st BN
IN ATTACK ON BEST

506 REG'T ATTACKED
& SEIZED
EINDHOVEN 1300—
CONTACT WITH
MAIN BRITISH
FORCE AT
1900   NUNEN

WOENSEL

EINDHOVEN

Left: The US divisions suffered few casualties in the delivery stage but the fighting was fierce. This photo shows one of the landing crashes, the result of two gliders colliding in midair above their LZ. Men of 506th PIR rushed to help.

Centre left: It looks bad but is probably just taken mid-roll. Nevertheless, many paratroopers sustained leg injuries during a drop.

Below left: The Germans fought with a tenacity that can be attributed to training, propaganda and education, honour and duty, the summary justice meted out to those who would not fight, and not wanting to let their mates down.

Below: Landing gliders was always more akin to crashing than anything else – particularly into soft ground when they easily flipped. On 17 September, the first day of Operation Market, 120 CG-4A, 13 Hamilcar and 345 Horsa II gliders landed.

MARKET GARDEN CASUALTIES

The casualties in the Netherlands during the period 17–25 September were not limited to the military participants: the civilians suffered, too. It's difficult to be precise because the events of September – specifically the Dutch railway strike – lead to German reprisals that caused the awful Hunger Winter of 1944–45 when upward of 20,000 civilians died. The usual figure given for Dutch civilian casualties in the operation is 453.

The American casualties (as given in a 1950s report) are shown below. More recent figures give 1,432 (82nd) and 2,118 (101st). The British lost over 13,000 all told – many of them made PoW: 1st Airborne lost 1,446 dead (including 229 glider pilots) and 6,414 WIA/MIA/PoW; the Poles lost 97 dead and 111 WIA/MIA; XXX Corps lost 1,480; VIII and XII Corps 3,847; aircrew deaths were 474.

The German losses have always been conjectural: the official figure of 3,300 was given for the Arnhem area (including 1,300 dead). Realistically, the total figure is 7,500–10,000 higher when the whole of the corridor is included.

US CASUALTY DATA

Day	82nd area			101st area		
	Jump/Landing	Battle[1]	Enemy[1]	Jump/Landing	Battle[1]	Enemy[1]
D-Day	124	165	1,079	114	95	24
D+1	–	279	336	26	162	13
D+2	–	206	342	70	232	615
D+3[2]	–	420	1,006	–	10	110
D+4	–	–	–	–	16	8
D+5[3]	–	–	–	–	68	250
AB phase	124	1,070	2,763	210	583	1,020
Totals	1,194		2,763	793		1,020
Link up to relief	1,848		2,704	2,107		–
Grand total	3,042[4]		5,467	3,301[5]		–

[1] All causes including missing and captured.
[2] 101st A/B phase ended this day.
[3] 82nd A/B phase ended this day.

[4] Includes all causes, 640 missing and captured.
[5] Includes all causes, 398 missing and captured.
Source: *WSEG Staff Study No. 3*

Medical Detachments

Casualties are a fact of war, and jumping out of aircraft behind enemy lines, often in the dark or difficult conditions, means on the spot medical facilities are vital. Every country ensured its paratroopers had adequate medical men trained as paratroops, the American *FM31–30* outlines: 'a. The battalion medical section of a parachute battalion is composed of two medical officers, two noncommissioned officers, eleven company aid men, and two litter bearers. Each member of the medical section is a qualified parachutist.
b. The regimental medical detachment of a parachute regiment is composed of three battalion medical sections, plus a headquarters section which includes the regimental surgeon, a dental officer, an additional medical officer, and sufficient enlisted personnel to handle administration of the detachment and the medical needs of regimental HQ and HQ and service companies. ...[The] equipment taken into combat is limited to that which can be dropped by delivery units and carried by the men after [the detachment] reaches the ground.

'Two delivery units, type A-5, carry the medical equipment used in combat. These two containers are packed identically. Each contains two aviation kit bags to hold the contents after the container lands, blankets, canteen containing alcohol, small operating case, flashlight, splints, bandages, first-aid dressings, cotton, iodine, a box containing miscellaneous drugs and ampules, and a folding litter.

'All medical personnel jump with their individual kits attached. As the two pouch kits are too bulky and awkward to handle as issued they should be mounted as follows: remove the false bottom of one pouch and extend the pouch; pack the contents of the two pouches with the exception of the book of emergency tags in this one pouch; carry the pouch on the left side suspended by a web strap, such as a litter strap, passing over the right shoulder. Attach a thong similar to that on the pistol holster to the bottom. and tie it around the left leg to hold the pouch in place. The book of emergency tags is carried in a pocket of the jump suit.'

Above: Photographed from a B-17 set aside for the Press, this is 1/504th PIR from Cottesmore flying over the Netherlands and Overflakkee island toward DZ-O. Coy B captured Heumen Bridge which proved to be XXX Corps' key to Nijmegen. Note the flooding below. The Germans made use of every possible tactic to delay the Allies during the Dutch and Rhineland campaigns.

Left and Below left: Men of 82nd Airborne's Div HQ climb aboard and take their seats. Note the SCR-536 'handie-talkie'at **A** (see p211).

Opposite, Left: A last-minute briefing from a cloth map. Note 82nd Airborne cloth badge on the officer's left shoulder, and the mass of personal equipment.

Opposite, Right: Gavin puts on his main parachute. Note Jumpin' Jim's trademark M1 Garand rifle. He made four combat jumps—Sicily, Italy (Salerno), Normandy, and the Netherlands—and was a tough and aggressive divisional commander.

It's easy to be wise after the event, but hindsight has shown that the plan was flawed. While the presence near Arnhem of two Panzer divisions is often cited, neither was near full strength (Hohenstaufen had 2,500 men and no tanks; Frundsberg had less than 3,000 men). In fact, the defence was made up of ad hoc units, who were well handled by disciplined and trained officers. The crux of the defence was that the Germans were able to flood the area with reinforcements. Two key armoured units – Panzer Brigade 107 and Sturmgeschütz Brigade 280 – were heading for Aachen by train but rerouted to the defence; and 14 King Tigers of sPzAbt506 also arrived by train on the 24th, the rest continuing to Aachen.

Another major problem was the tail wagging the dog. Brereton, commander of the First Allied Airborne Army, thought the airborne operation 'an outstanding success' which rather missed the point. Being overcautious at the start – only allowing single-tows of gliders and one lift a day because of September's reduced daylight – meant that the bad weather that came in on D+1 caught the airborne troops on the ground in Arnhem seriously short of men. The decisive factor was that it took four days to deliver the three divisions who also had to set aside troops to protect the LZs and DZs over this period. Polish airborne commander, Maj-Gen S. Sosabowski, said pithily, 'an airborne operation is not a purchase in instalments.' Additionally, there would be no tactical air missions while other air operations were taking place. One wonders what difference air support would have made to 1st Airborne as it slogged its way towards the bridge.

The final nail in the coffin was the fact that XXX Corps' attack down a single highway was easily disrupted. In spite of the best efforts of the 82nd and 101st Airborne, 'Hell's Highway' was cut a number of times; the bridge at Son was blown and had to be rebuilt; that at Nijmegen wasn't captured until D+3, by which time it was already too late for the brave men holding the 'bridge too far'.

Continued on p99.

Above: The 82nd had a difficult set of tasks for Operation Market. First, it had to secure the bridge at Grave (**Below**, seen later guarded by the Prinses Irene Brigade), then ensure that it opened the way to Nijmegen for XXX Corps—the Heumen bridge over the Mass-Waal canal proved the key. The division took and held the bridge there while, all the while, holding back serious German attacks from the Reichswald. The Groesbeek Heights, where the division's glider troops arrived, was the main battleground. The division was hard-pressed for a number of days and it was only after XXX Corps had helped fight through the city that Nijmegen bridge was taken. But that could not happen without a spectacular act of bravery as the 504th PIR assaulted across the Waal in flimsy storm boats.

Above: Nijmegen bridge fell too late to save the British paras at Arnhem. Even if XXX Corps' tanks had advanced on the evening of the 20th, it is unlikely that the outcome would have been different.

Below: The seizure of the city – the 88mm at **A** was a big obstacle – allowed the taking of the bridges and the crossing of the Waal, 19–20 September.

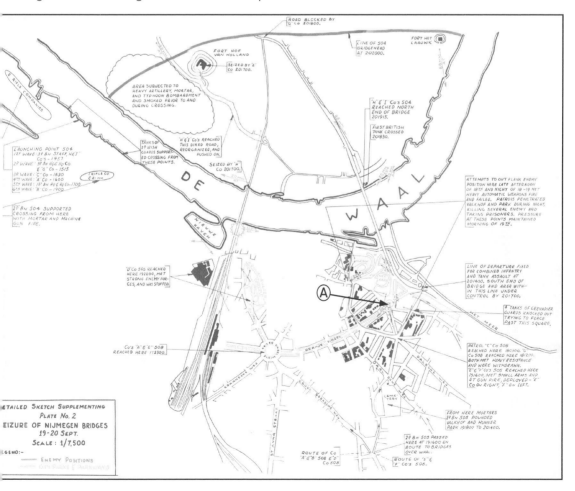

PHYSICAL OBJECTIVES AND ACHIEVEMENTS – MARKET[1]

Planned assault objective	Planned time allowed	Actual time required
101st Airborne		
Seize city of Eindhoven	6–8 hrs	8 hrs 05 min
Seize bridge over Wilhelmina Canal near Son	D-Day	Bridge blown. Area taken 1 hr 05 min
Seize bridges over Dommel River at St. Oedenrode	D-Day	3 hrs 30 min
Seize bridges over Aa River and Willemsvoort Canal near Veghel	D-Day	3 hrs 5 min
Secure and maintain continuous road corridor from Eindhoven north to north of Veghel (D+1)	D+1 to end operation	D+1
82nd Airborne		
Seize and secure bridge across Maas River at Grave	D to D+1 (am)	4 hrs
Seize and hold highway bridge across Waal River at Nijmegen	Noon D+1	75 hrs
Seize, organize and hold High Ground between Nijmegen and Groesbeek	D-Day	3.5 hrs
Deny the roads in the Division area to the enemy	D-Day	4 hrs
Dominate the area bounded on north by line running from Beek west through Hatert, SW to Eindschestraat, S by River Maas and Mook-Ricthorst Highway, E by Cleve-Nijmegen Highway and Forst Reichswald, W by line running north and south through Eindschestraat	D-Day to end operation	5 hrs
1st Airborne		
Seize and hold highway, railroad and pontoon bridges at Arnhem with protective bridgeheads to north[3]	D+1 (night)	North end highway bridge

[1] Edited excerpts from WSEG Staff Study No. 3 *Historical Study of Some World War II Airborne Operations*

[2] The 'time for use' is determined for this purpose by the time at which the 'Garden' forces actually first reached or were in position to use the objectives in question.

[3] Information on 1st British Airborne Division and 1st Polish Brigade objectives and their experiences are taken from a 1st Airborne after-action report.

Objective dealt with at planned time?	Objective held at time for use[2]	Planned assault objective
No	Yes	'Garden' forces were behind schedule to the extent that this degree of lateness did not affect their progress
No	No	'Garden' forces were delayed by necessity to build heavy vehicle bridge
Yes	Yes	
Yes	Yes	
Yes	In part	Corridor was initially cleared and held for the planned time but was cut twice later, once for a period of 36 hours. 'Garden' forces halted forward progress each time and resisted in reopening corridor
Yes	Yes	'Garden' forces arrived at 08:20, D+2
No	No	'Garden' forces arrived and participated with airborne units in unsuccessful attack on highway bridge D+2. Bridge taken by assault river crossing by 504th PIR, attack from south and by a battalion of 505th PIR and Grenadier Guards, this objective was given priority over No. 2 in point of time
Yes	Yes	
Yes	Yes	
Yes	Yes	This area received several heavy coordinated attacks but was successfully defended throughout the period of the operation. Enemy penetrations were reduced in all cases within a short time
In part	No	One company reached and took north end highway bridge in 7 hrs. Bridge demolition charges were removed. The RR bridge was blown by enemy and pontoon bridge neutralised by removal of centre sections by enemy. Garden forces did not reach south side of river until small elements arrived night D+5. South side river not reached in strength until night D+7. Units at north end highway bridge were out of ammunition and food and decimated. At about 05:00, D+4 survivors were ordered to attempt escape. 'Garden' forces never crossed river in force and did not attack south end of highway bridge

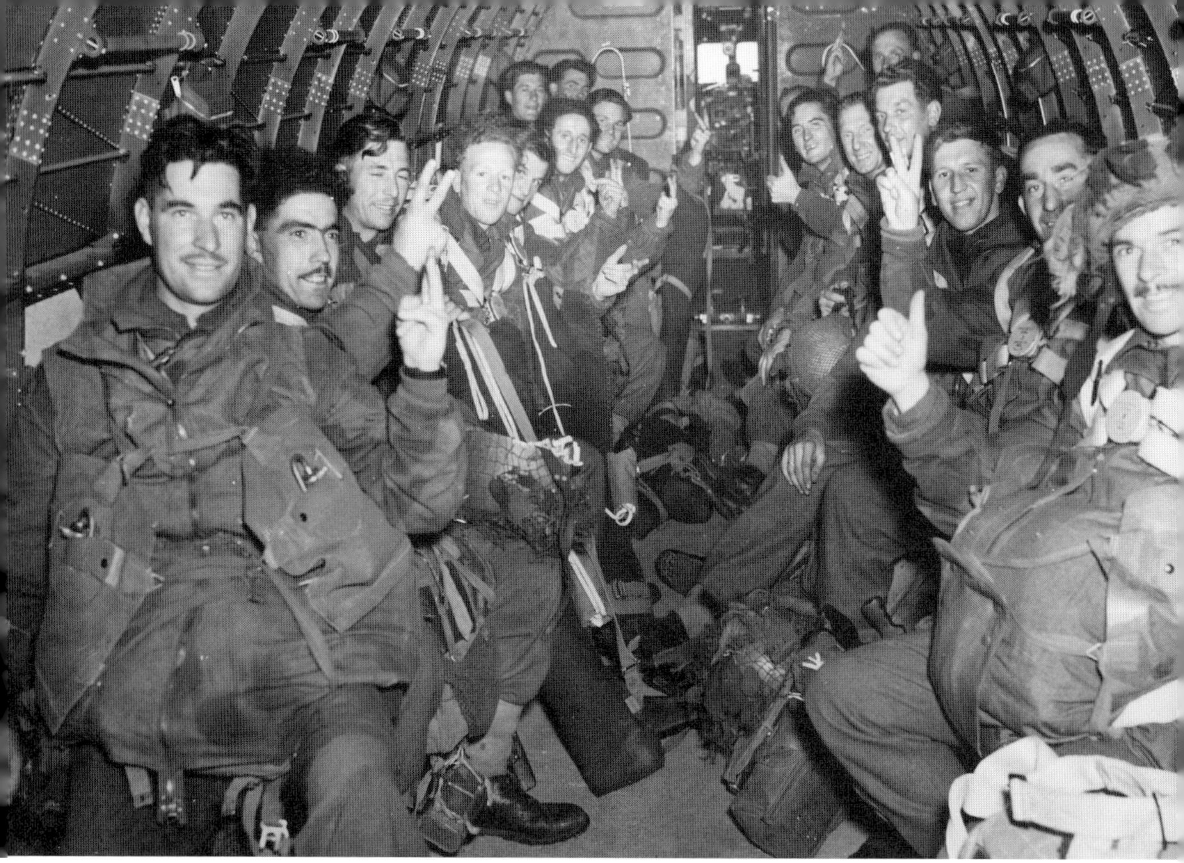

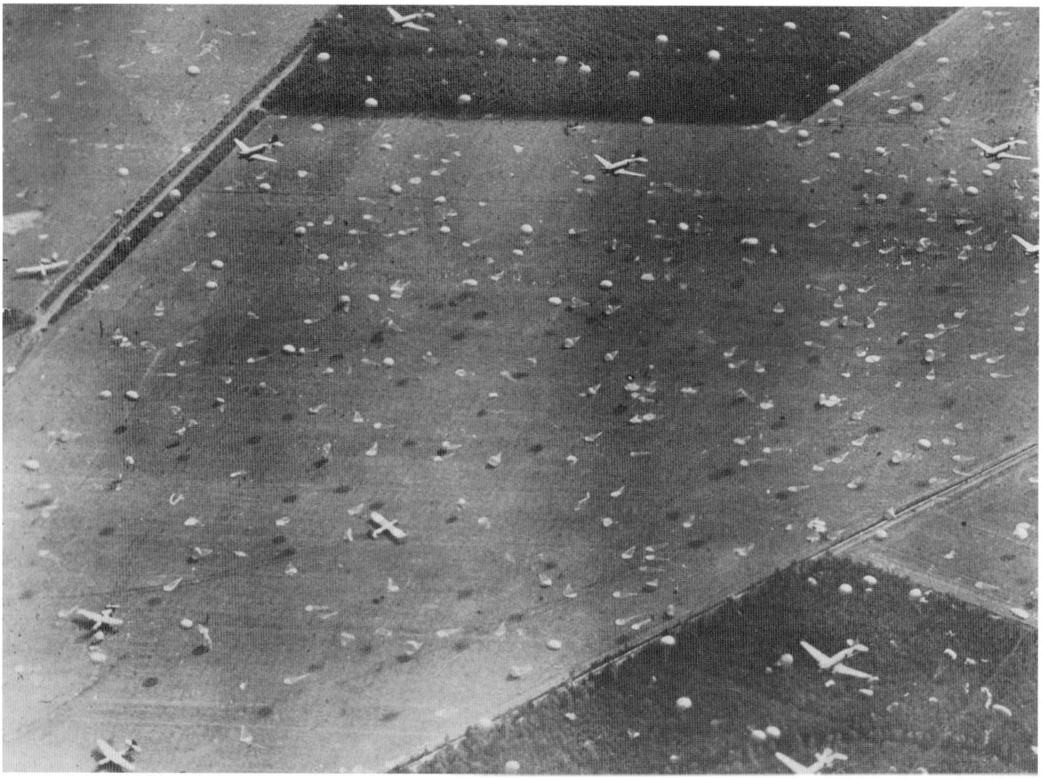

It had started on a wave of optimism engendered by the successful invasion of France, the defeat of the Germans in Normandy, the helter-skelter rush to the borders of Belgium, the Netherlands and Germany itself. But the German defence had begun to coalesce along the canals and waterways of the Low Countries. Fifteenth Army slipped away from the chasers and over the Scheldt from the Breskens Pocket. The war was not going to be over by Christmas. The first British landings were the gliders on LZ-S and LZ-Z bringing 1st Airlanding Brigade. They were followed in the afternoon by the paradrop of 1st Para Brigade on LZ-X. However, the second lift on D+1 was delayed five hours by bad weather and this meant the British paras were understrength at the critical moment of the battle.

Continued on p102.

Opposite, Above: V for Victory from 5 Pl, S/1st Para Bn on board a USAAF C-47 of 61st TCG at Barkston Heath. The man at left (Sgt P Kelly) isn't wearing his parachute yet. He became a PoW as did the platoon OC, Lt B. J. Gick, who ended up in Oflag 79, Braunschweig (Brunswick). 1st Para left DZ-X and headed by a northerly route into Arnhem.

Opposite, Below: DZ-X on 17 September. 2,283 paras of 1st, 2nd and 3rd Para Battalions jumped and 645 parapacks were dropped. Accuracy was as close to perfect as any para drop could be.

Below: Photo looking SE. The railway line (**A**) divided LZ-S and LZ-Z. DZ-X was alongside LZ-Z. 134 gliders were due to land on the LZ-S and 132 did so. LZ-Z saw 116 land on the zone and 27 nearby.

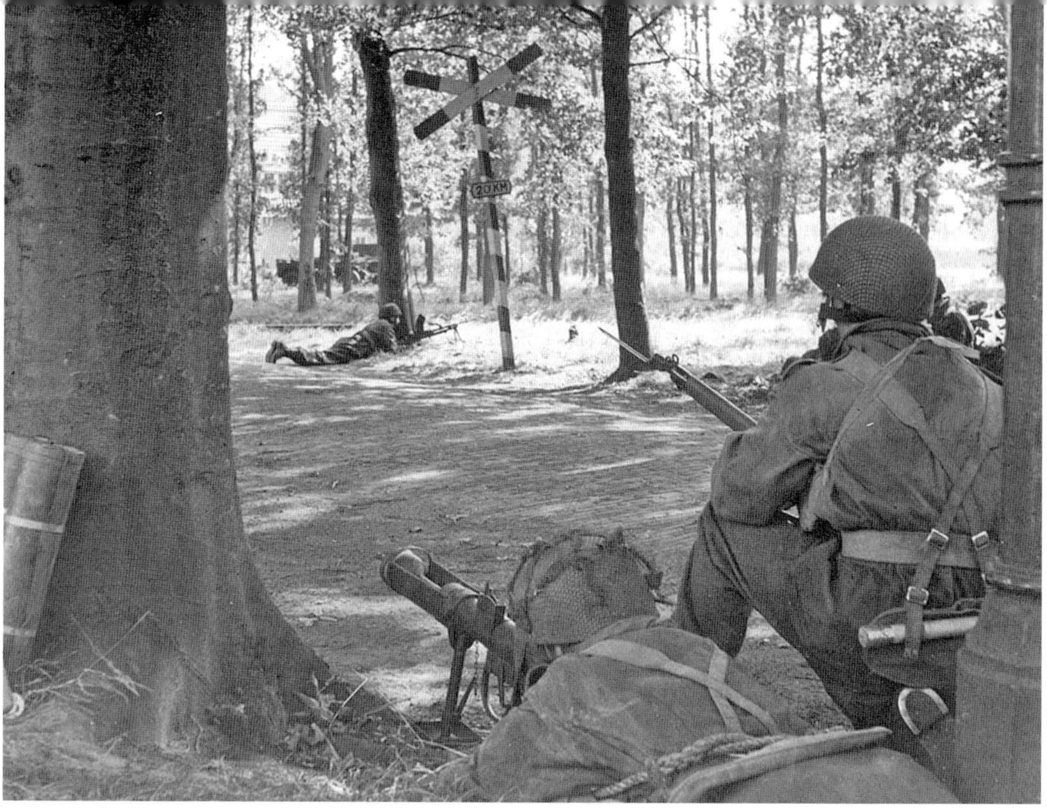
20 KM

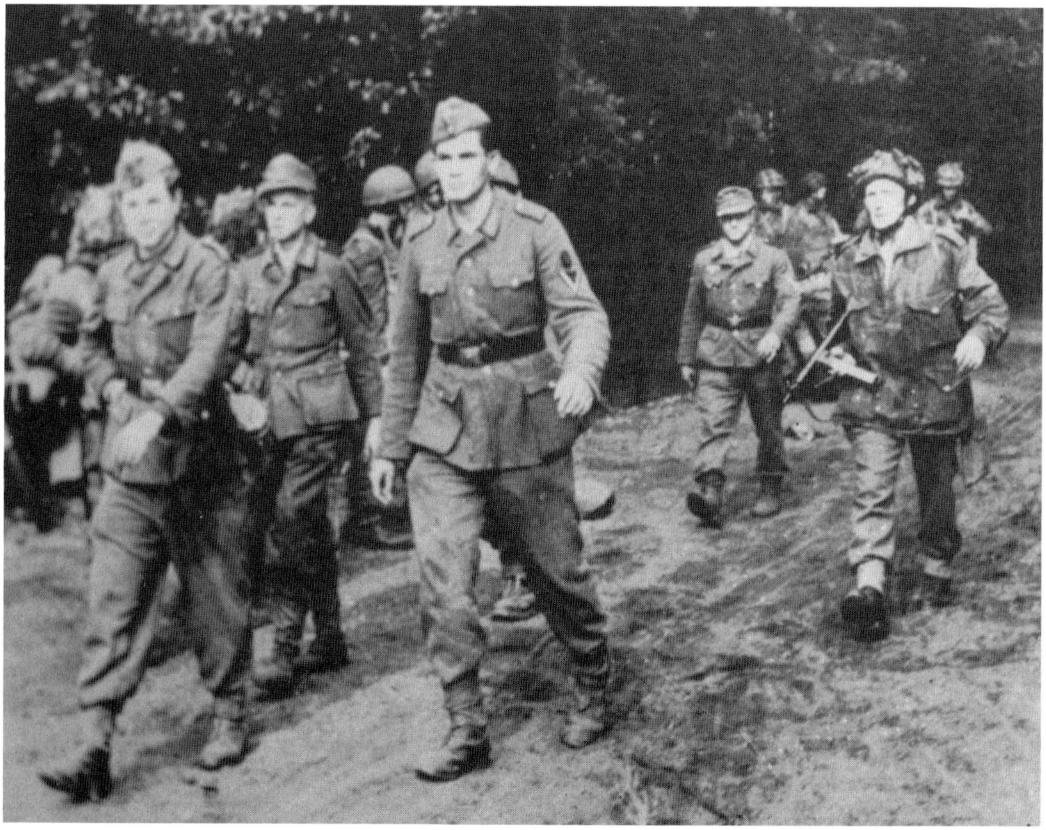

Opposite, Above: Men of the Recce Squadron near the railway line from Wolfheze to Deelen airfield. Note the PIAT. It might look like a Heath Robinson device but it was reasonably effective at ranges under 100yd. Postwar analysis of accuracy showed a marked drop-off on advancing vehicles (for obvious reasons) but it was as accurate and effective as most hand-held anti-tank weapons and extremely useful when used against infantry targets. It also had no give-away backblast?

Opposite, Below: The prisoners were taken to a PoW area at Wolfheze.

Above: StuG-Brigade 280 was instrumental in beating back attempts to reinforce the paras at the bridge. On its way to Aachen, it was redirected to aid the German defence. Internal lines of communications were critical in the defeat of the British at Arnhem.

Right: Around 750 men of Col John Frost's 2nd Para Bn held the bridge. The wrecked vehicles belonged to the Hohenstaufen (9th SS-Panzer) Division's Recce Bn knocked out on D+1.

Cut to ribbons on the 18th and 19th as they tried to force their way to the bridge, the men of 1st Airborne Division were pushed back into a perimeter around Oosterbeek. All hope of joining up with Frost at the bridge had gone, but there was still a chance that the arrival of XXX Corps could reinforce them and maintain a bridgehead on the north bank. To this end, the remnants of the division dug in and spent six days in an heroic defence that ended on D+8 when Operation Berlin saw 2,400 men escape over the river. They left behind 1,485 dead and 6,500 PoWs. There were two VC actions – the first by Lance Sgt John Baskeyfield of the South Staffords on the 20th, when he knocked out a number of armoured vehicles (almost certainly misidentified as Tigers in the citation), the second by Maj Robert Cain, of the Royal Northumberland Fusiliers (attached to the South Staffords) less than half a mile to the west of Baskeyfield's position. Cain knocked out a Stug III (again misidentified as a Tiger) with a PIAT. The attackers – in the east 9th SS Panzer Division units – included armoured vehicles, although the heavy Tigers and King Tigers didn't arrive until the 24th. The biggest problem for the defenders was that they lost the high ground above the river to the southwest. Once that had fallen, resupply and reinforcement became extremely difficult. Spare a thought for the attempted resupply missions that saw 35 aircraft lost.

4

1 One of the classic Oosterbeek photographs: the 1st Borders 3-inch mortar position of Cpl Jim McDowell and Ptes Norman Knight and Ron Tierney.

2 The Hartenstein Hotel – today the location of an excellent museum – was the centre of the defensive perimeter set up on 20 September and the location of General Urquhart's HQ. This defender has a US M1 carbine.

3 Another classic shot of a para patrol near the Hartenstein.

4 41 C-47s of the 315th TCG from Spanhoe dropped 560 men of 1st Polish Independent Parachute Bde at DZ-O (Overasselt) on D+6 (23 September). They were due to follow the

82nd Airborne glider drop but arrived before the latter had finished. Four days later than anticipated, mainly thanks to weather, 82nd Airborne's 325th GIR, 80th AAA battalion, two companies of 307th AEB and divisional troops – 3,385 men were dipatched in 406 CG-4As. Four of the glider tugs were shot down and 96 damaged as Flak and other exigencies led to a dispersed drop. Around 75% of the regimental strength was able to leave the landing grounds for Groesbeek with most of the missing turning up in the next two days. These men could have allowed the 82nd to take Nijmegen bridge earlier when there was still a chance the operation could have been successful.

5 On the night of 25–26 September those who could made their way across the river: in all about 2,400 – another 140 made their way across later. They were given a meal and then slept. Here some are seen recovering their weapons. 1st Airborne had suffered 50 percent casualties and it would take some months before its next operation – Doomsday, the postwar occupation of Norway where its most difficult job would be identifying war criminals. Greenway (2004) talks about arrests of 31 male and 17 female prisoners who had been staff at the Grini concentration camp; the apprehension of Finn Kaas, the 'Norwegian Lord Haw-Haw' and the commander of the Gestapo in Norway.

5

Operation Manna

One of the less well-known airborne operations, Operation Manna saw British paras of the 2nd Independent Parachute Bde – who had remained fighting as conventional infantry in Italy when 1st Airborne Div returned to the UK – drop into Greece on 12 and 14 October 1944. The German forces in Greece were in danger of being cut off by the Red Army's thrust towards Bulgaria and Yugoslavia. They prepared to pull out which would have left a vacuum that Churchill didn't want to see filled by Greek communists. So, on the 12th, 14 C-47s of No 10th Sqn, RAF dropped paras and nine Halifaxes dropped supply containers. On the 12th, the troops dropped were C/4th Bn and A Troop, 2nd Para Sqn, RE – the engineers to repair the airfield to enable airlanding operations to follow.

Next, on 13 October, nine C-47s, each towing a CG-4A glider, flew to Megara from Manduria in Italy to land bulldozers, engineers and jeeps. On 14 October, 68 transports (C-47s of 51st TCW, 12th US Air Force) loaded with paratroopers and supply canisters, with 20 additional aircraft towing CG-4A gliders arrived. It had been planned to land, but cratered runways led to para dropping from 800ft. There were further drops – in seven successive days 126 officers and 2,025 troops came in along with 69 jeeps, 44 trailers, 9 motorcycles and 327 tons of supplies and equipment. There were no losses of aircraft. Some of the gliders were returned to Italy with the casualties from the first day's drop. Subsequently, Kalamaki was also opened and aircraft flew in there on 17 and 18 October.

The paras may have thought they were going to harry the retreating Germans. They certainly did that, but in reality they had been sent there to accompany the Greek government back home and step in to ensure that there wasn't a communist takeover. The British found themselves between the communist EAM/ELAS movement and the royalist EDES party, fighting in Athens. They may have provided a semblance of order but it was fragmentary: the Greek Civil War restarted in 1946.

Opposite: Note the leg bags hanging below the paras as they drop over Megara (example circled). Having let the bags loose in a controlled way, they dangled below the paratroop and would hit the ground first, be quickly retrievable and contained weapons, ammunition and personal equipment.

Above: Megara, 12 October. A medic of 127th Para Light Field Ambulance tends to a para of the 2nd Independent Parachute Bde. Winds were high over the DZ and 97 jumpers were injured and 3 killed.

Right: En route to Megara.

Operation Varsity

The airborne component of Operation Plunder, the Rhine crossing by 21st Army Group, was commanded by the CG of XVIII Airborne Corps, Lt Gen Matthew Ridgway, with Lt Gen Richard Gale 2IC. On 24 March 17th (US) AB Div (Maj Gen William Miley) and the British 6th AB Div (Maj Gen Eric Bols) dropped some hours after the amphibious crossing had started.

17th Division's casualties were relatively light (159 KIA, 522 WIA and 164 MIA). IX TCC lost 41 KIA, 153 WIA and 163 MIA.

6th Airborne suffered 1,400 casualties during the day. The glider pilots had been well trained: the losses at Arnhem had been made good with RAF pilots – but there was a lot of flak. *By Air To Battle* says of the gliders: '90 percent touched down in the LZ; but of the 416 which reached the battlefield only 88 landed undamaged. Of the remainder, all were hit, mostly by light flak and small arms fire, and 37 were completely burned out.' Casualties among the glider pilots were 20–30 percent.

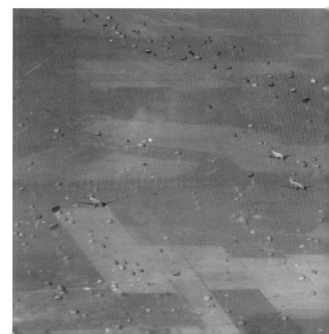

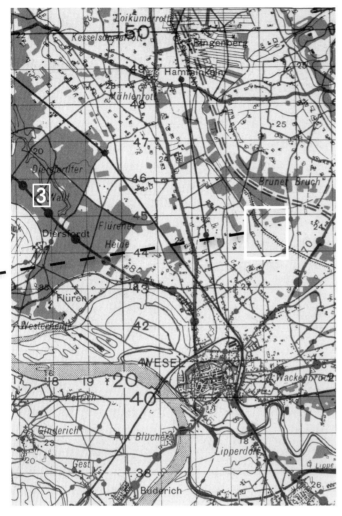

1 72 C-46s, 836 C-47s, and 906 CG-4A gliders (many double-towed) took 9,387 US troops to Germany.

2 and 3 The US LZs/DZs were north and northwest of Wesel. This is LZ-S covered with CG-4As alongside the Ijssel. The US preferred the smaller CG-4As to the larger Horsas, which accounts for the difference in numbers used.

4 6th Airborne used nearly 800 aircraft and 420 gliders, carrying over 8,000 soldiers. Here 5th Parachute Bde drops on DZ-B.

5 Men of HQ Bty, 466th PFAB prepare their equipment. They flew in 42 C-47s (27 offr and 356 men) and 17 CG-4As (2 offr and 55 men) to support 513th PIR. They suffered 107 casualties including 2 offr and 44 men KIA, most from C Bty. Jumping at 10:25, 13 howitzers were in position by 17:00. 12 were dropped by parachute and 3 brought in by glider. 1,550 rounds of 75mm ammo also arrived. The unit won a Distinguished Unit Citation.

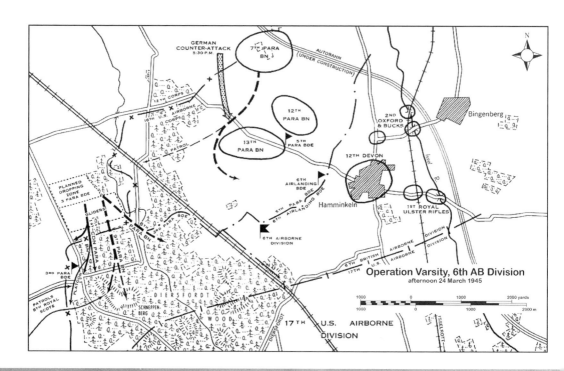

Operation Varsity, 6th AB Division
afternoon 24 March 1945

Above: 6th Airborne on the afternoon of the 24th. Casualties were high but the airborne troops achieved surprise and did their job, taking Diersfordt Forest and key bridges over the Ijssel. 3rd Para (8th, 9th and 1st Can Battalions plus elements of 3rd Airlanding ATk Bty) cut the road to the forest; 5th Para (7th, 12th and 13th Bns with 4th ATk Bty) took other road junctions; next came 6th Airlanding Bde (2nd Ox & Bucks, 1st RUR, and 12th Devons + elements 3rd ATk Bty), who took Hamminkeln with help from 513rd PIR who had been misdropped.

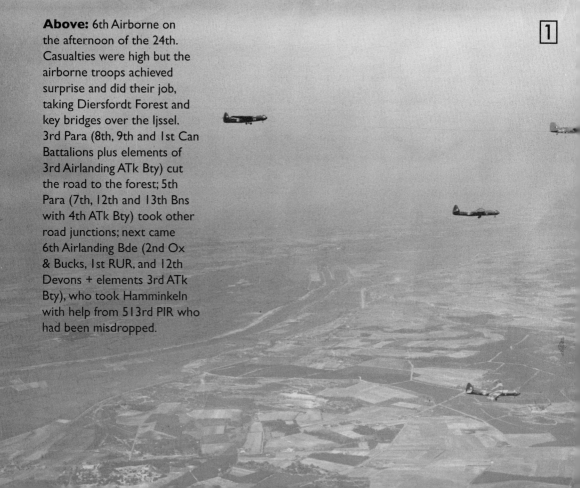

1 C-47s tow Horsas of British 6th Airlanding Bde towards Wesel.

2 Photo call on 25 March – of a 6th Airlanding Brigade 6pdr anti-tank gun in Hamminkeln.

3 Hamminkeln station littered with glider wreckage. German prisoners are grouped between the tracks. Smoke over the battlefield and heavy AA fire saw many gliders land badly.

4 Men of British 5th Para Brigade in Hamminkeln.

John Warren said of 'Varsity': 'the defenders had anticipated an airborne assault in the Wesel-Emmerich sector and had prepared for it. They appear to have had at least 10,000 men in carefully organized defensive positions in the Diersfordt area. An initial attack by one airborne division or less might have been resisted stubbornly, as was the assault at Rees. Instead the unprecedented and unexpected weight of the blow overwhelmed resistance and shattered the precarious morale of the defenders.'

'The degree of air superiority which enabled the United States and Great Britain to send 10,000 sorties over France and western Germany on the day of "Varsity" while the Luftwaffe could make less than 100 sorties against them made it possible to protect an airborne mission very thoroughly.'

Hardcore Fallschirmjäger with a DFS230 glider in the background. Note the MG above the cockpit, his FG42 and ammo bandoleer. The rescue of Mussolini was one of the great raids of the war.

5 German Operations After Crete

After Crete there was a hiatus before any major German airborne operations, with Student's plans for the invasion of Malta put on hold (see p165). Hitler's decision signified a change of role for the majority of the Fallschirmjäger. They became renowned as gritty, tough infantrymen: 'firemen' serving on every front, always with distinction – though sometimes clouded with darker war crimes (see p116). Hitler did not formalise his decision and disband them. Good examples of their new role in 1942 were the use of the 1st Fallschirm-Division on the Eastern Front in the Rzhev sector; the deployment of Ramcke's Brigade Group to the African desert in October 1942; and rushing FJR5 to Tunisia in November 1942. Under Student, who never gave up hope of using them as paratroops, the Fallschirmjäger continued to expand and develop, their numbers actually increasing. In 1943 each regiment of 7. Flieger-Division was used as the nucleus for expansion to divisional size and these new divisions (Fallschirmjäger-Divisionen 1–5) were the last to receive full airborne training. In the final years of the war eight more parachute divisions were created, their titles only reflected their Luftwaffe source of origin. They were given no full formal parachute training and were instead used exclusively as infantry.

In this enforced interim the problem of dropping without weaponry was to some extent alleviated with the introduction in 1942 of the revolutionary Fallschirm-jägergewehr 42, a light machine gun that fired standard rifle ammunition from a 20-round magazine in single rounds or bursts. The FG42 is considered one of the most advanced weapon designs of war and influenced the evolution of the modern assault rife. There was also a more powerful parachutable 4.2cm PaK anti-tank gun to succeed the 3.7cm version.

However, with Germany on the defensive and suffering from a shortage of manpower and equipment, no large airborne operation was ever seriously considered again. In the battle for Sicily on 12 July 1943, 1,400 Fallschirmjäger of FJR3 were airdropped successfully onto the Catania plains in reinforcement of German forces already on the ground – the largest German airdrop of the later war. Instead, the Fallschirmjäger returned to their tactical roots: small fast daring raids of up to battalion size to achieve specific goals or to reinforce isolated units. Half a dozen of these smaller operations were carried out before the end of the conflict, with 1943 the stand-out year for success. These

Above: The operation was planned with 12 gliders but only 10 were used. The flight crew of each was 10 men (9 combat troop men and 1 pilot). The DFS230 was excellent at short landings, and to improve things the Fallschirmjäger wound barbed wire around the skids to increase friction. Additionally, the DFS230B had a braking parachute.

Below: A good view of the Fallschirmjäger combat equipment: the camouflage smocks, para helmets – some with scrim, some with covers – and baggy grey Luftwaffe trousers. Note the grenade launcher on the Kar98k (**A**) and FG42 muzzle (**B**).

successful operations – such as Unternehmen Student (capture of Italian HQ at Monterotondo), Eiche (the rescue of Mussolini), Goldfasan (Elba), Eisbär (Kos), Leopard (Leros) – also demonstrated that Student had absorbed the tactical and doctrinal lessons of Crete and corrected all of them by 1943. Missions and objectives were tailored to the paratroops' capabilities and limitations, and paratroopers now always jumped with their weapons, with increased firepower, and on safer drop zones.

After the Axis retreat from Sicily the Allied invasion of the Italian mainland was only a question of when and where, so the Germans also had a contingency plan codenamed Unternehmen *Achse* (Axis) for the military occupation and disarmament of its former ally after its inevitable surrender. When this occurred on 8 September 1943 the bulk of FJD2 entered Rome on the ground in Unternehmen *Student*, and after some brief heavy fighting at the city's southern gate, they overcame and disarmed the Italian troops and occupied the city. Early the next morning a fleet of 50 Ju52s dropped II./FJR6 in the vicinity of the Italian Army HQ at Monterotondo, 20km to the north-east of Rome.

After a short, sharp firefight (the Germans lost 56 KIA/MIA and 79 WIA) they succeeded in capturing the complex and forcing the Italian General Staff to order an immediate ceasefire. By the 10th with the ceasefire agreed and Rome declared an 'open city', most of FJD2 then returned to defend the coast, which the Germans were scrambling to reinforce after the Allied invasion at Salerno on 3 September. Unternehmen Student had a wider resonance beyond its immediate tactical successes, for it enabled the Germans to smoothly assume territorial control of what would turn out to be a traumatic battleground for the Allies.

Unternehmen Eiche (Oak)

Just a few days later, on 12 September, came another spectacular operation: the rescue of Mussolini from pro-Allied Italian forces. Personally ordered by Hitler, while

KURT STUDENT

A WWI ace, during the 1930s, Student was involved in R&D for parachutes, aircraft, engines and gliders and expanding parachute training. He was given command of the paratroops and formed 7. Flieger-Division training his men on Ju52s which were organised into airlift transport units, *Kampfgruppe zur besonderen Verwendung* [Special Duty Bomber Groups]. Unlike the British and Americans with whom airborne forces were army units, the Luftwaffe controlled all German airborne troops, and Student commanded the glider infantry when 22. Luftlande [Airlanding] Division was created. He was badly wounded on 14 May 1940 and took many months to recover. After the Phyrric victory of Crete he was never able to convince Hitler to allow another major operation. Instead he commanded the 1. Fallschirmjägerarmee that did so much to hold up the Allies after the invasion.

Above: Hitler greets Mussolini on 14 September at the Wolf's Lair, near Rastenburg.

Left: The Hotel Campo Imperatore on the Gran Sasso d'Italia massif in the Apennines.

Below: General Student decorates some of the Fallschirmjäger who took part in *Unternehmen Eiche* (Operation Oak). There were a lot of medals: the pilot of the Storch (Hptm Heinrich Gerlach), three glider pilots (Oblt Johannes Heidenrich, Lt Elimar Meyer and Obfw Hans Neelmeyer) Maj Otto-Harald Mors (who commanded the operation), Hptm Gerhard Langguth and Oblt Georg Freiherr von Berlepsch (who led the landing) as well as Skorzeny (Knight's Cross) and Student (Oakleaves).

SS-Hauptsturmführer Otto Skorzeny and his SS commandos took the credit, in fact the operation was planned and executed by the Fallschirmjäger of 2. FJD under the command of Maj Otto-Harald Mors. Since his arrest Mussolini had been moved regularly between different locations. The Germans had been trying to find him and after a few near misses he was finally tracked down to the Campo Imperatore Hotel, a ski resort on a plateau in Italy's Gran Sasso, high in the Apennine Mountains 150km from Rome. 'Eiche' was then planned by 2. FJD and approved by General Student. A parachute drop wasn't practicable, so gliders were chosen to land on the plateau while another battalion would travel in vehicles to secure the lower end of the hotel's funicular access railway. Early on 12 September 12 DFS230 gliders – carrying 82 paratroopers of the Fallschirm-Lehr Battalion and 26 SS commandos including Skorzeny – set off. They also had an unwilling Italian general with them, Ferdinand Soleti, to control the 200 Italian troops guarding the Duce.

With surprise complete, the raid went perfectly. Only one glider crash landing causing minor injuries; not a shot was fired and the general did his bit ordering the Italian soldiers to stand down. Mussolini was whisked away immediately by Skorzeny, flown first to Rome and then Vienna, meeting with Hitler in Berlin just two days later. This propaganda coup was milked remorselessly by Himmler and Goebbels crediting it entirely to the SS, whose input in fact had been minimal. Skorzeny and the SS went on to complete a number of airborne operations (see p117).

Unternehmen Goldfasan (Golden pheasant)
On 17 September 1943, after a short preliminary bombing, 600 Fallschirmjäger of III./FJR7 were dropped onto the island of Elba to take control in case the Allies tried to use it as a jumping off point for an attack behind the German front lines. The operation was a complete success with the Italians uninterested in fighting and capitulating quickly, but the operation was rendered virtually pointless when the Allies chose Anzio for their assault. Following the Italian surrender the Germans also moved swiftly to seize their island possessions in the Dodecanese, while the British sought to intervene and support pro-Allied Italian forces. The most important island, Rhodes, fell to Sturm-Division Rhodos by 11 September, but the Brits occupied Kos, Samos and Leros.

Unternehmen Eisbär (Polar bear)
On 3 October the island of Kos, whose defence had been reinforced by a para-drop of 11th Para Bn, 1st AB Division, was attacked by sea and air in 'Eisbär'. With its defences – particular air support – restricted by Eisenhower (the Americans were more suspicious of British intentions in the Balkans than prepared to pursue the liberation of the eastern Mediterranean) – the British and Italian defenders were unable to withstand the

assault that included a para-drop of a battalion of I./FJR2 south and west of Antimachia airfield and a company of the Brandenburger Regt. From the sea came a Kampfgruppe of 22. Luftlande-Division, and it was men of that division who carried out the massacre of 100 Italian officers. Its OC, Gen Friedrich-Wilhelm Müller, would later be shot for similar crimes on Crete. Losing Kos and its airfield had disastrous consequences for British operations in the Dodecanese, for in the face of German air supremacy they were unable to hold on to any of them, suffering heavy losses in men and ships in a campaign that lasted two months and resulted in one of the last major German victories in the war.

Unternehmen Leopard

The Fallschirmjäger were next used in the battle for the island of Leros. Following an extensive 50-day bombing campaign against the badly organised British and Italian defence, in the early hours of 12 November and in conjunction with seaborne assaults from east and west I./FJR2 was dropped in the centre on Mt Rachi, cutting the island in two. This critical isolation of Allied forces decided the matter and after some bitter and complicated fighting over the next few days, the Allies surrendered on 16 November. With the fall of Leros, Samos and Kos, the other smaller islands were evacuated by the Allies, the Italians surrendered and the Germans completed their conquest of the Dodecanese, which they held until the end of the war.

Continued on p119.

WAR CRIMES

Mark Mazower's excellent *Inside Hitler's Greece: The Experience of Occupation, 1941–44* addresses the difficult issue of Fallschirmjäger war crimes. While nowhere near as frequent as other German units, especially the SS, the Fallschirmjäger were often responsible for war crimes and Cretans especially still remember the many civilian deaths on their island.

'Outraged by the part the islanders had played in resisting the invasion and attacking German paratroopers, ... Student ... ordered "Revenge Operations", and explained to his troops what these were in terms that left no room for ambiguity: "1) Shootings; 2) Forced Levies; 3) Burning down villages; 4) Extermination (Ausrottung) of the male population of the entire region". ... In Student's words: "All operations are to be carried out with great speed, leaving aside all formalities and certainly dispensing with special courts. ... These are not meant for beasts and murderers." '

Greek sources put the total civilians casualties at this time as around 2,000. That may be an exaggeration, but many crimes took place. For example, on 2 June 1941, Fallschirmjäger from III./Luftlande-Sturm-Regiment 1 (OC Oblt Horst Trebes) murdered up to 60 men in Kondomari – an event captured on film. The next day the same unit killed 180 at Kandanos because, as a sign erected at the time said:

'Kandanos was destroyed in retaliation for the bestial ambush murder of a paratrooper platoon and a half-platoon of military engineers by armed men and women.'

Allied soldiers were also murdered (for which Student was convicted postwar) and later in the war the occupying Wehrmacht killed over 500 more civilians between 14 and 16 September 1943 – a crime for which Gen Friedrich-Wilhelm Müller would be executed postwar.

Heavily armed men of SS-Fallschirmjäger-Battalion 500 after having dropped on Drvar during Unternehmen Rösselsprung. Tito got away and the Fallschirmjäger losses were high.

SS AIRBORNE OPERATIONS

The Fallschirmjäger were not the only German airborne forces. There was a range of other units that saw airborne delivery as the best way to undertake their missions. The most significant – and successful – of these was the airborne attack on Vassieux in the Vercors mountains of southeastern France. Part of Unternehmen Bettina, whose aim was to clear the area of maquis, on 21 July 1944 22 DFS230 gliders of II. Gruppe/KG200. – the Luftwaffe's special operations unit – landed on the Vercors plateau near Vassieux. Two days later 17 more arrived. At all times assisted by ground support missions, the airborne component of the operation – 220 men landed on the 21st, 50 more on the 23rd – was commanded by Oberlt Friedrich Schäfer. Heavy weapons and supplies came in on Go242A gliders. The airborne troops held a perimeter, beating off all attacks until relieved by Panzergrenadiers on the 25th. The German forces also included Reserve-Gebirgsjäger and a company from an Ost-Bataillon. SD men were also there – with the result that captured maquis and many civilians were executed.

Probably the most advertised of the SS air-drop operations were those undertaken by Otto Skorzeny and SS-Fallschirmjäger-Battalion 500 (renamed 600 in autumn 1944). Apart from his involvement in Unternehmen Eiche (pp113–114), Sorzeny's main operations were summer 1943's 'François' in Iran; an attempt to kidnap Tito – 'Rösselsprung' on 25 May 1944, the Yugoslav partisan's birthday, 'Panzerfaust' – the successful kidnap on 15 October 1944 of Hungarian Regent Admiral Miklós Horthy's son to force the regent to keep the country on the Axis side; and, finally, 'Greif' during the Ardennes offensive.

'François' involved a para drop, as did 'Rösselsprung' (Knight's move) on 25–27 May 1944. This attempt to capture or kill Tito involved around 900 SS paras who had to be delivered in three waves because of the paucity of aircraft and gliders. The first was a para drop on Drvar (c300 men); the second, simultaneous, a glider coup de main mission on the Citadel cave complex where Tito's HQ was (c100 men) and other targets (c250 men); the third a reinforcement mission (c200 men).

The SS attacked bravely but were badly mauled, especially the gliders at the cave complex. When finally relieved, only 200 were fit, with 576 dead and 48 wounded.

As was often the case – it was true in both Sicily and Normandy – the wide dispersal of a parachute drop may negate the primary mission, but the confusion generated was out of all proportion to the number of men involved. This was true about *Unternehmen Stösser* when reports of German paratroops caused 18th (US) Infantry Regt and a combat command to be used to search for them. Commanded by von der Heydte, the primary mission for the Fallschirmjäger was to hold an important crossroads for 12. SS-Panzer-Division *Hitlerjugend*. 1st (US) Infantry Division intelligence reports said ,'In spite of this distinguished leadership, however, the plan [Stösser] went awry. None of the paratroopers had been told of his mission, other than that further instructions would be given him once he landed. The NCOs only knew that they were to hold certain road junctions; beyond that they knew nothing. A cross wind and bad briefing of the Ju52 pilots scattered the units and their weapons and equipment over an area far wider than planned. Much of the equipment was lost during the fall and more was broken; the radios were knocked out and reorganization was sketchy. With no secondary mission, those paratroopers who managed to reassemble hid out in the woods, harassing isolated vehicles and taking a few prisoners. They were entirely unable to block the arrival of reinforcing troops.'

1 Fallschirmjäger before *Stösser*; 2 Men of US Coy F 3/18th Inf Regt searching for paratroops; 3 A German parachute found; 4 Oberst Freiherr Friedrich August Freiherr von der Heydte (right) jumped with a broken arm and finally surrendered on 23 December.

It was a hollow victory. Elsewhere, late 1943 and 1944 saw the Allies advance towards the Reich from every direction. Realistically, Germany no longer possessed the resources or the offensive power to carry out significant airborne operations. The Fallschirmjäger became infantry (see Chapter 9). But no one could accuse the Führer of being realistic, and in his desperate last pathetic gamble in the West he would throw away his final reserves of men with tragic abandon.

Unternehmen Stösser (hawk)

The final Fallschirmjäger operation of the war occurred during the 1944 winter offensive in the Ardennes and was an unmitigated disaster from the start. Scrambled together within a fortnight with whatever resources could be gathered, a 1,000-man Kampfgruppe commanded by Oberst von der Heydte was tasked with the seizure of a number of vital road features ahead of the advancing Panzer columns. His untrained men were poorly delivered and scattered over hundreds of miles. One company was even dropped over Bonn. The one-week preparation time was inadequate, as the few remaining parachute-trained men were scattered in units all over Europe, and there were essentially no remaining Ju52 pilots or crews with experience in parachute drops. Von der Heydte himself reached the Baraque Michel crossroads with men and ammo for one fight. He delayed await-ing the arrival of the Panzers but they never came. On the 19th, D+2, his men headed back to German lines, von der Heydte being captured on the 23rd. The operation was a complete fail-ure, except that their presence tied US rear area security into knots, and a rumour that German para-troops were planning to kidnap Eisenhow-er caused two U.S. infantry divisions to be diverted to guard his HQ miles behind the front.

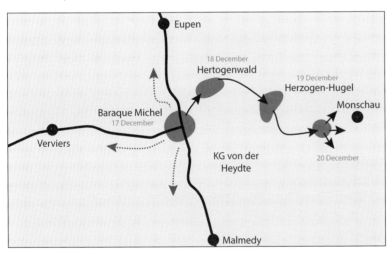

70 aircraft in two waves dropped paratroopers on Langoan airfield from a height of about 600 feet. They were dropped about 5 miles from the airfield but widely scattered by the AA gunfire.

6 Airborne Operations in the CBI and Pacific Theatres

The Japanese set up training schools for army and navy paratroops in 1940. The programme was assisted by German instructors – about 100 by autumn 1941 when there were 14,700 trainees in nine centres. The naval troops were formed into two battalions, designated the Yokosuka 1st and Yokosuka 3rd Special Naval Landing Forces (SNLF). They later came to be known as the Hariuchi (Karashima) and Fukumi forces.

The first-ever Japanese airborne assault was by the IJN paratroops against Langoan airfield near Menado in the Netherlands East Indies on 11 January 1942. The Japanese objective was to secure an airfield that could then provide aerial support for the amphibious forces which invaded the island at the same time. The 334 paratroops came from the Yokosuka 1st SNLF which consisted of two companies commanded by IJN Commander Toyoaki Horiuchi. Airlifted from Davao in the Philippines by 28 Mitsubishi G3M 'Nell' aircraft of the 1001st Daitai (IJN air squadron), the paratroops jumped from 500ft,

Japanese airborne operations 1942–45. Menado or Manado is on the Minahasa peninsula of the Celebes (today's Sulawesi). Once taken, it became the HQ for General Korechika Anami's 2nd Area Army (see p124).

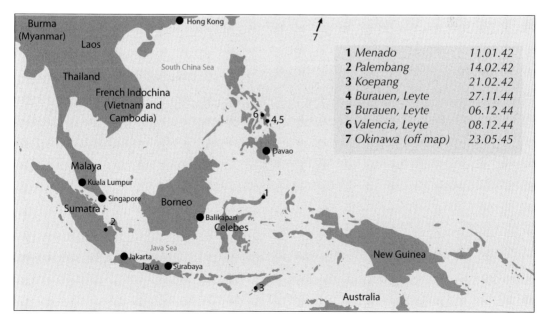

1	*Menado*	*11.01.42*
2	*Palembang*	*14.02.42*
3	*Koepang*	*21.02.42*
4	*Burauen, Leyte*	*27.11.44*
5	*Burauen, Leyte*	*06.12.44*
6	*Valencia, Leyte*	*08.12.44*
7	*Okinawa (off map)*	*23.05.45*

Above: Palembang – a scene reminiscent of Goro Tsuruta's painting *Divine Soldiers Descend on Palembang* in 1942. Japanese paratroops were used heavily for propaganda and soon there were songs, movies and the like describing (as Melzer (2020) put it) 'Japanese transport aircraft with their "magnificent silver wings" carry the "warriors of the sky" ... their "pure white parachutes" opened like big flowers in the cerulean sky, and, one after another, the paratroopers descended from heaven.' These are 'Topsy' – Mitsubishi Ki57 – transports.

Below: *Japanese Parachute Troops* describes their equipment thus: 'The paratroopers were dressed in greenish-khaki uniforms and wore gloves and crash helmets. They were armed with rifles, pistols, submachine guns, and light machine guns. In addition to rations they carried cigarettes, money, and water.' Note the 10-pocket cartridge bandoleers slung over the shoulder.

at about 09:00. Taken by surprise – the Dutch focus was on the seaborne invasion – the defenders were quickly overrun. A second drop of 185 men took place from 18 G3Ms the next day, 12 January, and contributed to Japanese success – but at some cost. The 1st Yokosuka SNLF suffered high casualties. They also murdered a numer of PoWs once they had secured the airfield.

Success in the Celebes was followed on 14–16 February 1942 by an attack on the airfield at Palembang and the oil refineries nearby at Pladjoe and Soengei Gerong. This task was assigned to the IJA 1st Parachute Force, and two waves were sent in, one of around 270 paratroopers from the captured airfield at Kahang in Malaya. The transport aircraft for this attack force were 34 Ki57s of the 1st, 2nd and 3rd Chutais (IJA air squadron), with 7 Ki56s dropping weapon and supply containers. Two other drops were made: one at Pladjoe refinery (60 men) and the other (30 men) southwest of Pangkalanbenteng airfield (called P1 by the British). The oil refineries were taken and then lost and the oil stores were set on fire. However, the paras had been able to remove the main demolition charges and the Japanese could bring the refinery back on line quickly. This oil supply was of considerable assistance to the Japanese in future operations.

The attack on P1 didn't go well with high casualties. The problem of tasking separate aircraft with the equipment drops was highlighted when one was shot down. Nevertheless, the Allies had also lost ground and sustained casualties, and after further drops (100 men) on the 15th, the airfield fell. That afternoon Palembang town was taken and the paras linked up with the invading amphibious force, elements of the 229th Regiment, 38th Division.

A week later, on 21 February 1942, the next parachute drop was by the 3rd Yokosuka SNLF (Lt Cdr Koichi Fukumi) on Timor as part of an attack that included the 228th Regimental Group of 38th Division. The Japanese force was dropped on the 20th (308 men in 25 G3Ms from Kendari airfield) and the 21st (323 men). Dropped some distance from the airfield they were tasked with taking, they had a long march – the defence of Langoan airfield had made the Japanese rethink their tactics.

The attack on Timor was even harder on the 3rd Yokosuka SNLF than Menado. At Usua ridge the battle ended with an Australian bayonet charge. The Japanese forces took the island, but as many as 550 paratroopers died. As an horrific side note, while the Australian guerilla operations continued into January 1943, the Japanese killed large numbers of civilians. By the end of the war as many as 70,000 are said to have died.

This was the last significant operation by IJN paratroops. The IJA, however, continued to maintain its airborne arm and look at possible operations, although there would not be another until 1944. There was a string of cancelled attacks, that on Lashio in April 1942 on Chinese 66th Army coming closest to fruition. As with so many Allied operations in 1944, the pace of the attacking Japanese forces and poor weather stopped the mission, cancelled as the paras flew towards their objective.

Operation Gi

The Kaoru Airborne Raiding Detachment took part in Operation Gi on 26/27 November 1944. The unit was composed of Takasago volunteers from Formosa and had its HQ at Menado (captured in the first Japanese parachute operation). The Kaoru detchament (named after the commanding officer) left Lipa airfield (Manila) in four Showa L2D aircraft (codenamed 'Tabby') to attack North Burauen and South Burauen airfields on Leyte. The aircraft were rigged with explosives. The attack was a complete failure. One came down in the sea near Dulag airfield; one on the beach near Abuyog airfield; one was shot down as it neared the target airfields and all aboard were killed; and one landed near Ormoc, its passengers joining nearby Japanese troops. Here, men in one of the L2D aircraft: note swords and the white sash worn by officers and NCOs.

Below: All paratroopers used containers for heavy weapons and the Japanese were no exception. With different coloured chutes, and dropped by separate aircraft (with all the problems that would cause), the containers carried everything from light machine guns to Type 100 flamethrowers. Note at left the paratroop version of the Type 99 (1939) 7.7mm LMG. One type of container carried 110lb of gear, was c42in long, made from aluminium. One end had a canvas-covered cushion; the other the parachute pack. However, not all weapons were carried separately. The paratrooper landed with a special version of the standard Arisaka rifle, the Type 2, which separated using a screw-in wedge that held the two halves together. This and the LMG were carried in a canvas bag on the chest, the reserve chute clipping on the top.

The next operations were against the American troops fighting to regain the Philippines – three took place in November and December 1944 against the airfields around Burauen. The first, Operation Gi, was on the night of 26/27 November – as described in the box (Opposite). A complete failure, this didn't put the Japanese off.

Their next attempt was on 5/6 December, at the three airfields near Burauen – San Pablo, Bayug, and Buri – and against those at Dulag and Tacloban. In all, around 500 men from the 3rd and 4th Raiding Regts and 40 aircraft were involved. Some dropped paras, others planned to crash-land their men. The attack was linked on the ground with 16th Division. M. Hamlin Cannon assessed the plan 'The Japanese parachutists were well drilled as to

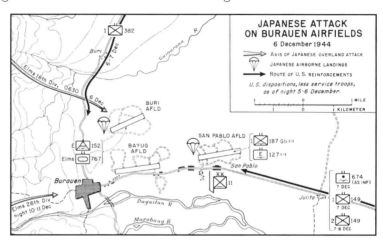

their mission. The operation was to be divided into five phases. The first phase was to begin with the jump-off. The men, immediately after landing, were to attack and destroy aircraft on the ground, and one element was to attack the barracks and communications. This phase was to end when the moon rose. In the second phase, ending about 2230, the troops would destroy matériel, ammunition dumps, bridges, and remaining barracks. During the third phase, from 2330 to 0300, the paratroopers were to destroy the remaining aircraft and installations. In the fourth phase, lasting from 0300 to 0600, they were to build defensive positions. In the fifth phase, from 0600 on, preparations were to be made for future operations.'

The attack didn't go exactly to plan. About 60 men dropped on the Buri strip and 250–300 near the San Pablo strip. Defence of the area was by elements of 11th (US) Airborne Division. The Japanese failed to achieve any major objective. They destroyed minor fuel and supply dumps and a few American aircraft, but could not delay the Leyte operation. The air transports to Tacloban were destroyed by AA fire, while those destined for Dulag crash-landed, killing all their occupants. The 77th (US) Division landings at Ormoc saw this operation cease. General Suzuki, the CG of the 35th Japanese Army ordered that all troops make for the Ormoc Valley. This is where the last of the airdrops took place. On 8–14 December some 500 men from 4th Air Raiding Landing Unit parachuted onto Valencia airfield. They were unable to achieve anything and retreated, collecting stragglers and repeatedly attacked by Filipino guerillas.

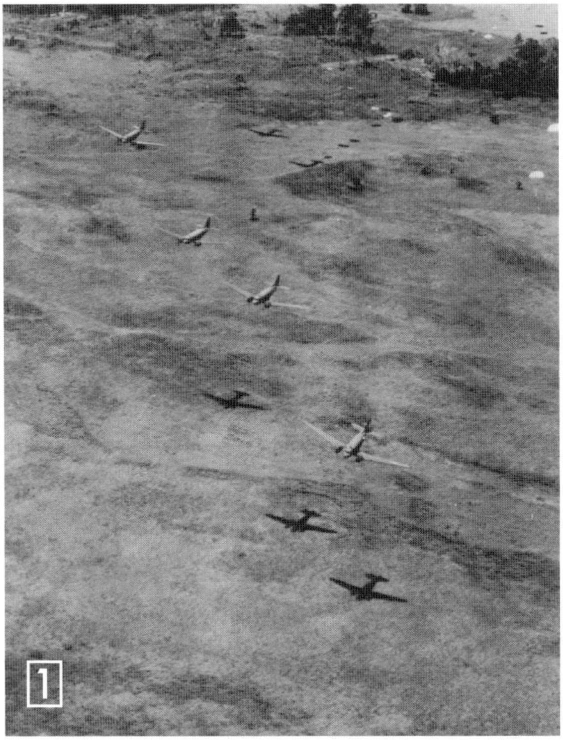
1

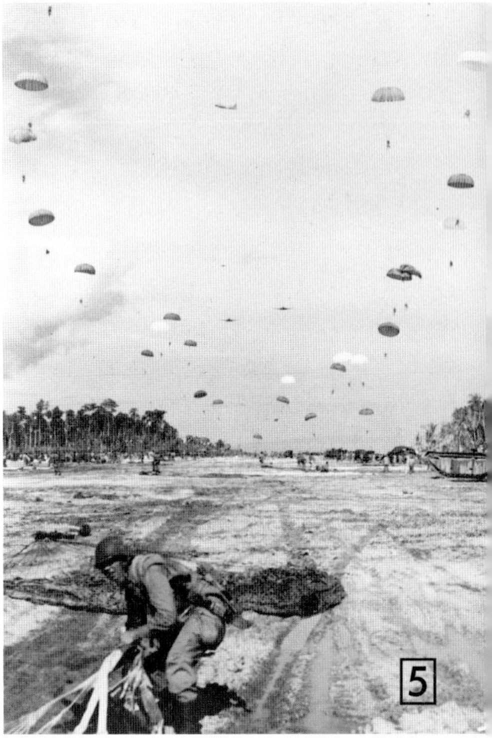
5

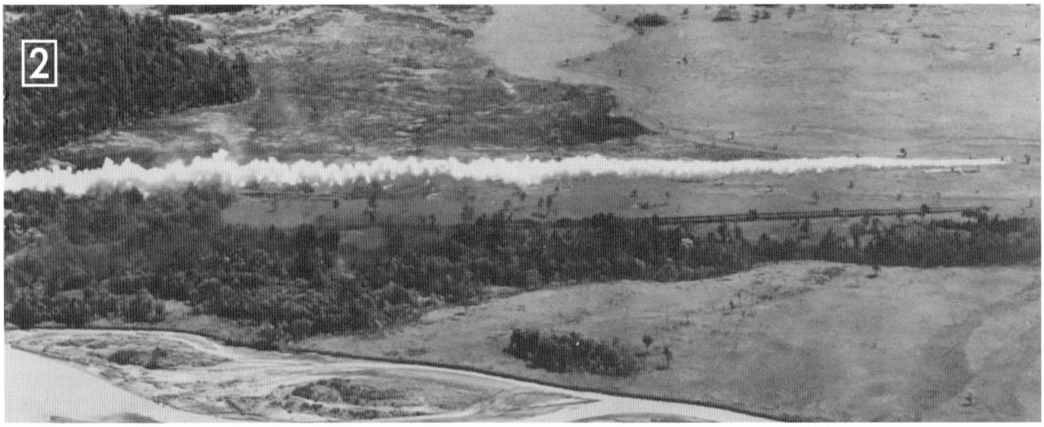
2

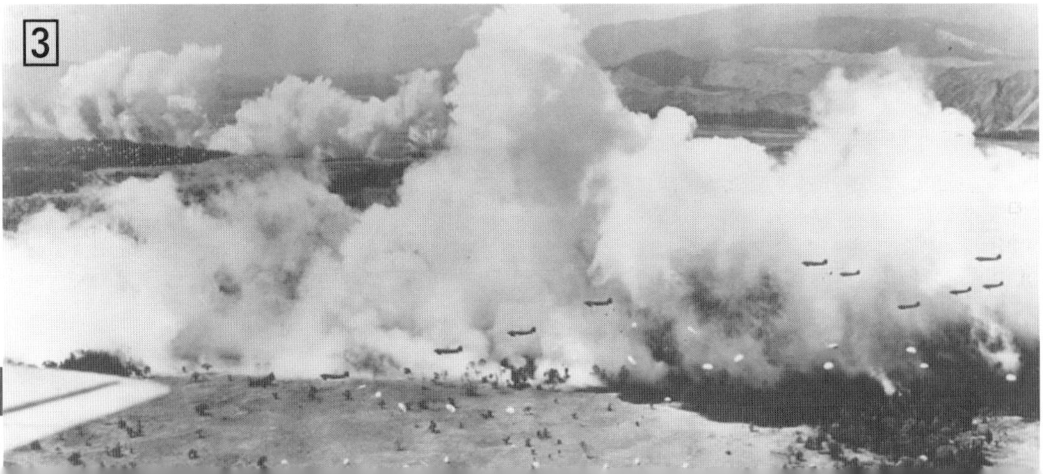
3

US airborne actions in the Pactic theatre

These involved USMC 1st Parachute Regiment, and the US Army's 503rd Airborne RCT and 11th Airborne Division. The Marines didn't manage a combat jump but were involved in PoW rescue operations and fought alongside their amphibious colleagues. The lack of transport aircraft and the long distances between objectives militated against their use in major airborne operations.

The first action was by the 503rd in the Markham Valley, 4–16 September 1943, part of the series of operations towards taking Rabaul. A heavy practice regime ensured the regiment was more than ready on 4 September. The successful drop – which included a number of Australian gunners after only one practice drop – at the Nadzab Emergency Landing Strip allowed the capture of the airfield and its preparation by Aussie engineers for the arrival of the 7th Australian Division by air. There was no opposition on the ground and the first C-47 landed at Nadzab on 6 September. By the 16th, 420 had done so and the Australians were able to take Lae. The textbook success of the operation – following so closely from Husky II – allowed Gen Swing to incorporate the lessons into recommendations for future airborne operations. At a time when so many influential leaders were having doubts about airborne operations, the success of the 503rd – under the eyes of Gen McArthur circling overhead in a B-17 – had a profound impact.

The next airborne operation in the Pacific took place on 3/4 July 1944. Operation Table Tennis saw 1 and 3/503rd jump on the Island of Noemfoor in Dutch New Guinea. It was chosen because it wasn't heavily manned and there was little AA defence; it also had a large number of airfields. These proved helpful for subsequent operations against Borneo

The 503rd jumped from 400ft on six separate drop zones around the Nadzab airstrip (**1**), the way having been prepared with six A-20 Boston bombers laying a smokescreen (**2**).

3 The attack at its height, with one battalion of paratroops descending from 54th Troop Carrier Wing's C-47s in the foreground, while in the distance (left) another battalion descends against another smokescreen. The regiment left the aircraft in less than five minutes. The drop was remarkably free from mishaps although, unfortunately, there were 3 deaths and 33 injuries.

4 Digger meets para (note Aussie Owen SMG).

5 Noemfoor gave a rough landing: nearly 130 of the 2,000 who dropped sustained injuries.

and elsewhere. As it happened, the para-drop was all but unneccessary. They had more problems with the low-altitude drop than the enemy, as the field had already fallen. With 128 non-battle injuries incurred in two drops, 2/503rd was delivered by sea.

Next, 11th Airborne Division's 511th PIR and 457th PFAB jumped on Tagaytay Ridge in Luzon (in the Philippines) on 3 February 1945 to capture road junctions on the way to Manila, while the 187th and 188th GIR fought alongside the amphibious invasion.

The 511th PIR didn't benefit from pathfinders – although the division's Recce Platoon had set up smoke signals – but problems with cloud in the dropping area meant that these weren't visible. Nevertheless, the drop went ahead with no opposition and the division made its way to Manila.

On 13 December 1945 the 503rd RCT landed by sea on Mindoro Island in the Philippines, alongside elements of Sixth (US) Army. Two months later, on 16 February 1945, the same 503rd RCT, launched an airborne assault on Corregidor. Their assault on the 'Rock' saw them land on two extremely small DZs: one, the old parade ground, was 460m long with a width varying between 60 and 210m; the other, the old golf course, was also 460m long varying in width between 140 and 210m – as tight a regimental drop as any in the war. To keep the Japanese away from the drop zone, the island was heavily bombed – over 2,000 sorties between 23 January and 16 February.

Brought from Mindoro by the 317th TCG on 16 February, the first stick was blown back onto the cliffs after dropping from 600ft, so the altitude for succeeding aircraft was cut to 400ft. Aircraft needed to make three passes to drop their full complement of paras and it took an hour for the first drop. That hour saw 1,007 men dropped – three infantry companies, a 75mm pack howitzer battery, a

USMC PARACHUTISTS

Looking very different to any other paratroops in the Pacific, the short-lived USMC experiment with airborne troops withered on the vine some three years after the first volunteers had reported for training in October 1940. Always short of transport aircraft, the lack of enthusiasm from the top was obvious: one company was instituted in March 1941, but by March 1942 there were only 500 men. Gestation may have been slow, but once they were sent to the Pacific (along with 1st Marine Division in June 1942) they saw action quickly: at Gavutu on 7 August and Tasimboko, attached to the 1st Raider Bn. Their next action was a year after that, Choiseul on 28 October 1943, but after taking part in the invasion of Bougainville on 1 November 1943 the 1st Parachute Regt was recalled and furled its colours on 29 February 1944. Many of its men joined 5th Marines and three of them were on Mt Suribachi raising the flag in 1945. The unit had never jumped into combat. Note Marine raider 'frog skin' camouflage and M50 Reising SMG.

Above: 11th Airborne Division para-drop near Aparri on Luzon in the Philippines. Unneccessary it may have been, but it did give an opportunity for gliders in general and a single CG-13 glider (see p186) to see action for the first time in the South West Pacific Area.

Below: Men of the 11th Airborne Division assemble after their arrival at Aparri. Note the CG-4As at left.

50cal. MG platoon, elements of an engineer company, Bn HQ and elements of the regimental HQ. Luckily, surprise was complete. A notable immediate casualty was the Japanese island commander whose OP was either hit by bombing or by the paras.

The second drop saw 51 aircraft bring in nearly 1,000 more men and equipment, and there was a resupply drop of ammunition, rations and water later that afternoon. The third drop – due for 17 February – was cancelled because of the high winds and 1/503rd came in by sea. 2,069 men dropped in total and casualties were surprisingly light: 231 – of whom 13 were killed (3 malfunctions, 2 impacts and 8 enemy action). That figure rose to 209 killed, 725 wounded and 19 missing by the time the island was captured, the fighting having included banzai charges and suicide bombers.

The Los Banos Internment Camp was the site of another jump when the 511th – fighting alongside Filipino guerillas – were tasked with freeing the prisoners. They were joined by the rest of the division in Amtracs which were then used to evacuate the internees safely. The operation went ahead on 23 February 1945 and was completely successful, although it led to the enraged Japanese massacring local inhabitants in revenge.

On 23 June 1945 the final jump took place – although, as Robert Ross Smith says, 'The airborne operation had proved both useless and unnecessary.' The very day – 21 June – that Gen Krueger ordered the 511th PIR to drop near Aparri, US forces entered the town unopposed. Some 1,030 men, including the reinforced 1/511th PIR and Bty C, 457th PFAB dropped from 54 C-47s, 14 C-46s, and 7 gliders. The dropping ground was Camalaniugan Airstrip.

Right: Paratroopers of the 511th PIR prepare for their jump to on Los Banos. In the end 2,147 Allied civilians were released from internment. Three men of US 8th Inf Div and four Filipino guerillas died – and the Japanese subsequently massacred over 2,000 civilians in retaliation.

Below right: The survivors from Los Banos were brought to safety by use of LVTs. Each of the 60 vehicles could carry around 30 people and had to make two round trips across the 25-mile long Laguna de Bay.

The American and Japanese weren't the only paratroops in the Pacific theatre. The Australians formed their own unit – the 1st Parachute Battalion – in 1943. Most of these men had seen action and their training reflected this – it was not just learning to use parachutes but demolitions as an engineer troop was also raised, and tactics. In August 1944 a 25pdr mountain artillery battery was added to the order of battle.

In late 1944 the battalion was prepared to drop into Borneo. It also practised amphibious landings. It was then prepared to attempt a prisoner rescue at Sandakan. Cancelled for lack of aircraft – a perennial problem – the unit was ready to take part in the range of operations that didn't take place following Japan's surrender. Frustratingly, the battalion only entered Singapore as an honour guard before disbanding.

The British Indian Army set up and trained a number of airborne units, usually composed of a mixture of British, Indian and Gurkha troops. The 50th Parachute Bde (set up in 1941) was first used for IS duties, in July 1942 when elements were dropped north of Hyderabad to help supress an insurgency by the Hurs in Sindh.

Left: Australian paras didn't have a chance to drop in anger, in spite of their heavy training schedule.

Below: Australian armed forces in Singapore at the end of World War II. Personnel of the First Australian Parachute Brigade march to the Cenotaph on Armistice Day 1945.

The 1st Air Commando Group was formed to support long-distance operations behind Japanese lines in Burma. Activated in India on 29 March 1944, it's best known for Operation Thursday, the second Chindit mission. The 6,300ft strip at Lalaghat handled the transport and gliders for resupply of the Chindits, initially to landing strips Piccadilly, Broadway and Chowringhee; later to two others – Aberdeen and White City. A 2nd Air Commando was raised later and the pair were used in Operation Dracula against Rangoon.

During 1944 they were used to combat the Japanese attack on India (Operation U-Go). The 50th Parachute Brigade fought at Sangshak 20–26 March 1944, delaying the Japanese advance, inflicting heavy casualties (and sustaining them) before retreating. Their six-day battle, in awful conditions, with air-dropped resupply operations going to the Japanese, was nothing short of heroic. They had given time for the positions at Kohima and Imphal to be prepared, ensuring that the Japanese attack foundered there.

The only parchute operation in Burma took place as the monsoons of 1945 neared. It was essential that Rangoon was captured. The Japanese received their supplies through the port and the advancing Fourteenth Army would need to do the same. As part of the plan – Operation Dracula – the coastal defences around the mouth of the River Rangoon needed to be neutralised. To effect this, the Composite Parachute Battalion of 44th Indian Airborne Division was dropped on Elephant Point. The drop went well and the attack on Japanese batteries – in spite of blue on blue attacks by their air support – was swiftly prosecuted. The Gurkhas did their job with light casualties.

73161A.

The Composite Parachute Battalion was made up of Gurkhas from 2nd and 3rd Gurkha Bns. It had time to conduct hurried training and a rehearsal before 40 Dakotas (one carrying pathfinders) of 1st and 2nd US Air Commando Groups flew them to the DZ. These photos show the drop. Note the container drop (**Opposite, Above**) and the containers just visible under the aircraft (**Opposite, Below**). The aircraft were those of the unit that had towed gliders for the second Chindit expedition (see p133) – but had no previous experience in parachute drops. They did a remarkable job, flying for 400 miles in bad visibility and poor flying conditions. that steadily got worse. Nevertheless, the drop was a huge success with only five minor injuries – whereas the Gurkhas lost 15 killed and 30 wounded to misbombing.

A 1930s view of Red Army paratroopers wearing jump helmets and carrying 7.62mm DP light MGs. Glantz (1984) pithily remarks: 'The ambitious plans of he Soviet High Command for successfully employing their massive and varied forces in battle foundered on the rocks of incompetent leadership, inadequate weaponry, and the lack of equipment as sophisticated as the Soviet force structure.' Nowhere was this more true than Soviet airborne forces – the VDV.

7 Russian Airborne Operations

Russian preeminence in the theory of airborne warfare in the 1930s fell victim to Stalin's purges that left the Red Army a shadow of its former self. 'The brain of the army,' as Glantz put it, 'dulled, and imagination and initiative failed.' The Russians had examined vertical envelopment before other countries. Mikhail Tukhachevsky, CO of the Leningrad Military District, held exercises and proposed the T/O&E for an airborne motorised division. On 2 August 1930, 12 paratroops armed with MGs dropped on Voronezh airfield from 500m and 300m. This led to the creation of a 164-man unit in the Leningrad district that could be deployed by 12 TB-1s and 10 R-5s. The tactical concept was that the paratroops would seize airfields or airstrips to allow airlanding forces to be transported in. On 5 January 1932 a *Revoensovet* (Revolutionary Military Soviet) report mandated the creation of four aviation motorised detachments, one in each of Moscow, Leningrad, Belorussian and Ukrainian military districts along with a TB-1 squadron to carry them. Only the Leningrad unit and a platoon in the Ukraine were formed. On 11 December 1932 the Revoensovet ordered the creation of an airborne brigade. Larger and larger exercises took place 1934–37.

Tukhachevsky would play no further part in this development, however. On 2 May 1937 he was arrested as part of the purges. He was tortured into making a confession that he was a German spy and executed on the night of 11/12 June. His wife and brothers were executed, too; three of his sisters were sent to the gulag as was his daughter when she reached adulthood – his family's fate a microcosm of the purges.

The airborne forces continued to expand. By 1939 they were:

Unit	MD	Unit	MD	Unit
201st AB Bde	Leningrad	211th AB Bde	Kiev	1st Rostov Regt
202nd AB Bde	Far East	212th AB Bde (later Odessa)	Far East	2nd Gorokhovets Regt
204th AB Bde	Kiev	214th AB Bde	Belorussian	3rd Voronezh Regt

Source: Sukhorukov via Glantz

They gained combat experience: 212th AB Bde fought at Khalkhin-Gol; the 201st and 204th fought in the Soviet-Finnish War of 1939–40. In June 1940 – admittedly against little or no opposition – the same three units were dropped in Romanian Bessarabia and secured the cities of Bollard, Ismail and Kabul.

The reorganisation by S.K. Timoshenko that took place after the debacle against Finland saw Russian airborne forces' missions defined – Glantz lists: disruption of army command and control and supply functions; destruction of communications routes; interruption of enemy troop, arms, and supply movements; capture and destruction of airfields and bases; seizure of coastal areas in support of naval landings; reinforcement of troops in encirclement and of mobile units operating in the enemy's rear; and fighting against enemy airborne troops in one's own rear.

The airborne forces were expanded and the new T/O&E of the airborne brigade was expanded to 3,000 men:

Para group	Airlanded Group
2 × parachute battalions 546 men each of 3 × rifle companies (3 × rifle pl; 1 × 50mm mortar pl); sig pl, recce pl, engr pl, supply pl, med squad, sigs coy	2 × airlanded battalions (546 men organised as per para group)
	1 × mor coy (9 × 82mm)
	1 × air defence coy (12 × HMGs)
Glider group	1 × tk coy (11 × T40 or T38 tanks)
2 × glider battalions (546 men organised as per para group)	1 × arty Bn (1 × 45mm bty, 1 × 76mm bty)

In April 1941 five airborne corps were created from the cadre of the 201st/204th/211th/212th/214th bdes. They were

1st (Kiev Special MD)	3rd Odessa MD	5th Pre-Baltic Special MD
2nd Kharkov MD	4th Western Special MD	

Each corps had 10,419 men, 50 tanks, 3 × AB Bdes of 4 para bns.

In June 1941 the VDV were separated from the control of the Red Army Air Force and by the time they went to war, on paper they looked impressive: five airborne corps, one airborne brigade and other units totalling 100,000 men. Whether, however, the armaments, leaders or training – or indeed manpower levels – were worth more than the paper they were printed on remained to be seen.

Corps	Bde	MD
1st	1st, 204th, 211th	Kiev Special
2nd	2nd, 3rd, 4th	Kharkov
3rd	5th, 6th, 212th	Odessa
4th	7th, 8th, 214th	Western Special
5th	9th, 10th, 201st	Pre-Baltic Special

Immediately, everything went wrong. The German attack, the weaknesses of the Russian political and military leadership, the skill at arms and purpose of the attackers – all led to big losses, collapse and a desperate defence that was halted by the Russian winter on the doorstep of Moscow. The airborne troops were deeply involved

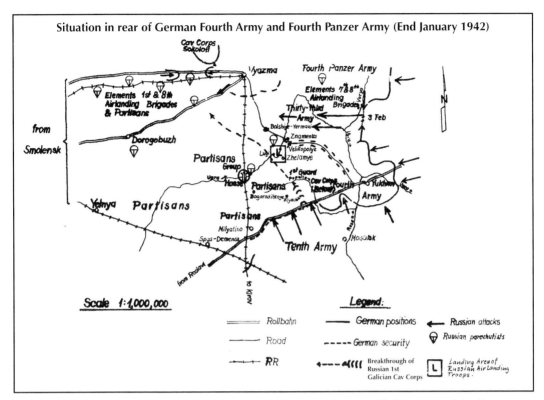

Situation in rear of German Fourth Army and Fourth Panzer Army (End January 1942)

Cav Corps Sokoloff
Vyazma
Fourth Panzer Army
Elements 1st & 8th Airlanding Brigades & Partisans
Elements 7&8th Airlanding Brigades
Thirty-Third Army
3 Feb
from Smolensk
Dorogobuzh
Znamenka
Velikopolye
Zhelamye
Partisans Group
Partisans
1st Guard Cav Corps
Fourth Army
Yelnya
Partisans
Milyatino
Spas-Demensk
Tenth Army
Mosalsk
from Roslavl
to Kirov
Scale 1:1,000,000
Legend:
Rollbahn
Road
RR
German positions
German security
Breakthrough of Russian 1st Galician Cav Corps
Russian attacks
Russian parachutists
Landing Area of Russian Air Landing Troops.

The first significant Russian airborne operation took place in January 1942 as part of the Russian winter offensive. German Fourth Armee had been flanked; there were strong partisan bands south of Vyazma and the key Rollbahn, the Moscow–Warsaw road, down which the logistic supplies came, was under threat. The plan was good – the problem was the execution. Without a successful drop the paratroops and partisans at no stage presented a strong enough threat and the Germans were able to weather the storm, albeit with some difficulty and some losses.

in attempting to halt the German attacks – but as infantry rather than airborne troops ,although there were a number of smaller operations around Moscow that were successfully prosecuted (see table on page 141)

This had been helped in September 1941 by the reorganisation that placed the airborne units that had survived – primarily 4th and 5th Corps – under direct control of the Stavka (Supreme headquarters). There was a new T/O&E, the original corps were reinforced and five more corps (6–10) were created. The biggest problem for their use by air was lack of aircraft and this issue would dog the Soviet paras when they were used for the first major paratroop operation on the Eastern Front.

Having seen the problems the Allies encountered on its first major airborne operation – Sicily – it's no surprise that the Russians, too, were incapable of delivering a sizeable unit and its equipment in one area at night. Insufficient aircraft, poor navigational aids and, once they hit the ground, lack of suitable communication aids meant that the drops

were fragmented. It was the start of a six-month campaign and of the 14,000 men dropped over this period, fewer than 4,000 returned. The idea was good: support for the deep incursions made into the German lines by the Russian winter offensive and an attempt to surround and cut off German Fourth Army, but too few heavy weapons and insufficient coordination of forces rendered the attack an irritant rather than a decisive blow and the Germans were able to weather the storm – prolonged though it was. A postwar study (Reinhard, 1952) by German generals talked about the German troops tied down dealing with the paratroops (four divisions of seven army corps) and the significant boost given to the cause of the partisans in the Germans rear but suggested this was never a strategic threat. By June 1942 it was over and the troops that remained in a cohesive unit broke out to the Russian lines.

In summer 1942 there were major changes to the airborne forces caused by the exigencies of the Russian strategic position: specifically, the fact that the Germans were knocking on the gates of Stalingrad. The Stavka needed to support their forces and used its strategic reserve – as Eisenhower did in the Ardennes in 1944 – sending the airborne corps into battle, converting them into guards rifle divisions. Other units were sent to the Caucasus. The airborne units – as with their western counterparts – performed well enough to justify this reallocation.

At the same time, the Stavka created new airborne corps (1st and 4th–10th) in autumn 1942. They were well trained and ready for another major operation. The opportunity arose in September as the Russian forces closed on the Dnieper – a major obstacle and a good place for the Germans to set up a defence line. As the Germans scrambled to get their forces across, the Russians managed to establish two small bridgeheads – blocked by elements of 19. Panzer-Division from Kiev in the north. If the Russians could bounce those defences with an airborne operation, they could get a substantial bridgehead across the river that the Germans would be hard pressed to hold. However, the opportunity went begging. As in 1942, the plan was better than reality – delivery and concentration of the airborne force was wanting: the drops had

Smaller Operations
(source: Glantz, 1984)

The Russians initiated a number of smaller airborne operations in late 1941– early 1942. Because they required fewer aircraft, less equipment and were shorter in duration, they were more successful.

Date	Location	Unit	Corps
14–15 Dec 41	Teryaeva Sloboda	One Bn, 214th AB Bde	4th AB
2–4 Jan 42	Medyn	One Bn, 201st AB Bde	5th AB
	One Bn, 250th Rifle Regt		
18–22 Jan 42	Zhelan'ye	1st and 2nd Bns, 201st AB Bde	5th AB
	250th AB Regt		
27–31 Jan 42	Ozerechnya- Tabory	8th AB Bde	4th AB
13–23 Feb 42	Velikopol'ye-Zhela'ye	One Bn, 8th AB Bde	4th AB
		9th and 214th AB Bdes	4th AB
16–17 Feb 42	Rzhev	4th Bn, 204th AB Bde	1st AB
26–18 Apr 42	Svintsovo	4th Bn, 23rd AB Bde	10th AB
29–30 May 42	10km S of Dorogobuzh	23rd AB Bde	10th AB
		211th AB Bde	1st AB

Opposite: White M3A1 scout car from the 3rd Guards Airborne Division reconnaissance detachment. Allied Lend-Lease played a huge part in equipping the Soviets. The 3rd Guards fought at the Demyansk Pocket, Kursk and won the Order of the Red Banner, it ended the war in Austria.

Below: Paratroopers armed with PPSh-41 SMGs. The 71-round ammunition drum was subject to misfires and was replaced by a 35-round box magazine.

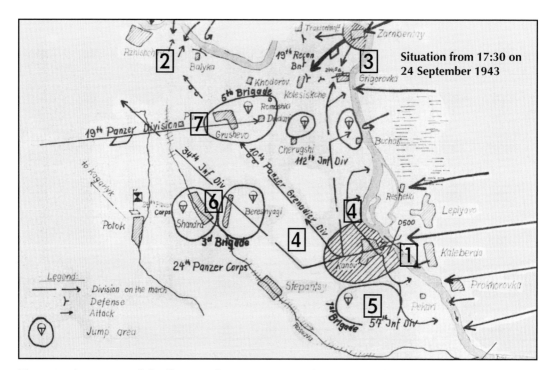

The critical moments of the Dnieper drop as seen on a German map (Reinhard, 1952). **1** German crossing point at Kanev: bridge finally demolished late on 23 September. Russian bridgeheads established on 23 September at Rzhishchev (**2**) and Velikyi Bukrin (**3**) but lack of bridging equipment means the Soviets cannot push enough men or armour across the river. German forces rush to negate bridgeheads (**4**). Airdrops of 1st Guards AB Bde (**5**), 3rd Guards AB Bde (**6**) and 5th Guards AB Bde (**7**) – in fact, they were much more scattered than this map indicates.

to be delayed from 23/24 September by a day – thus giving the Germans sufficient time to move their forces north from Kanev. The reason for the delay was a combination of the awful state of the railways (no stock and lines in disrepair) and bad weather. The Germans rushed north. The drop, when it happened, saw only 298 of 500 sorties on the first night. In total, only 4,575 men from 3rd and 5th Bdes were landed and the drop was badly scattered. The paratroopers that did drop were caught in the air or mopped up in small groups: many were killed immediately. However, by early October, sufficient men grouped together under Lt Col Sidorchuk (CO of 5th Bde) to create a coherent unit. Supplied with weapons, radios and acquiring more men, this force fought on until linking up with 254th Rifle Division when it crossed the Dnieper. On 28 November – two months after having been dropped – what remained of the heroic paratroopers were evacuated.

As with so many of the airborne operations of World War II, the paratroopers had proved themselves tenacious and brave warriors, but the command and control, delivery and logistics had proved too much.

KERCH PENINSULA 31 DECEMBER 1941

The winter of 1941 saw the Russians desperately trying to stem the German assault. Winter came to their aid, but not before the Germans had reached the Black Sea and invested Sevastopol. The attempt by the Red Army to retake the peninsula and relieve Sevastopol started with an amphibious assault on 26 December 1941. An airborne attack on Vladislavovka airfield was intended but called off because of bad weather. The amphibous attack was pulverised by the German response but on 28 December the Soviets landed in Feodosia forcing the Germans to retreat. As they withdrew, on 31 December, 250 paratroopers were dropped near Ak Monai from TB-3 bombers in dreadful weather conditions and harried by a German ammunition convoy. Nevertheless, the spread of the drop made the Germans think the force was larger than it was and the paras took a German artillery position and then harassed the retreat. It couldn't stop the Germans from setting up defensive lines and a visceral campaign started: it ended on 19 May when the Russians left the peninsula having suffered 352,000 casualties.

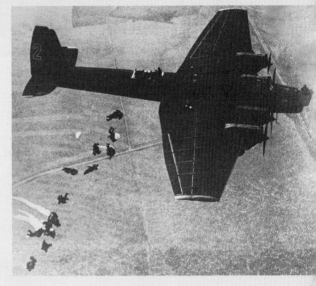

Above: It looks bizarre but Russian paratroopers jumped from the TB-3 by sliding down the wing surfaces.

1 *First amphibious landing at Kerch, 26.12.41.*
2 *Second amphibious landing at Feodosia, 29.12.41.*
3 *Para drop, 31.12.41.*

Left: The Kerch peninsula after it had fallen to the Russians. The attack petered out, however, and the siege of Sevastopol wasn't relieved.

Below left: This memorial commemorates the Soviet participants in the Kerch landing operation.

Below: Monument to the Soviet paratroopers who died on the waters of the Kerch Strait and Taman Bay in the battle for Crimea.

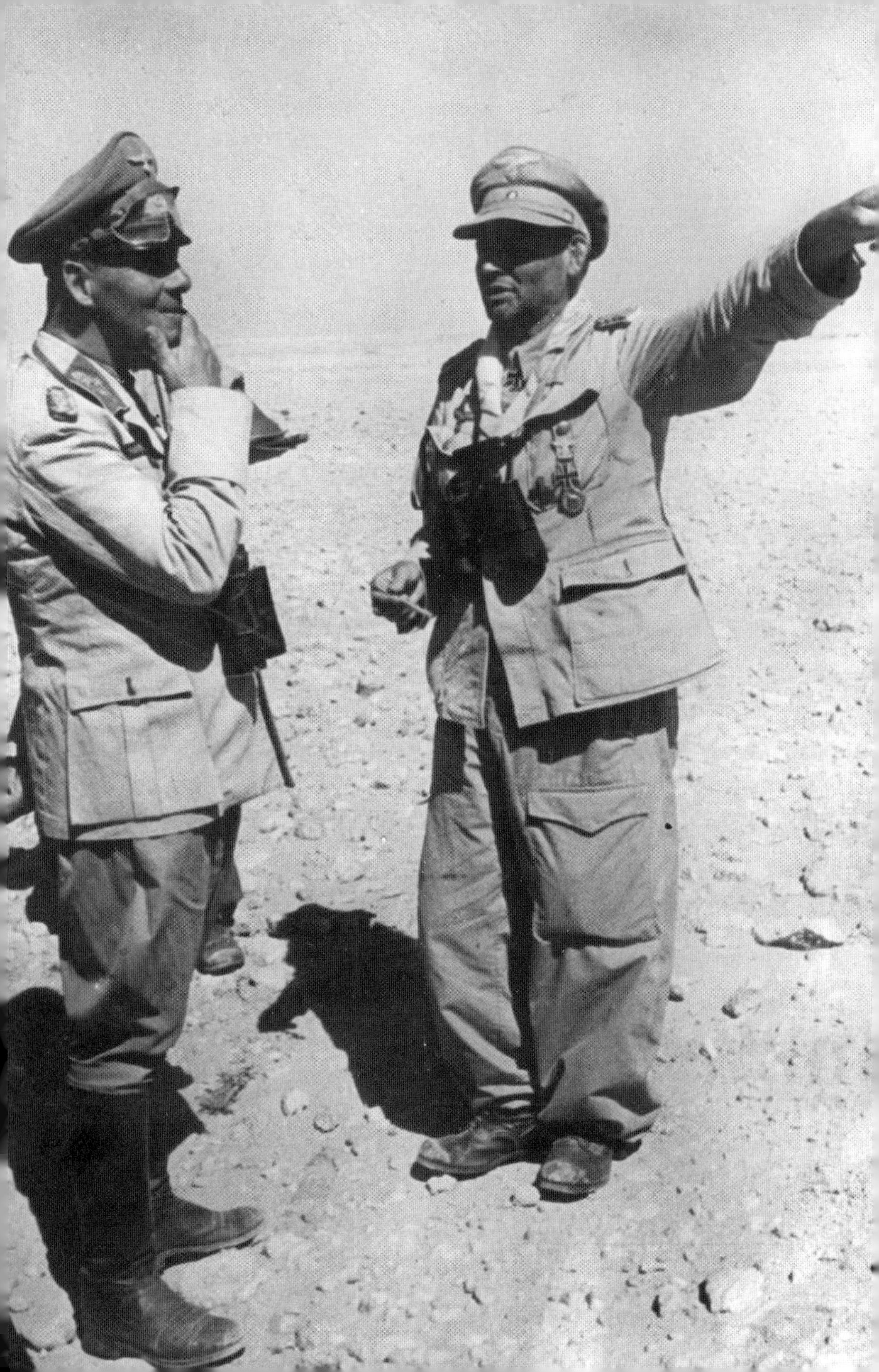

8 Paratroopers as Elite Ground Forces

After the close-run battle of Crete, in spite of Student's attempt to woo Hitler into a massive air envelopment of Malta, the Fallschirmjäger were mainly used in the ground role – one that they performed brilliantly but brutally in every theatre. It started in September 1941 when 7. Flieger-Division, reinforced and refreshed after the battle of Crete, was sent to Leningrad. It wasn't introduced as a single unit, however, but piecemeal, FJR1 and FJR3 in Leningrad and Kampfgruppe Sturm based on FJR2 on the River Mius. The freezing temperatures of their first Russian winter and the heavy casualties would become regular things in the future. From late 1941 till July 1942, 22. Luftlande-Division fought in the Crimea before taking up duties in Crete and ending the war in the Balkans. (The other Luftlande-Division – 91. – formed in January 1944 and fought in Normandy opposite Utah Beach and, later, in France.)

Late 1942 saw Ramcke's Brigade sent to North Africa and, in an attempt to hold Tunisia after Operation Torch, FJR5 was sent there. It and Tunisia were lost, as was the FJ-Pionier-Bataillon. In 1943, Ramcke's unit was rebuilt as 2. FJD in Brittany and then fought in Russia, 1. FJD (renamed from 7. Flieger-Division) was used to reinforce the Axis troops in Sicily. It was joined by 2. FJD and other units in Italy as Mussolini's fascist regime was toppled. 1. FJD would fight in Italy – memorably at Monte Cassino – until 1945, joining 4. FJD (who fought at Anzio) in 1944 to become 1. FJ-Korps.

2. FJD moved to Russia and fought there until returning to Germany for re-fitting in May 1944. It went to Normandy where it fought hard against the Allied invasion. FJR6 was cut to pieces in the Falaise Pocket; the rest of the division was lost when Brest fell. Reconstituted, it fought in Germany in 1945. 3. FJD (raised in France late 1943) fought in Normandy, forming – with 5. FJD – II FJ-Korps and was destroyed at Falaise. It was reconstituted and fought around Arnhem as part of Student's 1. Fallschirm-Armee, and then the Hürtgen, the Ardennes and into Germany. 5. FJD (the last to receive proper paratoop training) fought in Normandy, the

Rommel and Ramcke in the desert. A diehard Nazi, Hermann-Berhard Ramcke joined the Imperial German Navy in World War I. He joined 7. Flieger-Division in 1940 as an Oberst (colonel) and became a fully fledged paratrooper aged 51. After Crete – and promoted Generalmajor – he led a brigade that fought with distinction in Africa. As a Generalleutnant he commanded 2. FJD in Italy and on the Eastern Front before it moved to Brest. He took command of Festung Brest and refused to surrender until forced on 19 September 1944. He never recanted, was found guilty of war crimes and after serving his time continued as an outspoken supporter of the Nazi regime.

Netherlands and the Ardennes. Also formed to fight in Normandy in June 1944, one regiment of 6. FJD (the 15.) went to the Eastern Front while the rest (some of whom received jump training) fought in Normandy and the Netherlands. 7. FJD fought at Arnhem and in the west 1944–45.

Many other divisions were created using the Fallschirm title – 8., 9., 10., 11., 20., 21. – but none of them had paratroop training and were formed from Luftwaffe personnel, fighting as ground troops. 11., 20., 21. hadn't formed completely when the war ended.

Above left: Ramcke's men in the desert – the front two are carrying machine gun magazines for the MG34 or 42. The 7.92mm drum magazines came in two forms, the *Patronenkasten* 34 and 41. Both carried 50 rounds, the later, steel version was waterproofed with a rubber seal.

Centre left: This sleeping Fallschirmjäger has what looks like an 8cm GrW34 mortar bipod behind him.

Left: Having spotted the Allies' 'Torch' convoys, the Germans rushed reinforcement to Tunisia. The first were Stab, I. and III./FJR5 who had been training for an operation against Malta. By 16 November 1943 the Ju52s had brought them in and they were dug in around Tunis.

Opposite: Fallschirmjäger sing as they march through Tunis – perhaps their marching song 'Rot scheint die Sonne.'

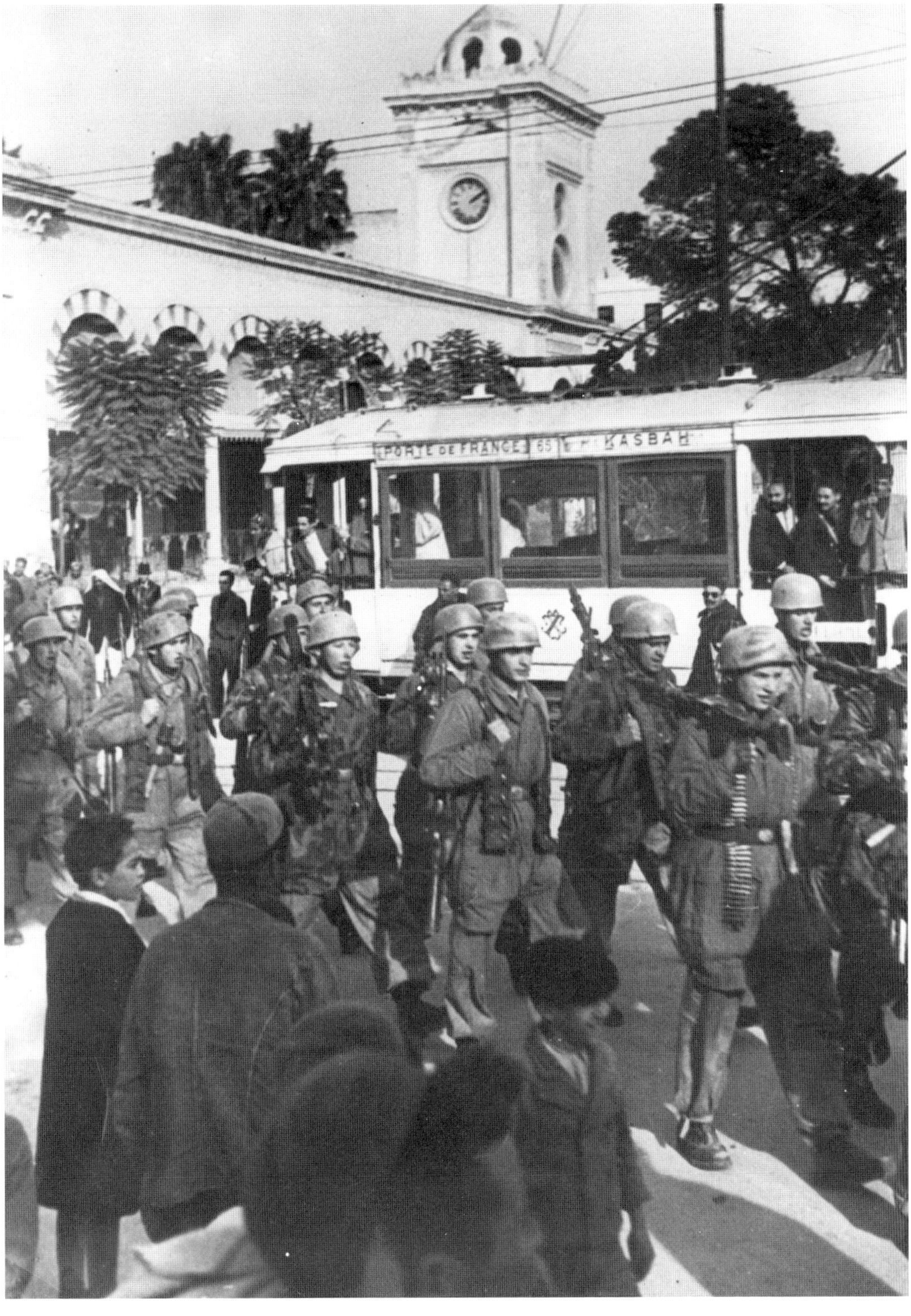
PORTE DE FRANCE
65
KASBAH

The Italian *Paracadutisti* didn't have much chance to put their parachute training into practice and spent the war as infantry. The most successful unit was the 185ª Divisione Paracadutisti Folgore, which made its name in the African desert. At El Alamein it performed heroically, and on into Tunisia. A second division – 185ª Divisione Paracadutisti Nembo – was set up in 1943 and sent first to Yugosla-via and, later that year, to Sardin-ia. When the Italian armistice (of Cassibile) took place – made public 8 September 1943 – some elements of the Nembo remained with the Germans as part of 4.FJD and were involved in the defence of Anzio.

Some of the Italian paras who changed sides, part of the Italian Co-belligerent Army, were involved in Operation Herring on 19 April 1945 (see photo **5**).

1 Fallschirmjäger in Italy – a typical scene shows a unit festooned with MG ammunition, both boxes and drums.

2 Ammunition of a different order – 8.8cm rounds for a gun crew on the Anzio front. Kesselring's forces oppos-ing the Allies included I. Fallschirm-Korps, 4. FJD – a new division that incorporated the 'Nembo' Battalion from the Royal Italian Army's 'Folgore' Regiment – was part of I.FJ-Korps.

3 Fallschirmjäger 8.8cm on its cruci-form mount – note the wheels at right. Those firing would need good ear protection in these city streets.

4 Italian paras from 4.FJD.

5 Operation Herring saw a small force – around 226 men from Italian F Reconnaissance Squadron and 184ª Divisione paracadutisti Nembo – parachute behind German lines. For 72 hours they created havoc, killing 481 German soldiers, taking 1,083 prisoners, and holding a number of bridges to facilitate the Allied offensive. Note the MAB38 SMGs, and British X-type parachutes and leg bags.

6 Men of 1. FJD with Italian paras from the 'Folgore' Division. Note the Beretta MAB38 SMG and the distinctive 'Samurai' magazine-holding vest which held 5 magazines on the front and 7 on the back along with 6 grenades in waist pouches.

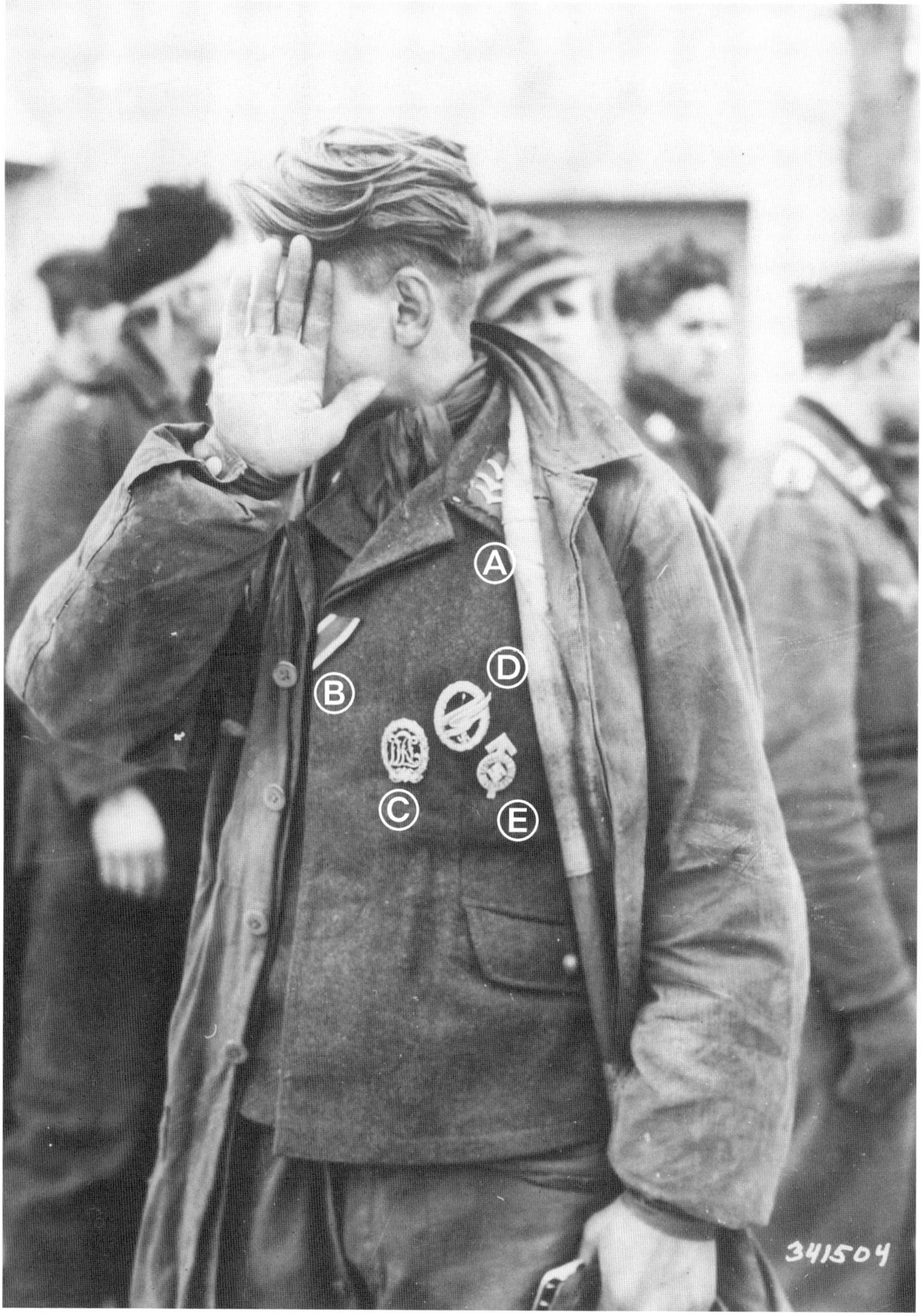
A
B
C
D
E
341504

Opposite: Fallschirmjäger, probably of 3. FJD, having been captured by 16th (US) Inf Regt (1st Inf Div) Waywertz, Belgium during the Ardennes campaign. Note the badges on this Obergefreiter: **A** collar rank; **B** Iron Cross Second Class; **C** German WW2 Sports badge, awarded by the German *Deutscher Reichsbund fur Leibesubungen* (DRL) in silver; **D** Luftwaffe Fallschirmschützenabzeichen (received for making six qualifying jumps); **E** Hitlerjugend performance badge in silver.

Above: Fallschirmjäger pass a KO'd M4A3. Note the Panzerfaust (**A**) and Panzerschreck (**B**).

Below: Men of FJR6 in Ste-Mère-Église. They earned a reputation as the 'lions of Carentan'.

Above: As with the Luftwaffe Fallschirmjäger, the SS paras were used as ground forces for most of the time. Here, General der Infanterie Gerhard Matzky, commander of XXVI. Armeekorps, decorates three stern-looking men of SS-Fallschirmjäger-Bataillon 500 with the Iron Cross after fighting near Klaipeda, Lithuania.

Below: Another view of SS-Fallschirmjäger-Bataillon 500 in Lithuania, this time supported by a StuG III Ausf G.

Above: Heavily camouflaged Fallschirmjäger Kübelwagen in Normandy.

Above right: During Operation Pheasant, as the Allies cleared North Brabant in October–November 1944, the 53rd (Welsh) Infantry Division fought three battalions from the Fallschirmjäger training regiment based at 's-Hertogenbosch. Note man carrying Panzerfaust has a captured M1 carbine.

Below: Another Beutewaffe put to use – in this case a US Army M1919 Browning .30 MG by Fallschirmjäger of 3. FJD during Operation Market Garden at Oosterbeek.

Above Well-stocked
Fallschirmjäger
position in Russia.
Note the profusion of
grenades, the Model
39 Eihandgranaten
(**A**), Model 24
Stielhandgranaten (**B**)
and rifle grenades (**C**);
Kar98k and ammo clips
(**D**).

Above left:
Fallschirmjäger dash for
cover on the Leningrad
front line.

Left: Russia –
camouflaged mortar
team with their 8cm
GrW 34.

Above: German paratroopers from 2. FJD on a Tiger I of 2. SS-Panzer Division Das Reich, near Zhytomyr, Ukraine, December 1943. Note reversible winter snow clothing.

Below: The Bulgarian Parachute Druzhina was formed in 1943. Uneasy allies of the Germans, the Bulgarians trained at Fallschirmschule 3 at Braunschweig-Broitzem where they were mistrusted by their trainers. When Bulgaria switched sides in late 1944, the unit was quickly involved and on 18 October 1944 played an important role in the Battle of Stracin, Yugoslavia. They suffered high casualties (35 KIA, 65 WIA of the c400-man unit). Here they are seen brandishing their MP40s.

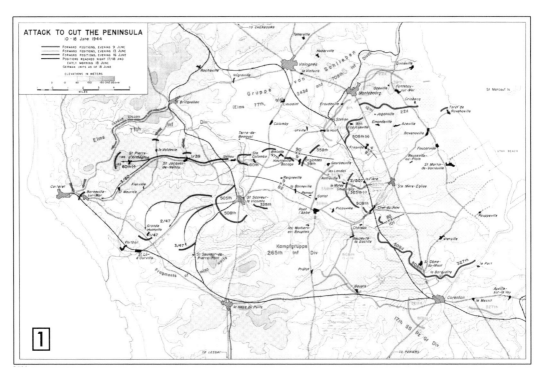

ATTACK TO CUT THE PENINSULA
10 - 18 June 1944

1 After the beachhead was secured, the US forces cut the Cotentin peninsula to stop any military assistance heading north. Having achieved this, the liberation of Cherbourg was made considerably easier.

2 St Sauveur-le-Vicomte has fallen: the the 508th PIR – the Red Devils – fought as infantrymen for 33 days after 6 June. They returned to England on 13 July after suffering 1,061 casualties with 307 KIA.

3 Paras from 2/506th PIR between Opheusden and Randwijk on the Betuwe.

4 Men of the 101st Airborne patrolling through Opheusden station.

5 1/505th's HQ Coy Mortar Pl in Nijmegen heading towards Groesbeek Heights on 29 September.

US airborne troops in the infantry role

After the initial Normandy beachhead had been secured, the 82nd Airborne fought through till July before returning to the UK for rest and recuperation. The 101st Airborne were pulled out earlier, in late June. Next up, as we have seen, came Operation Market Garden. After the battle around Arnhem ended with the British Paras retreating across the Lower Rhine, the 101st Airborne was tasked with defending the Betuwe, the Island between the Rhine and the Waal – low-lying, wet and 'the worst tank-going country of the world'. The 82nd joined the 101st on the island later in October and it was not until November that the two divisions moved out of the line.

Part of Eisenhower's SHAEF strategic reserve, the 101st and 82nd were recuperating around Reims at Camp Mourmelon after the rigours of Operation Market when they were called to action on 17 December. Rushing to the front, the traffic jams stretching out through pre-motorway France and Belgium, both divisions took up positions in time to affect the course of the battle.

Right: The main map on this page is dated 21 December 1944. 82nd Airborne's CG – Maj Gen Jim Gavin – was initially commanding XVIII Airborne Corps and his division was right in the path of Peiper's 1st SS-Panzer-Division Leibstandarte.

1 The 504th and 505th PIR held the southern flank as Peiper was stopped by the bravery of C/51st ECB blowing bridges in his face and by the tanks of 3rd Armored Division.
2 The 101st reached Bastogne in time to hold this vital crossroads. This map dated 25 December when Bastogne was surrounded (see p160). In the centre, Fifth Panzerarmee's main thrust, with 116. Panzer-Division in the van, headed for the Meuse through Houffalize and La Roche.
3 Elements of 3rd and 7th Armored and 325th GIR took position to fight delaying actions against Sixth Panzerarmee's 2nd SS-Panzer Division Das Reich.

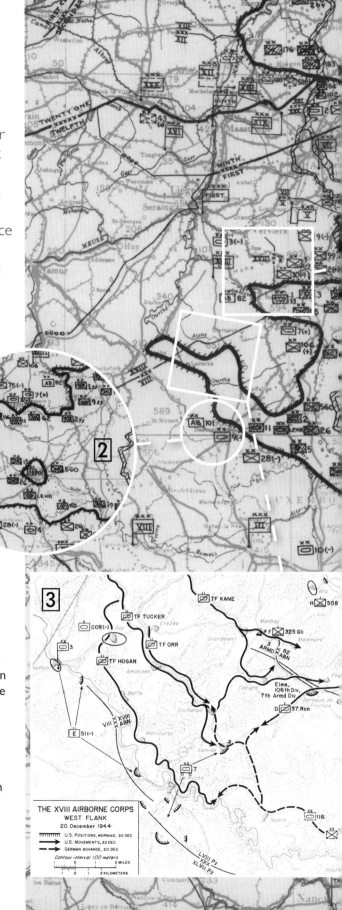

THE XVIII AIRBORNE CORPS
WEST FLANK
20 December 1944
U.S. POSITIONS, MORNING, 20 DEC
U.S. MOVEMENTS, 20 DEC
GERMAN ADVANCE, 20 DEC
Contour interval 100 meters
2 MILES
2 KILOMETERS

THE XVIII AIRBORNE CORPS MEETS KAMPFGRUPPE PEIPER
20–25 December 1944

U.S. FORWARD POSITIONS, EVENING, 19 DEC
U.S. ARMORED ATTACKS
U.S. INFANTRY ATTACKS
GERMAN ATTACKS
WOODS

Contour interval 100 meters

Below: This is Pfc Vernon Haught of 325th GIR which fought at the ferocious battle with Das Reich and, later, the Führer Begleit Brigade at the Baraque de Fraiture crossroad.

159

The 101st Airborne may have been involved in the major parachute drops over Normandy and the Netherlands, but it is for their actions in the defence of Bastogne during the Battle of the Bulge that many remember them best. Hurrying to the front to support the disintegrating 28th (US) Inf Div, the division reached Bastogne on the 19th, just in time. Supported by 705th TD Battalion, the 101st withstood all that the German attackers could throw at them, while awaiting Third (US) Army's relief operation that reached Bastogne on the 26th. Photos show men of the division in the town:

1 Note M9 bazookas at **A**, **B** and **C**; and 2.36in rockets at **D** and **E**.

2 Carrying MG ammo.

3 Command of the 101st fell to Brig Gen Anthony C. McAuliffe (R) until CG Maj Gen Maxwell D. Taylor returned from the USA after the siege. It was McAuliffe who replied 'Nuts' when the Germans suggested he surrender the town. Photo dated 5 January 1945.

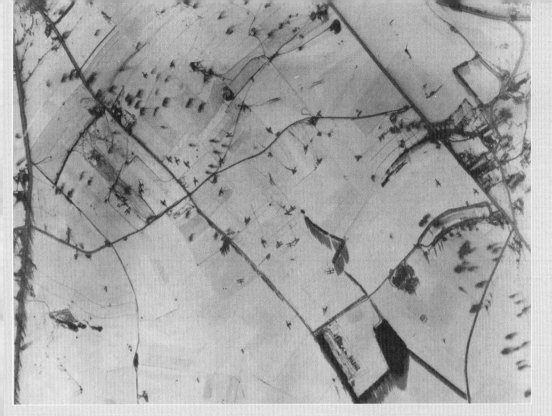

'Supply,' *FM31-30* reminds its readers, 'is a responsibility of command which cannot be delegated.' Resupply of forces in the field – particularly those in combat or in difficult situations such as the Chindits in Burma or besieged Bastogne – was undertaken by glider (as **Above**) and by paradrop (as **Below**). Reinforcements, food, water and ammunition were the most important resources that could be airdropped – and first on the *FM31-30* list. However, there were other essentials that were often desperately needed – such as batteries for radios and medical equipment. On 24 December a C-47 dropped whole blood, vaseline gauze, litters, blankets, atropine sulfate, tetanus toxoid, pentothal sodium, distilled water, syringes, and sterilisers. On 26 December 1944 two surgical teams were flown in to Bastogne by glider and landed safely at 16:00.

Right: It wasn't just American airborne troops who were involved in the Ardennes. Canadian, 1st Parachute Bn fought through to Bande, January 1945. Note the typical mix of airborne gear: smocks, toggle rope, scrim, para helmets and the range of weapons: two Stens, four SMLEs and a Bren gun. After taking Bande the battlion returned to the Netherlands where it had been fighting since 1944.

British and Canadian airborne units as infantry

On the east side of the Orne, the men of 6th Airborne Division accomplished their missions and then took up blocking positions to protect the flank of the British amphibious landings. They were quickly joined by Lord Lovat and men of the 1st Special Service Brigade, at midday on 6 June The arrival of 6th Airlanding Brigade by glider (see pp66–67) gave 6th Airborne enough men to hold fast against increasingly heavy German probes – by 8 June this included Panzergrenadier-Regiment 125 of 21. Panzer-Division who attacked the 12th Devons at Ranville. There was another major attack on 10 June that was beaten back by 7th Para Battalion and the tanks of the 13th/18th Hussars. The Canadian 1st Parachute Battalion meanwhile were feeling the pressure at le Mesnil crossroads on the Bavent ridge.

The culmination of the German attacks was the battle of Bréville. Once that village had been taken on 12 June the front remained fairly static until the breakout that started on 17 August. Nine days later, and the paras were on the Seine having advanced 45 miles. The division returned to England in September having suffered 4,457 casualties (821 KIA, 2,709 WIA and 927 MIA).

When the Germans attacked in the Ardennes in December 1944, 6th Airborne joined 82nd and 101st (US) divisions in heading towards the action. The 6th lined up along the Meuse between Dinant and Namur. When the threat diminished, having been stopped but a few miles from the river, 6th Airborne moved to the Netherlands and a stretch of the Meuse opposite FJD5. It didn't remain there long. By the end of February it had returned to England to prepare for the last major airborne operation of the war: crossing the Rhine – Operation Plunder – after which the paras sprinted 285 miles to Wismar, meeting the Red Army there.

Advancing northeast after crossing the Rhine, Churchill tanks of 6th Guards Armoured Brigade carry paratroopers of the US 17th Airborne Division through Münster (**Below**) on 24 March 1945 and then Dorsten, **This photo**) on the 29th on the way to the Elbe.

US paratroop kit didn't change massively over the period of the war. The men below wear the paratrooper boots and carry their First Aid bandages under the helmet scrim. However, note that they are carrying rifles. The lightweight M1 carbine had not been as effective in combat as had been hoped, so the number of M1 rifles carried was increased in new T/O&Es produced for Parachute and Glider Infantry Regiments in December 1944. Before, a PIR had 1,098 M1 carbines and 859 M1 rifles; after, 484 M1 carbines and 1,869 M1 rifles – a significant improvement in firepower. The other major change was that M18 57mm (**Right**) and M20 75mm recoilless rifles were introduced to replace the towed 57mm which had themselves replaced the original 37mm guns of 1942. First use was a soldier from 507th PIR who hit a German tank on 24 March.

Above: On 29–30 April 1942 Hitler, Mussolini and their staffs met to discuss Unternehmen Herkules – the invasion of Malta. They met at Klessheim castle, near Salzburg, half an hour away from the Berghof where this photo was taken: Keitel (**A**) Mussolini (**B**), Jodl (**C**), Hitler (**D**), Marshal Ugo Cavallero, Chief of the Italian staff (**E**), P. O. Schmidt, Hitler's interpreter (**F**), Kesselring (**G**) and General Antonio Gandin chief Italian planner of the operation (**H**).

Below: Ramcke (left) and Student (note his Pilot/Observer Badge in Gold with Diamonds awarded on 2 September 1941 above the Clasp to the Iron Cross) were sold on Unternehmen Herkules (attacking Malta) but the main man wasn't, so it didn't get the go ahead.

9 Cancelled Operations

Although carefully planned in great detail, there was little chance of the invasion by air of Malta taking place for one simple reason: Hitler was against it. He had a number of reasons. First, the German losses in the battle for Crete were so high. Second, the plan was predicated on Italian Navy support which Hitler thought was flaky. Third, his eyes were set on Russia and he felt any other operation would detract from that. Wayne Lutton ('Malta and the Mediterranean') quotes Hitler: 'I can assure you, though, that as soon as we begin our attack the Gibraltar squadrons will take to the air and the British fleet will set sail from Alexandria. You can imagine how the Italians will react to that. The minute they get the news on their radios, they'll all make a dash for the harbors of Sicily—both warships and freighters. You'll be sitting all alone on the island with your paratroopers.' On top of this, Rommel was clamouring for every bit of assistance possible in his push towards Alexandria.

The 'Herkules' plan had initially been put together by the Italians with help from Japanese amphibious operations experts. A meeting of 29–30 April between Mussolini and Hitler, however, put Rommel's attack on Tobruk ahead of 'Herkules' which was scheduled for July. However, by July it had been scrapped. It would have involved 30,000 airborne and 70,000 army troops. The main airborne element was for XI. Fliegerkorps to land gliders in the south to secure the landing site for Italian troops and an armoured division, capture airfields south of Valetta (RAF Hal Far and Safi Dispersal Strip) before a second para drop further north would attack Rabat, Mdina and the airfields at Ta'Qali and Luqa. The Axis airborne troops involved were 7. Flieger-Division, with additional Fallschirmjäger regiments, the Italian 1st Folgore Parachute Division and 80th Infantry Division La Spezia (an airlanding division). The German force was to be transported to Malta by 500 Ju52s, 300 DFS230s (carrying 10 men), 200 Go242s (carrying 21 men) and 24 Me321 Gigants (carrying 200 men). The Italians were transported in SM75s, SM81s and SM82s.

It wasn't the first airborne operation to be cancelled in the war, although some say that it was the most strategically important. Had Malta fallen, the resupply of Rommel's forces would have been that much easier. However, Hitler was more concerned about Russia. *Fall Blau*, the major summer offensive designed to knock the Soviets out of the war, was due to start in June. Hitler's Directive No 41 emphasised issues with resources available for his two-pronged offensive ambitions:

EXAMPLES OF CANCELLED ALLIED AIRBORNE OPERATIONS
(June–September 1944)

Codename	Planned Date	Drop Zone	Units*	Mission (reason for cancellation)
WILDOATS	June 14	Évrecy	1st	Clear way for 7th Armd Div attack/ prevent German retreat from Caen
BENEFICIARY	July 3	Saint-Malo	1st	Seize port (cancelled July 15: too heavily defended)
HANDS UP	mid-July	Quiberon	1st	Seize area (cancelled August 15: Naval objections)
SWORDHILT	late-July	Brest	1st	Seize port (cancelled July 29)
TRANSFIGURE	August 17	Paris-Orleans gap	1st, 101st, Polish, 52nd Div	Trap Seventh Armee (cancelled August 17 because ground forces overran objective)
AXEHEAD	August	Along Seine	1st, 101st, Polish, 52nd Div	3 outline plans to take Seine crossing points (cancelled August 19; ground forces overran objective)
BOXER	late-August	Boulogne	ditto	Seize port; V-weapons sites (cancelled August 26 because of mission shift)
LINNET	September 3	Tournai	ditto	Cut off retreating German forces and take Escaut crossings (cancelled September 2 because of weather)
LINNET II	September 4	Liège-Maastricht	ditto	Seize Meuse crossing near Aachen for US First Army (cancelled September 3 because of weather)
COMET	September 7/8	Arnhem	1st, Polish, 52nd Div	Seize bridges from Eindhoven to Arnhem (cancelled September 8 because of weather)
INFATUATE	September	Walcheren Island	1st	Help clear Scheldt Estuary (Brereton rejected because of Flak and terrain)
NAPLES I	September	Aachen	18th	Assist US First Army against Westwall (planning only)
NAPLES II	September	Köln (Cologne)	18th	Seize Rhine bridges for US First Army (planning only)
MILAN I	September	Trier	18th	Assist US First Army against Westwall (planning only)
MILAN II	September	Koblenz	18th	Assist US First Army in Rhine Crossing (planning only)
CHOKER I	September	Saarbrücken	18th	Assist US Third Army against Westwall (planning only)
CHOKER II	September	Mannheim	18th	Assist US Third Army in Rhine Crossing (planning only)
TALISMAN/ECLIPSE	September	Berlin, Kiel	Undetermined	In event of sudden German collapse, seize airfields/port

Units: 1st = BR 1st Airborne Division; 82nd = US 82nd Airborne Division; 101st = US 101st Airborne Division; 18th = US 18th Airborne Corps; 52nd = BR 52nd (Lowland) Infantry Division (airlanding); Polish = 1st Independent Polish Parachute Brigade

'In view of conditions prevailing at the end of winter, the availability of troops and resources, and transport problems, these aims can be achieved only one at a time.'

Other German cancelled operations include: *Seelöwe* – the air component was significant; *Felix* – assaulting Gibraltar and the Canary Islands (dependent on Franco entering the war); *Edelweiss* – attacking the oilfields in Baku; *Marita* (part of) – assaulting Lemnos; *Nordwind* (part of) – events overtook this and *Marita*.

Lack of resources hindered the Allies, too. However, most of their cancellations were like the Germans: because events on the ground happened faster than the long-winded planning process. Take Operation Effective in 1945. In this, US 13th Airborne Division would be dropped south of Stuttgart to seize an airfield over 50 miles behind German lines. SHAEF agreed the plan on 9 April 1945; the date was set for the 22nd – and then German resistance collapsed and Seventh Army no longer needed it.

Weather, too, was another significant factor that led to operations being cancelled in 1944 – its effect on the airdrops in Normandy and the restrictions they caused to the landings in Operation Market show this only too well. The failure of Market Garden was attributed to the weather – and the problems getting second-wave drops to the ground certainly meant 1st (BR) and 82nd (US) divisions had too few troops when they most needed them on D+1 and D+2.

Finally, of course, the end of the war against Japan curtailed the final air operations: the British air elements of Operation Zipper intended for the Malay peninsula and Mailfist (Singapore); and the US air component of Operation Downfall, the invasion of Japan.

A Fallschirmjäger and a Gebirgsjäger mourn their lost comrades on Crete. But while 'Merkur' and its high casualty figures is identified as having brought a halt to major Axis airborne operations, other aspects need to considered: first, large-scale airborne operation tend to be offensive in nature. 1943 saw the Axis on the back foot with fewer opportunites. Second, as the Allies found to their cost, too few transport aircraft and gliders also caused problems. Germany's paucity of both also militated against major airborne operations. Third, airborne troops are elite troops – the Axis needed theirs in the field, not training and honing their skills and waiting for the right moment. It was Fallschirmjäger – even if many weren't trained to jump – who stiffened defences in the Netherlands, Italy, Russia and Germany. Some would say that this was a better use of the elite than the huge operations of the Allies.

Appendices

1 Parachutes

Parachutes and parachute packing isn't simple. To begin with, parachutes are large and delicate – over 50sq yd of silk that has to be packed into a small package along with all its lines (the British X type had nearly 700ft in total). The notices proclaimed: 'Remember a man's life depends on every parachute you pack' to the WAAF, WAVE or WRNS packers. RCAF-WD's motto was 'We Serve that Men May Fly'. The job of the riggers didn't end once packing had taken place. Each time a chute was used it had to be repacked; they had to be tested regularly; and inspected for tears or holes from such things as insect damage.

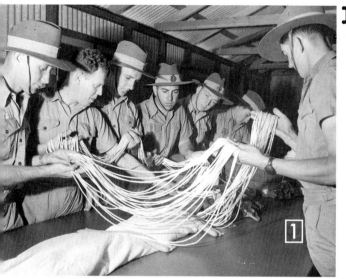

1 Australian trainees learn about parachutes.

2 Men of the 13th Air Cargo Re-Supply Squadron of the Seventh Air Force repack parachutes at the edge of Kadena Airfield on Okinawa. They would have packed the parachutes and containers necessary to supply the 11th Airborne Division who were destined to drop in any attack on Japan.

3 Women of the RCAF-WD demonstrate parachute packing technique at RCAF Station Rockcliffe, Ontario, 1943.

4 and 5 Fallschirmjäger were trained to pack their own parachutes. The Luftwaffe system – the Rückfallschirm, Zwangablösung – was nowhere near as good as that of the Allies. The worst aspect was that it attached to a point at the back (6, overleaf, as exemplified by Max Schmeling) that forced men to exit the aircraft by diving (see p178). This meant they had little or no control over their descent and had to endure a face-first landing requiring knee and elbow pads (7, overleaf preparing to drop on Leros).

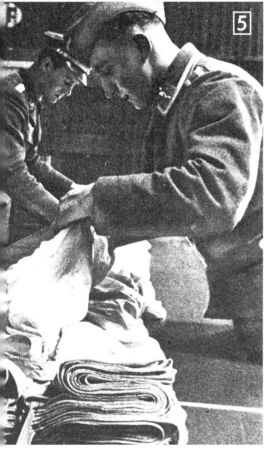

The main types – the RZ 16 and 20 – are described in *Enemy Air-Borne Forces*. They had '28 panels. Each panel has 4 gores (tapered sections), cut from a single piece of material in such manner that warp and weft are both at an angle of 45 degrees to the long axis of the panel. ... there are 14 rigging lines which pass through the top vent. ... Each line is 21m (69ft) long, ... a canopy 62sq m (648sq ft) in area ... When packed, the canopy and rigging lines fold inside the bag, which is fastened by means of a ring to the static line. The bag is then contained within the pack, which consists of a base (next to the man's back) and four flaps which close over the bag. A further bag, in which the whole parachute is kept during shipment, is included among the accessories, and is removed when the person enters the plane.

'The harness is made of webbing and consists of a belt with a large buckle in front, two braces, two thigh straps, and a strap across the top of the chest. It is connected to the rigging lines by hemp lift webs. Each web is so made that its lower end forms an eye which fits into the appropriate "D" ring of the harness, where it is secured by a screw, the free upper ends being joined to form two eyes. To each of the four eyes so formed, seven rigging-line ends are attached.

'The parachutes are automatically opened by a static cord, 6m (20ft) long, fastened to the inside of the plane, which pulls the bag away from the pack, releasing the canopy. (**8, overleaf** – as they get into the aircraft the Fallschirmjäger grip this between their teeth to leave their hands free). The cord then becomes detached, taking the bag with it. After a drop of some 24m (80ft) the parachute has become completely operative and the subsequent falling speed of a man and parachute is about 16ft/sec. The shock felt by the parachutist when he reaches the ground is comparable to that transmitted by a jump without parachute of from 16 to 18ft.'

9 (overleaf) One of Wolf Willrich's 'Soldiers of the Reich' series, this postcard shows one of the elite Fallschirmjäger *Luftlandepionier* (combat engineers). The insignia is that of 4.FJD. He's clutching a 3kg explosive charge.

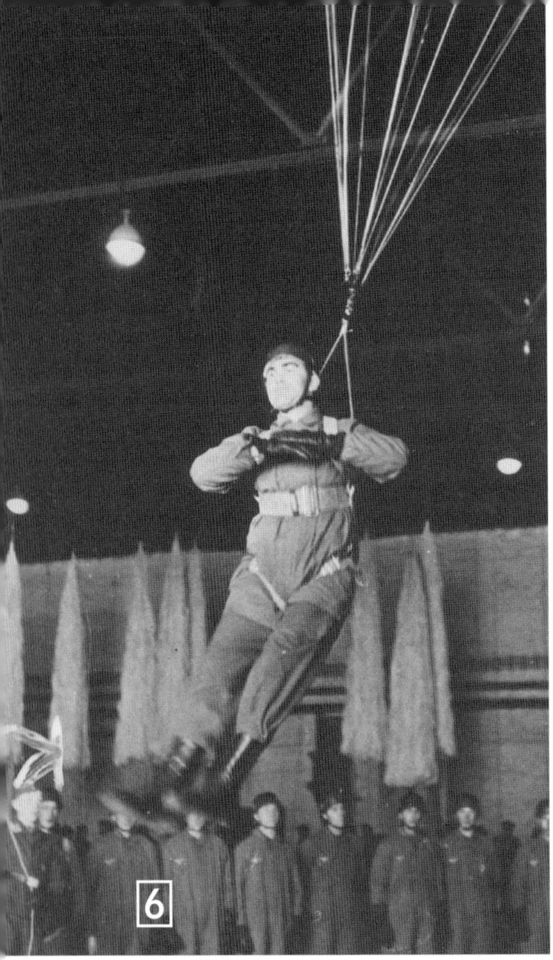

6

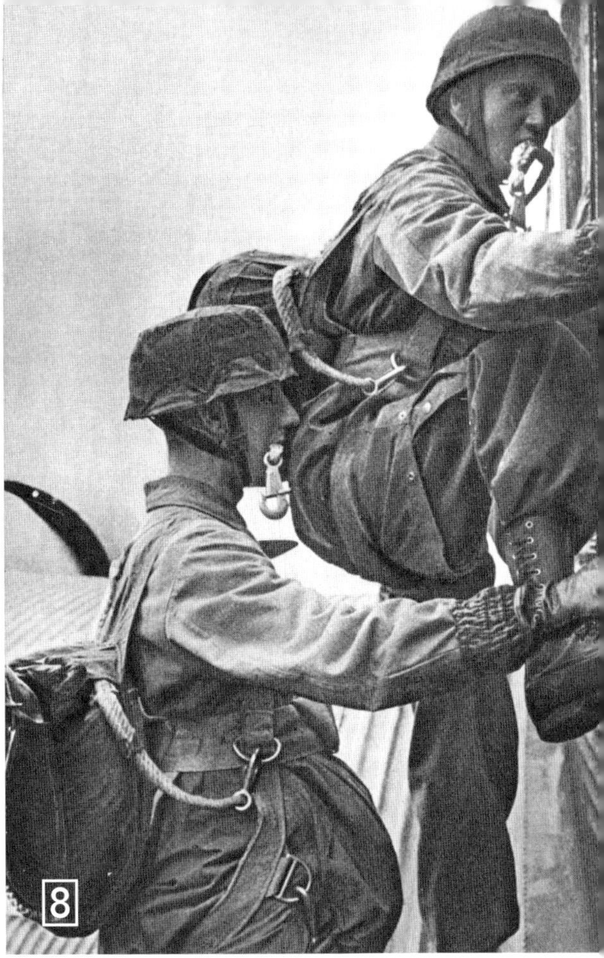

8

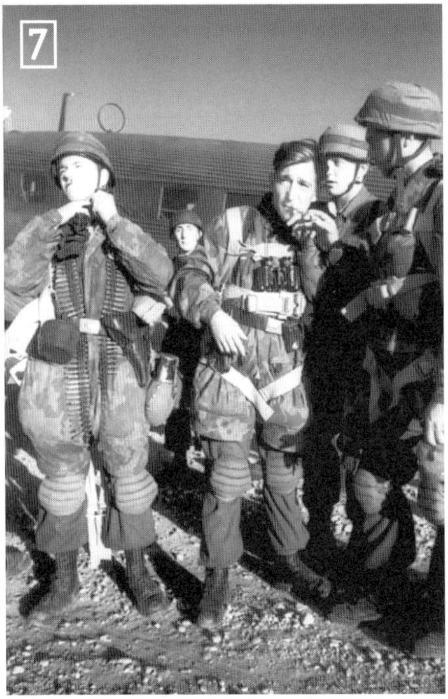

7

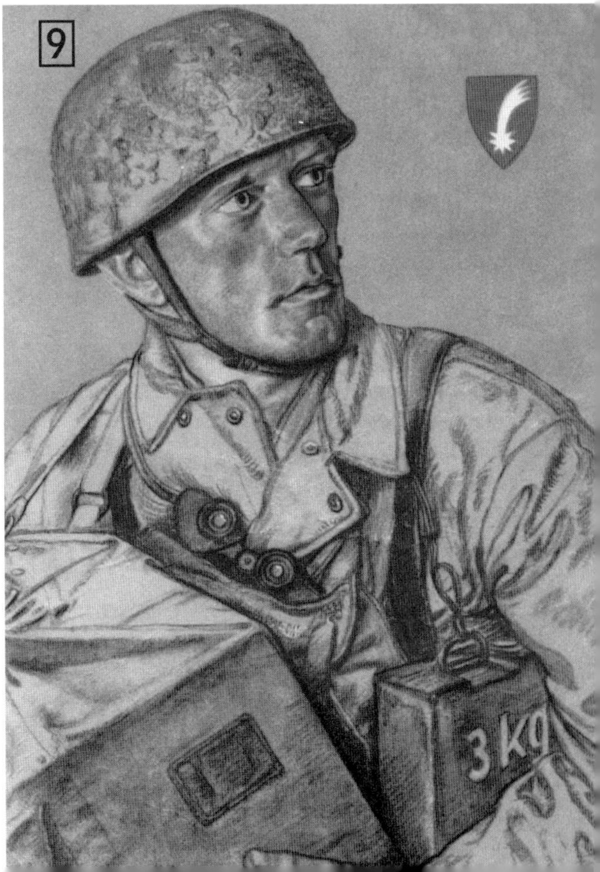
3 kg

9

Above: As we have seen in Chapter 7 (p136), Russia was ahead of the game when it came to the creation of a paratroop force but in the end a combination of Stalin's purges and military conservatism saw their airborne arm used almost exclusively as ground forces. The paras are about to board a TB-3 and are equipped with T6 parachutes and PPSh sub-machine guns. The Tupolev TB-3 was obsolescent by 1939 but would see service throughout the war. It could carry 35 paratroops.

Right: The Japanese used a back-pack, static-line operated parachute with a reserve at the front. Their paratroop-compatible aircraft were relatively few in number. They used Kawasaki Ki56 transport aircraft on the Palembang operation which had one unexpected side effect. The fact that the Ki56 was based on the US Electra meant there was confusion on the ground as the observers thought the incoming troopships were Allied Hudson aircraft. Another aircraft used for airborne operations was the Mitsubishi G3M 'Nell'.

The American T series started with the prewar T-3 that led to the 1940 T-4 specifically designed for airborne troops with a quick-release buckle. This was improved by 1942's T-5 (**1**), the preferred model after modifications, with no snap hooks and no quick-release. This proved a mistake and the T-7A was modified for Operation Varsity with a QR buckle. The T-5 had a 28ft (8.5m) diameter olive drab canopy with 28 silk and then nylon panels, each with a midway diagonal reinforcing panel (blowout) designed to halt any tearing. There were 28 x 22ft (6.7m) rigging lines coming from the reinforced edge of the canopy to the D rings on the four nylon reinforced canvas risers, integral to the harness. Like the British X-type, steering gave some degree of control when landing. The Americans, unlike others, consistently had a reserve chute resting just above the stomach (**3A** below). This also had pockets for extras and was deployed manually by pulling a red rectangular ripcord. There were three major flaws with the T-4. First, the canopy opened before the rigging deployed which resulted in a fierce 120mph 'nut-crushing' stop before descent proper began. Sometimes this could cause extreme pain and the loss of poorly secured equipment. Second, snap-hooks slowed release from the harness making the wearer vulnerable. These had replaced the Irvin QR buckles of the earlier types because they were not reliable enough having failed a number of times during testing. Third, the reserve chute took up space that would, perhaps, have been better otherwise utilised.

Designed and developed by the British GQ Parachute Co and the Irvin Air Co, the X-type (**5**) was the finest military parachute of the war. The canopy was 28ft (8.5m) in diameter with the panels made alternately from silk, ramex (cotton) or nylon. There were 28 x 25ft (7.6m) rigging lines from the reinforced edge of the canopy to four D rings each attached to a web riser, an integral part of the heavy-duty X-strap harness (clearly visible above **4**) with its quick-release turn and press (hit!) round buckle, crutch straps and over and under shoulder straps to the canopy bag. Unlike the American T series the British system didn't have a reserve chute, first because it was considered safe and reliable and second because the Brits jumped from a lower height with no time to deploy a reserve. On jumping from the aircraft (**6**), the static line extracted the chute and risers before the canopy opened. This was generally a smoother but slower procedure than other systems. With a descent speed of 23ft/sec (7m/sec) the landing had a degree of steer by manipulation of the risers to spill air. It was still a hard landing!

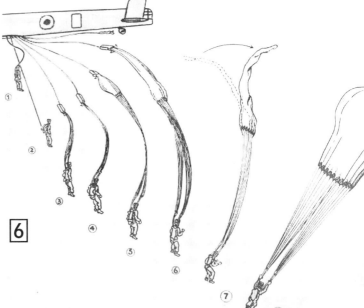

2 Aircraft

COMPARISON OF C-46 AND C-47 IN OPERTION VARSITY

		C-46	C-47
Group		313rd	315th
Sorties		72	81
Losses:	Aircraft	19	14
	Aircraft damaged	38	42
% of aircraft unharmed		21%	31%
% of aircraft hit that were lost		33%	25%
Losses:	Personnel		
	KIA and MIA	33	26
	WIA and IIA	22	8
	Total Casualties	55	34
Percentage of personnel unharmed		82%	90%
Troops dropped		2,038	1,235
Equipment dropped (lbs)		126,834	79,030
No. of A/C needed to do same job		72	133

Above: C-47s from RAF Spanhoe carry D Coy 2/504th PIR towards DZ-O as part of Operation Market, 17 September 1944.

1 and 3 Horsas and CG-4As await take off from airfields in England prior to D-Day, June 1944.

2 The Curtis C-46 Commando is best known for its use in the CBI theatre where it proved a useful workhorse. It was less successful in Europe as a paratrooper. Here one is seen dropping parapacks during Operation Varsity.

DC-47 SKYTRAIN

'Vomit comet', 'flying truck', 'Gooney bird' in the Pacific or Dakota to the Brits, the military version of the DC-3 commercial airliner was the Allied workhorse worldwide throughout the war, carrying all types of cargo – troops, paratroopers, glider-tug, POL, casualties or 21 stretchers (litters), supply drops, equipment, vehicles, mules – anything that could be airported. Another DC-3 development, the DC-53 Skytrooper was created specifically for paratroops but didn't catch on – it lacked the reinforced cargo floor, large cargo door and hoist attachment of the C-47 which did the same job.

An unarmed twin-engined low-wing monoplane, the C-47 was vulnerable to air attack and ground fire but could take punishment. It had a crew of four – pilot, co-pilot, radio operator and loadmaster. It could carry 28 fully armed troops or 18–20 paratroops and their equipment with bucket seats down either side.

The C-47 also acted as a tug. When operational, the tug crew and glider crew were a team, communicating via radio, telephone (wire along the towline) or hand/flag/flashlight signals. The tug pilot determined the release, sometimes with fatal consequences, Operation Husky being a classic example. Neither the Allies nor the Axis ever fully solved communications between glider and tug.

The glider tow-line for the C-47 was made from the newly manufactured nylon, 100yd (91.4m) long with a stretch factor of up to 25% on take-off theoretically contracting slowly as optimum speed was achieved. The telephone cable attached allowed for this but quite often it broke.

Length: 63ft 9in (19.43m)
Wingspan: 95ft 6in (29.11m)
Height: 17ft (5.18m)
Speed: 185–230mph (298–370kph) depending on cargo and altitude

From the start, the British used bombers to drop paratroops and to tow gliders. In the early days some were converted with a hole in the floor, for paratroop training (see p191). Lack of suitable aircraft in sufficient numbers meant that they couldn't do without these, although most paratroop dropping was – as the Americans – from the ubiquitous C-47 Dakota. With side doors the Dakotas were better equipped for both training and drops. Nevertheless, Albemarles carried the Pathfinders on D-Day and also delivered elements of 1st Canadian and 9th Para Bn as well as HQ/3rd Para Bde.

For Operation Market, British 1st Airborne gliders were towed by various types of aircraft – Stirlings from Harwell and Keevil; Halifaxes from Tarrant Rushton; Dakotas from Broadwell, Fairford, Down Ampney and Blakehill Farm; and Albemarles of Nos 296 and 297 Squadrons from RAF Manston (**Above**).

Below: Tarrant Rushton, 6 June 1944. Operation Mallard delivered 6th Airlanding Brigade to LZs W and N (see pp66–67). The first two gliders lined up are Horsas, the rest are Hamilcars. Towing aircraft are Halifaxes of Nos 298 and 644 Squadrons, RAF. It was from here that the Operation Deadstick Horsas took off.

ARMSTRONG WHITWORTH ALBEMARLE

Twin-engined monoplane recce and transport (converted from bomber during design); entered service 1943.

Crew: 4–6

Defence: Boulton-Paul turret with 4 x .303 Browning MGs

Adapted: Glider-tug, mainly for the Horsa, but also the Hamilcar and a few Hadrians. Could also carry 10 paratroopers. As they exited through a hole in the floor they had to careful that they didn't break their nose ('ringing the bell') on exit!

Use: Pathfinder and other para drops for 6th Airborne on 6 June 1944; glider-tugs for 1st Airborne at Arnhem

Built: 600

Below: Paratroops of 6th Airborne Division climbing into an RAF Albemarle aircraft at RAF Harwell, 5 June 1944.

HANDLEY PAGE HALIFAX

Four-engined monoplane bomber; entered service 1941. Many variations.

Crew: 7

Defence: Ventral and rear turrets (each 4 x .303 Browning MGs); 1 x Vickers K MG in nose

Adapted: Many. Glider-tug for the Hamilcar

Use: D-Day and many other operations

Built: 6,000+

SHORT STIRLING IV

Four-engined monoplane heavy bomber. Entered service 1941 but used in other roles from 1943

Crew: 7

Defence: Originally three gun-turrets

Adapted: Mk IV had nose and dorsal turrets removed for use as glider-tug (Hamilcars and Horsas) and Para drops

Use: D-Day, Arnhem and elsewhere

Built: 2,380

1 5. Gebirgsjäger wait to emplane for Crete.

2 The Ju52 was as ubiquitous for the Germans as the C-47 was for the Allies. Losing 170 on Crete did much to curtail paratroop operations.

JUNKERS Ju 52

The 'Tante Ju' was a low-wing corrugated duralumin-skinned tri-motored monoplane transport aircraft with fixed undercarriage. It was the Luftwaffe's standard transport tug throughout the war and reliable in all weather conditions.

3 Heinkel He111Z *Zwilling* towing an Me321 glider.

4 and 5 Apart from its size the biggest drawback of the Ju52 was that paratroops had to dive out head first, curtailing the gear they could carry with them.

Crew: 3–4
Defence: 3 × MG15
Adapted: Could transport 15–20 fully armed troops, supplies and, with stretcher fittings, wounded, or 12 Fallschirmjäger exiting via side doors with supply containers dropped from the bomb-bay.
Towing ability: 1 × G 242 or up to 3 × DFS230
Use: A jack of all trades best known for getting supplies into Stalingrad and the wounded out, also all Fallschirmjäger operations such as 'Hannibal', 'Merkur', etc.

For night towing each tug had eight shielded formation lights on the upper rear edge of the wings which could only be seen by the glider pilot when he was in the correct towed position.

A slow top speed of 165mph (265kmh) made the Ju52 vulnerable to ground and air attack. Huge losses during the 1940 invasion on the Netherlands could well have had some influence on the postponement of Operation Sealion, the invasion of England. Certainly the losses of Ju52s on Crete did little to help resupply operations in Russia. In spring 1942, the Luftwaffe was able to resupply the troops in the Demyansk Pocket, but lost over 200 aircraft and crew doing so. By the time of the encirclement of Sixth Armee in Stalingrad, there just weren't sufficient transports to deliver the needed supplies. The Germans also lost nearly 500 transports trying to do so.
Built: Just under 5,000.

OTHER GERMAN TUGS

The main one was the Heinkel He111. Its strangest form was as the He111Z *Zwilling* (twin fuselage – see **3**) with five engines. Three Bf110s were needed to pull a 40-ton fully loaded Me321 Gigant off the ground even when wing-rocket assisted. 129 crew and occupants died when three Bf110s and an Me321 crashed in 1941 – the worst aviation disaster at the time.

Above: The tri-motor Savoia Marchetti SM82P was used as a bomber and a transport by both the Italians and Germans (over 100 in 1942–43). It was roomy – it could carry up to 40 men on two levels, the upper level holding seats for 32. They were used extensively to shuttle in reinforcements to North Africa.

Below: The Antonov TB-3 is noteworthy for its Heath Robinson undercarriage and cantilevered wingspan – an immense 137ft (42m). It made up 25% of the Russian bomber fleet in 1941.

3 Gliders

Gliders were developed in the 1930s as a logical method of deploying troops into landing environments that would be too perilous for aircraft. They also allowed the carriage of heavier weapons than para-troops. Gliders were superseded postwar by the helicopter and have universally fallen out of favour. A brilliant aid to learning flying skills – many of the Luftwaffe pilots trained on sporting gliders – they proved to be excellent for stealthy small-scale coup de main operations (as was shown so well at Eben Emael and, later, Pegasus Bridge). However, they were extremely vulnerable to landing-denying obstacles on the ground – such as inundations or poles dug into possible landing fields – and also to small arms or artillery fire, whether the enemy's or indiscriminate friendly fire made little difference to the crew and passengers in an unarmoured glider. Following the debacle during Operation Husky when lack of experienced glider and tug pilots saw hundreds of airborne troops dropped into the sea and friendly fire incidents also kill many soldiers before they reached their objectives, later operations proved more successful, especially those conducted in daylight such as Operations Mallard and Market. Night drops proved more difficult (D-Day) as did those when smoke obscured the landing areas (Varsity).

Above: The most extensively produced glider during the war was the US Waco CG-4A or 'Hengist' in British parlance – nearly 14,000 in total.

Below: The Japanese came up with a number of glider concepts but few were produced in any quantities. This one, the Kokusai Ku-8-II, saw the largest numbers, around 700. Developed from the Ki59, codenamed 'Goose' it carried 20 equipped troops and was used operationally in the Philippines.

Bottom: Gliders aren't as expensive to manufacture as aircraft but parachutes are a much cheaper option than gliders unless the latter are reused. The US armed forces tried to make them reusable. Teams were sent in after operations to identify those still in one piece. They were then picked up by the simple expedient of a C-47 trailing a towing hook. Unfortunately, local pilferage and battle damage meant that few were retrieved.

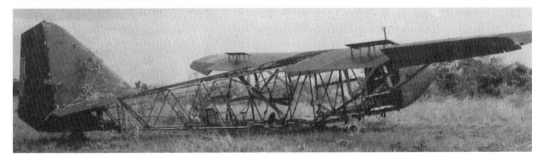

1 I The wingspan of the DFS230 is well illustrated in this North African photograph – 10ft wider than the Gotha Go242 (**5**).

2

DFS 230 Assault Glider

Operational from 1939, over 1,600 were built. They only carried nine fully armed men and pilot in an extremely cramped interior (**2 and 9**). Five and pilot faced forward; four back. The four rear seats could be taken out to provide more space for cargo. The wheels were usually jettisoned after launch, leaving sprung skids front and rear for landing. Unlike the Allied gliders it was armed – with one MG15 above the pilot (**7**). Made from doped fabric (or plywood) over welded steel tube, the DFS230 proved stealthy enough for coup de main operations. It had a long-release glide for a silent approach (**3**). However, with a landing dive angle of 80 degrees and a parachute brake assistance (**4**), it was capable of a short landing. Its tug was usually the Ju52/3m.

Wingspan: 70ft (21.1m)
Length: 37ft (11.30m)
Max towing speed: 130mph (210kmh)

Glide speed: 100mph (160kmh)
Load: 2,740lb (1,240kg)

5, 6, 8 The DFS230 was, latterly, used as a cargo carrier – this one came a spectacular cropper in Belgrade in 1945 (**8**) – but couldn't carry a large payload. The Gotha Go242 (**5**), of which 1,500 were built, came in two versions: A-1 cargo (8,500lb/3,855kg) and A-2 troop-carrying (20+ fully armed men and two pilots). This one is burnt out in North Africa. The largest of them all was the Me321 Gigant developed for the invasion of Britain. 200 + built, the largest glider ever made. It could carry (allegedly) 200 fully armed men or a PzKpfw IV, StuG or up to 50,000lb (22,7000kg) of other cargo. 200 powered versions were also built (**6**) – they were used extensively ferrying to Africa.

3

4

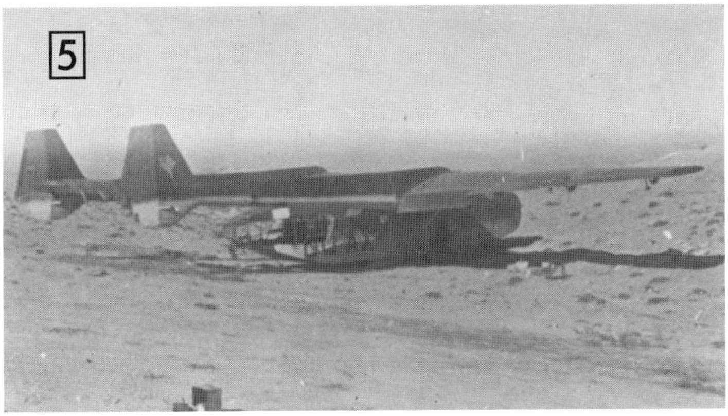
5

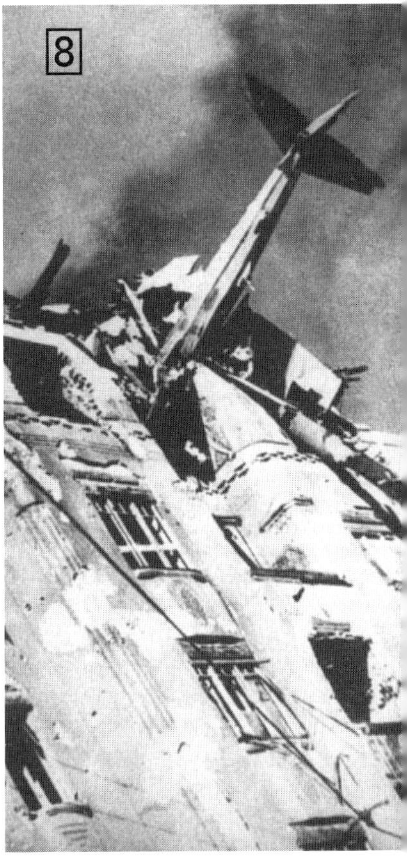
8

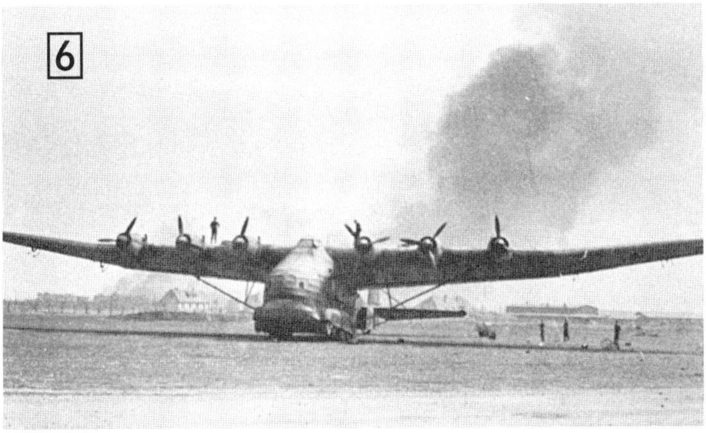
6

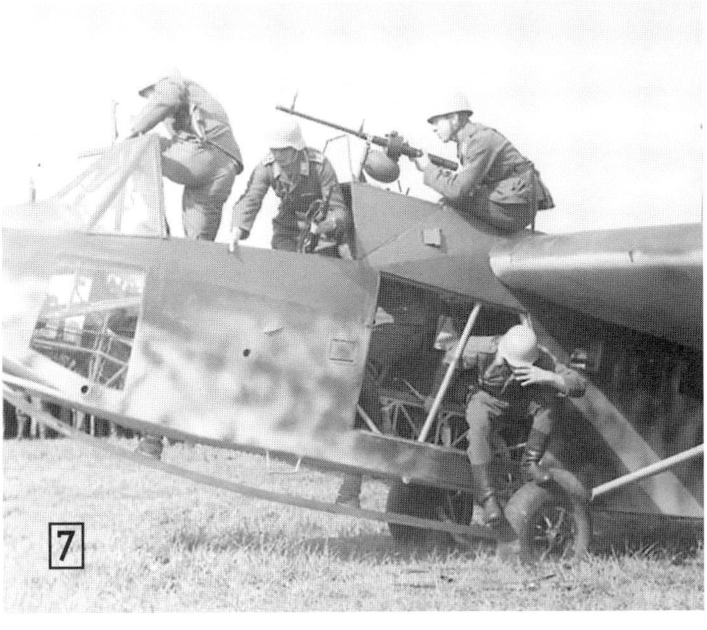
7

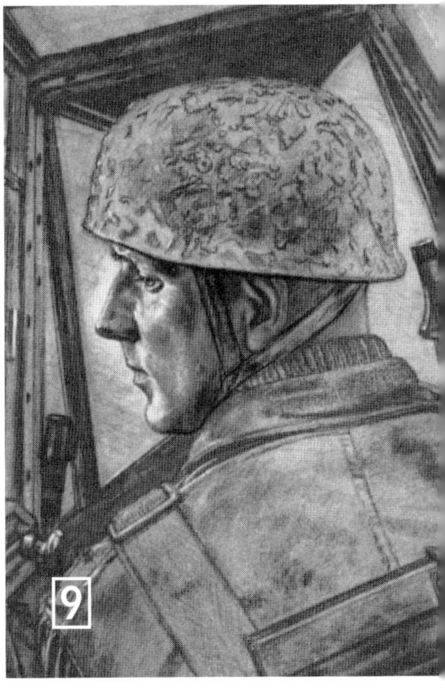
9

GAL Hamilcar Mk I

The largest glider built by the Allies, it was designed to transport heavy equipment or 40 fully armed troops. The first were delivered in 1943. The Americans showed an interest but pulled out. It had a wooden, steel-reinforced frame and a canvas-covered plywood outer skin; fixed undercarriage with forward hydraulic pressure release to lower for unloading; armoured cockpit, above the fuselage, and wings allowed maximum cargo space. 344 were built. A safe glider – from 2,800 tows only three accidents involved injury or loss of crew life.

Wingspan: 110ft (34m) with large air-bottle assisted flaps to control speed and angle of descent
Length: 68ft (21m)
Approach speed: 100mph (160kmh)
Landing speed: 52–80mph (84–130kmh) for a short landing distance
Load: 17,500lb (7,938kg)

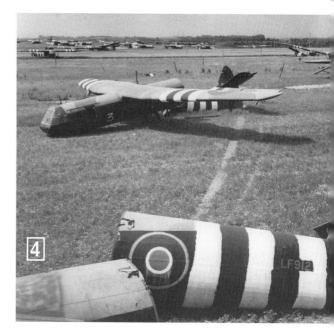

The Hamilcar could carry a light tank either the Tetrarch (as in this photo showing the arrival of 6th Airborne Armoured Reconnaissance Regiment on the evening of 6 June) and, later the Locust (see p 219).

The Glider Pilot Regiment

The British trained their glider crew both as pilots but also as infantrymen unlike the US pilots about whom the army would complain that after landing they got in the way – even when relegated to PoW guard duties. Formed in 1942, the GPR's first major mission was Operation Husky. They lost 57 pilots, many drowned along with their passengers when they landed in the sea. At great risk from obstacles on the landing grounds, the pilots were also at risk from shifting loads as well as AA gunfire: the wooden gliders had no bullet-proofing. The regiment distinguished itself in Normandy and subsequent landings, particularly Arnhem where they fought alongside the 1st Airborne troops in the northwestern sector of the Oosterbeek perimeter (1,200 pilots in total: 229 KIA; 469 WIA/PoW) and Operation Varsity: of the 416 gliders that landed near Hamminkeln (of 440 planned – 390 Horsas and 48 Hamilcars) only 88 were undamaged, which accounts for the losses to pilots noted below.

| Sicily | 57 | S France | 1 | Rhine Crossing | 100 |
| Normandy | 34 | Arnhem | 229 | Other operations | 127 |

1 The benefit of the larger gliders was that they could carry artillery and jeeps – things that airborne forces particularly needed. The Horsa could carry a jeep and a 75mm pack or 6pdr AT gun.

2, 3, 4 While the CG-4A could carry 13 men, the Horsa – as here – carried 22–25. A quick release joint allowed the tail to be removed for speedy egress. The later Mk II had a hinged nose as well and carried 28 men.

AIRSPEED AS.51 Mk I and AS.58 Mk II Horsa

Conceived, trialled and accepted within 10 months, Horsas were first used in November 1942 for Operation Freshman (see p43). A high-wing cantilever three-sectioned monoplane built almost entirely from wood and 'skimmed' with glued plywood, the Horsa was considered disposable after landing. It sat 22–25 fully armed men on canvas benches down either side with some on a rear bench. Alternative loads included two jeeps – or one with an ammo trailer and any medium-sized piece of ordnance needed for its task. Around 3,600+ were built of both marks. All were unarmed.

Wingspan: 88ft (27m)
Length: 67ft (20m)
Max towing speed: 150–160mph (241–257kmh)
Glide speed: 80–100mph (160kmh)

Landing distance: within 330ft (100m) or longer subject to weight carried.
Load: Mk I—6,340lb (2,876kg); Mk II—7,380lb (3,348kg)

The greenhouse perspex (Plexiglass) cockpit windows gave the two pilots in the front section excellent vision; the other two sections held the cargo. Originally the rear section was detached using cordtex but this was considered too dangerous, so it was replaced with quick-release bolts and wire-cutters. A bottom-hinged freight door allowed entry into the aircraft behind the pilots. The later model, the AS.58 (Mk II) had a hinged nose for direct loading and unloading as well as a reinforced floor and double nose wheels for the extra weight carried. Operationally, the fixed tricycle undercarriage could be ditched before landing, leaving sprung skids instead.

WACO CG-4/CG-4A

The CG-4 and CG-4A (CG = Cargo Glider) is better known as the Waco after the first of the 16 constructors who made the glider. It was dubbed the Hadrian in British use. Less complimentary names were also used such as the 'vomit comet' and 'flying coffin'. It was certainly the most widely used American glider and over 14,000 built from 1942. It was a high-wing monoplane with fixed landing gear (two main wheels and tail wheel). Skids were added later as was a parachute brake. It was made from plywood but had a welded steel tube frame that made it sturdy enough for reuse. The frame was covered with doped canvas. The hinged nose lifted for loading/unloading (**3** and **4** below). It carried no armament. Its main drawback was its size – it held only 13 fully armed infantry and 2 crew, or a jeep and 6 men, or a 75mm howitzer, ammunition and crew. This was a distinct drawback. For example, to get a glider field artillery battalion into combat required 66 Wacos: 14 for HQ Bty and 26 for each of the howitzer batteries. It could also carry the small Clarkair Crawler CA-1 bulldozer, but the blade had to be delivered separately to reduce weight.

Wingspan: 83ft 8in (25.5m)
Length: 48ft 8in (14.8m)
Max towing speed: 150mph (241kmh)
Glide speed: 60mph (96kmh)

Landing distance: 600–800ft (180–244m) or longer subject to weight carried.
Load: 3,600lb (1,633kg) – emergency load is +1,500lb (680kg)

1 CG-4A interior – 1 towline release; 2 trim tabs; 3 parachute release; 4 spoiler control; 5 rudder pedal; 6 toe brake; 7 nose release; 8 interphone system; 9 instrument panel.

2 The CG-13 was a larger design that could carry 40 men. It entered service in 1945 and only one glider flew a mission.

3 and 4 The nose of the CG-4A hinged upwards. Here (**3**) a 75mm howitzer is stowed, one of a sequence of photos taken in Morocco of an 82nd Airborne unit – on its strength were the 319th and 320th Glider Field Artillery Battalions, and the 376th Parachute FA Bn.

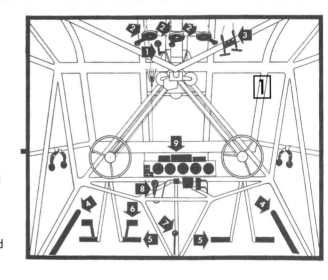

5

5 The main problem with gliders was that landing was like a controlled crash – with the controlled part being disputed. Landings weren't helped by obstacles and inundation of the area. As 'The Glider Riders' says:

> *Once I was infantry, now I'm a dope*
> *riding in gliders, attached to a rope*
> *safety in landing is only a hope,*
> *and the pay is exactly the same.*

6 CG-4As were used for cargo carrying as well as combat landings. The load-bearing capacity of the floor allowed the CG-4A to carry 3,600lb of cargo.

7 Inside a CG-4A, the tubular construction is obvious. Here an 82nd Airborne 75mm gun and crew.

6

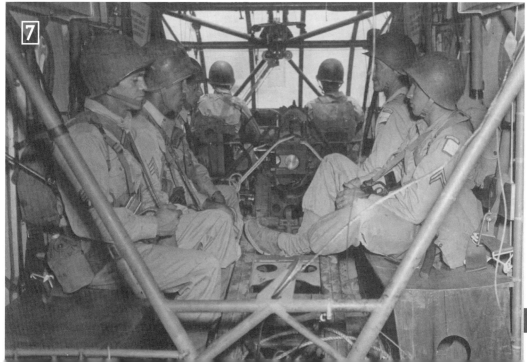

7

1

1 and 3 Attaching the tow rope to a CG-4A. The tow ropes had a telephone cable wound around (note the black cable). They were then pulled out to be attached to the tugs (4). 'The CG-4A,' the manual identifies, 'was not designed as a sailplane. It is simply a cargo-carrying airplane without engines.' To take off, the pilot simply released the brakes, allowed the tug to take up the slack, made sure his glider didn't nose into the tarmac and then lifted off (6) when travelling at 15mph above the stall speed (49mph with a load of 7,500lb). The glider took up a position above the turbulance created by

NORMAL SINGLE TOW POSITION

2

3

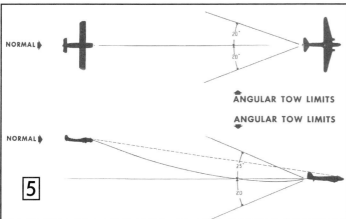

the tug and allowed the latter to take off before adopting its normal tow position (**2, 5, 7**). Double-towing (when the tug pulled two gliders at once) required careful flying. One glider had a tow rope 75ft longer than the other and the closer glider couldn't see the one behind. Once a glider dropped the tow, the pilot made a standard approach and then, if necessary, deployed the tail parachute (but not above 140mph IAS) and landed as safely as possible in the melee.

4 Training

Paratroops are elite troops. Delivering them to the battlefield is just one aspect of their training. Physical fitness, excellence with weapons, tactical flexibility, courage and determination: all these factors are important. FM13–30 identifies training requirements:

6. TRAINING. a. Commanders and staffs Commanders and staffs of airlanding troops are specially trained in the following:
(1) Logistics of enplaning troops, equipment, and supplies.
(2) Planning and execution of tactical operations requiring unusually precise coordination with air forces, parachute troops, and other supporting arms.
(3) Communication with supporting aviation, parachute troops, and task force headquarters.
(4) Administration, supply, and evacuation of units under conditions when normal transportation faculties are lacking.
b. Troops Airlanding troops are trained in the following:
(1) Enplaning/deplaning, including the loading and securing of equipment.
(2) Technique of operating weapons, particularly those found in the rifle platoon and company. It is essential that all individuals be proficient in use of the rifle or carbine.
(3) Destruction of materiel and installations, such as enemy weapons of large caliber, bridges, communications, and public utilities.
(4) Operation of captured enemy weapons, transportation, and equipment.
(5) Treatment to be accorded hostile civilian population.
(6) Communication with supporting aircraft by means of panels, pyrotechnics, radio, and prearranged signals, with emphasis on proper designation of targets and methods of identifying themselves to supporting aviation.
(7) Independent operation of small groups which may become separated from their organizations.
(8) Execution of missions to be performed immediately upon landing.

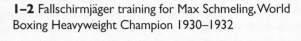

1–2 Fallschirmjäger training for Max Schmeling, World Boxing Heavyweight Champion 1930–1932

3 Fallschirmjäger trainees await their jump from a Ju52.

4 and 5 Many countries started their parachute training with a tower. In Britain, the RAF Training School, Ringway, had tethered balloons in Tatton Park (where today there's a memorial). After jumping from these, the trainees progressed to aircraft such as the Albemarle (**6**) or Whitley from which 1st Canadian Parachute Bn paratroops prepare to jump, October 1943 (**7**).

4

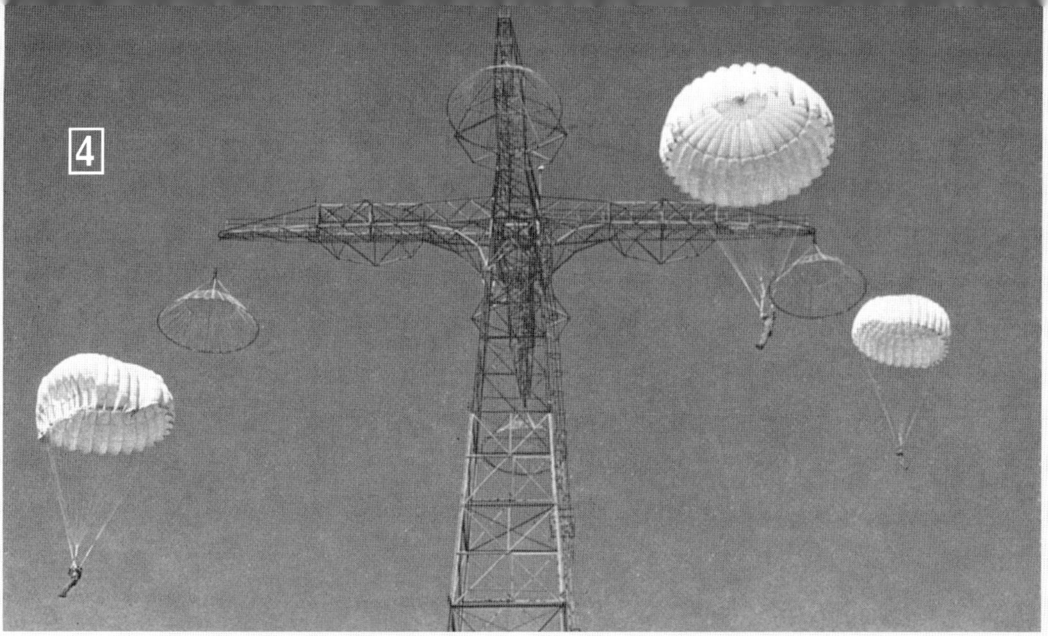

5

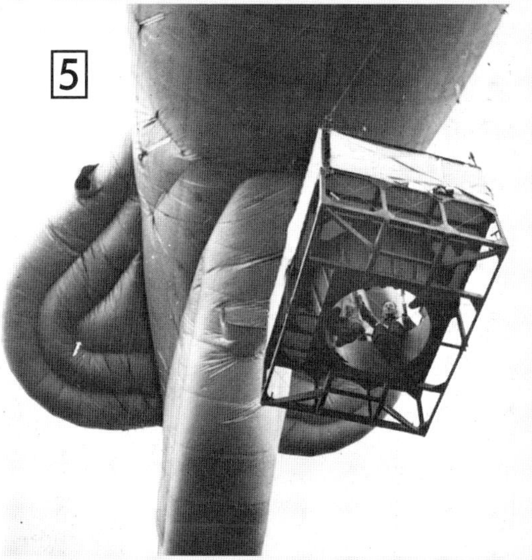

6

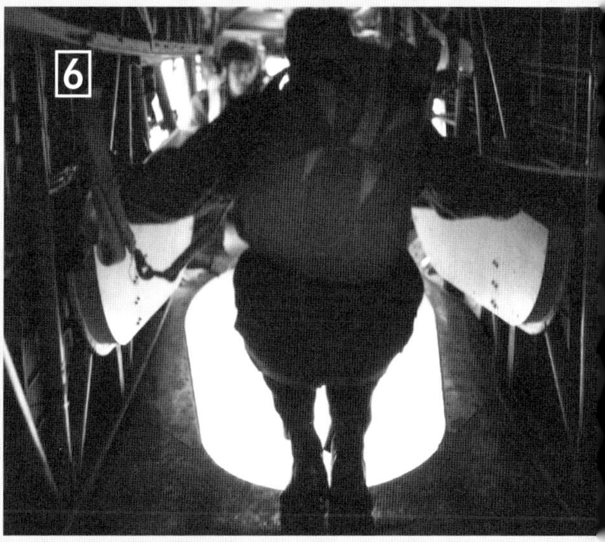

7

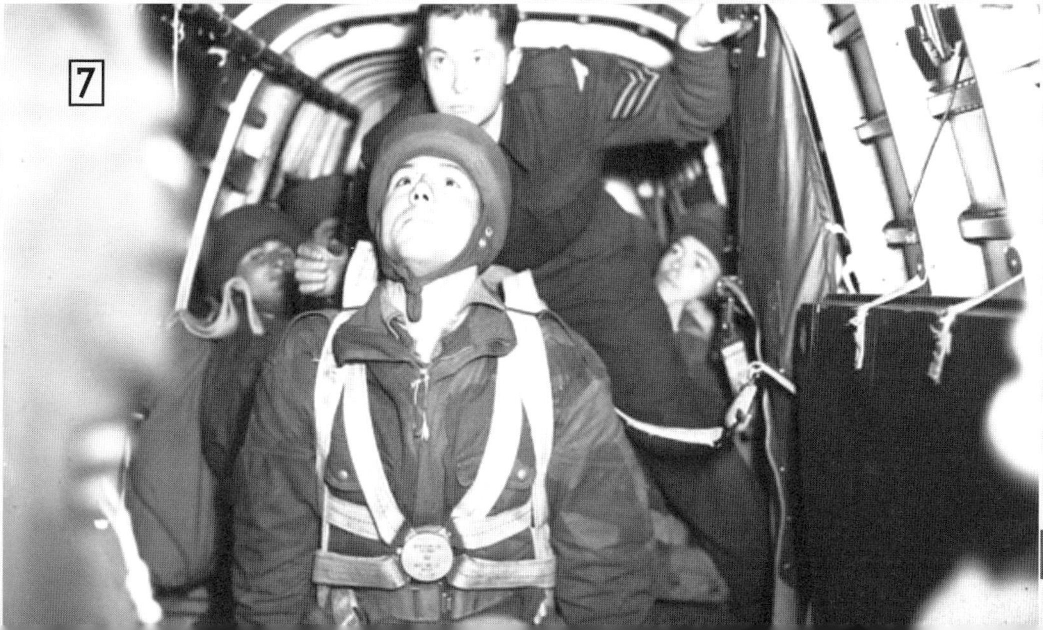

1 Men of 1st Canadian Parachute Battalion prepare for a practice jump at the Royal Air Force Training School, Ringway, Cheshire, England, 4 April 1944.

2 and 4 Glidermen train in a CG-4A – this one named 'Sadsack'. Over 6,000 men trained as glider pilots – 509 gliders landed on D-Day of which 57 glider pilots died or were missing. Some 4,000 infantrymen and 95 pieces of artillery landed in these CG-4As.

3 Australia's 1st Parachute Battalion never dropped in action, but they trained hard and were ready had the call come.

5 Practice for 101st Airborne en masse on 23 March 1944 over RAF Welford near Newbury, England. The latter was a huge display by 1,500 paratroopers in front of Prime Minister Winston Churchill, Gen Dwight Eisenhower, Lt Gen Omar Bradley and the 101st CG, Brig Gen Maxwell Taylor.

81. PHASES OF TRAINING.—Training of parachutists is divided into four phases: basic training, individual technical parachute training, unit training, and combined training. The basic training of a parachutist corresponds to that of all infantry soldiers and is normally given at an infantry replacement training center. Because of special equipment and materiel required for individual technical parachute training, this phase normally should be conducted at the parachute school or parachute training center. Combined training of parachute troops, air force elements, and airlanding troops will be conducted at every opportunity.

82. GENERAL.—Unit training of parachute troops closely approximates that of rifle regiment units of comparable size, particularly in mechanical training with weapons, range practice, combat principles, and the basic training subjects. It differs principally in that all parachutists must be qualified to handle all platoon weapons, and receive training in such specialized subjects as care, maintenance, and packing of the parachute, and parachute jumping. In addition, parachute troops must be trained in executing demolitions. The men most proficient in this subject are available for use on special demolition missions. Concurrently with the technical and tactical training of parachute units, an intense and continuous physical training course must be conducted. This training tends to minimize the number of landing injuries and prepares the unit for arduous field service normally incident to parachute operations. When the training of a parachute unit is sufficiently advanced, joint training should be undertaken with air corps units, first with transport units flying in tactical formations, and later with both transport and supporting combat units. Problems of reconnaissance, transport of troops, liaison, supply, preparation bombing and machine-gun fires, and continuous support during ground operations can be solved only by joint training during the advanced training phase. Parachute units should also train with airlanding troops, since they will usually work with these units in combat.

3

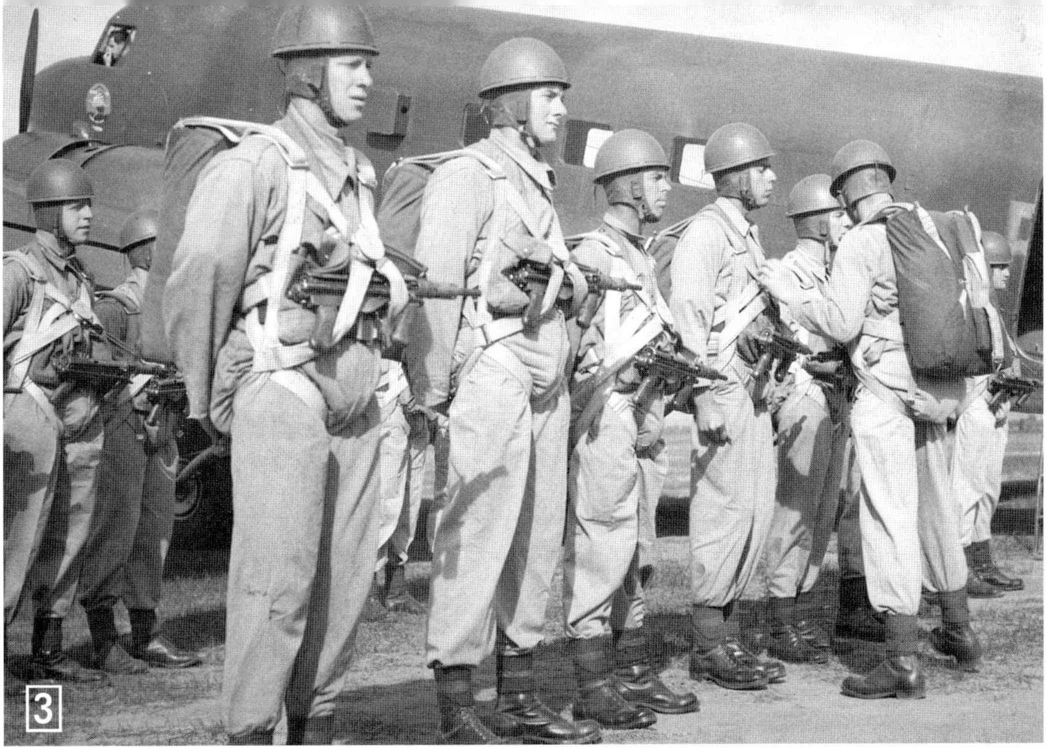

4

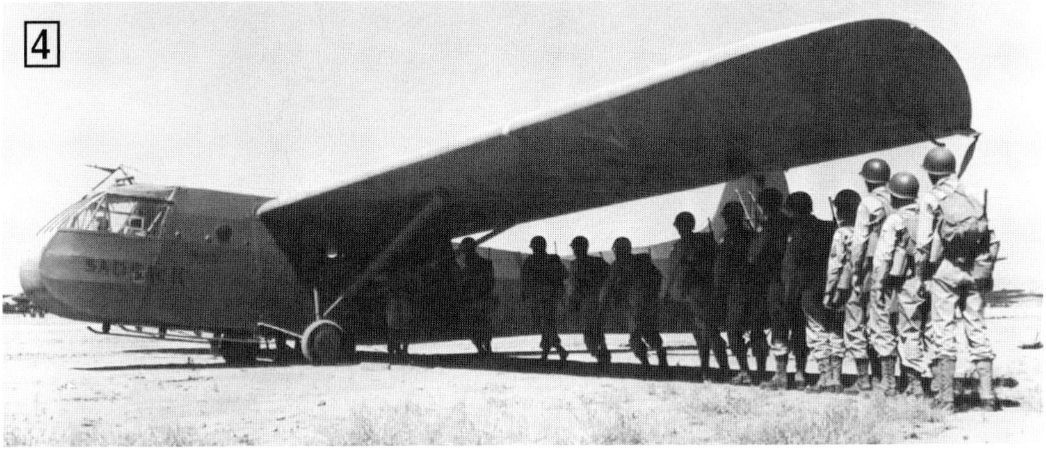

5

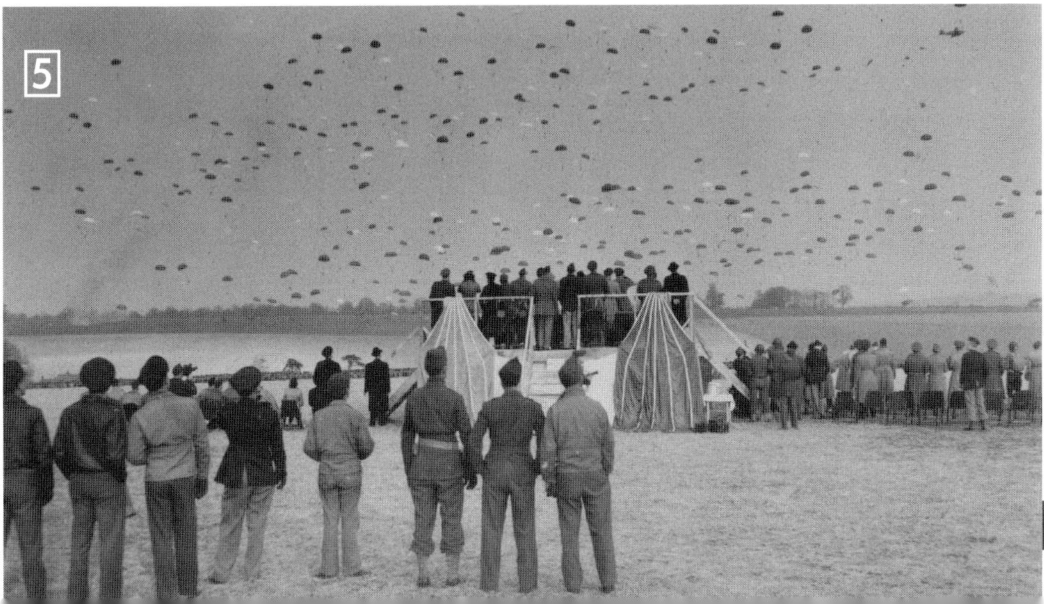

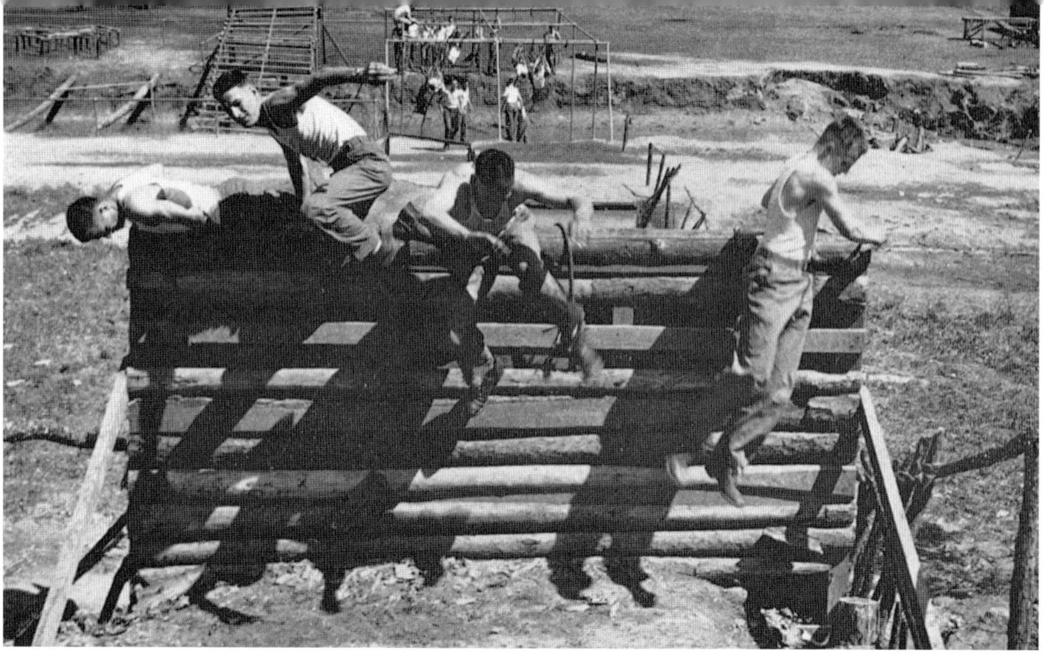

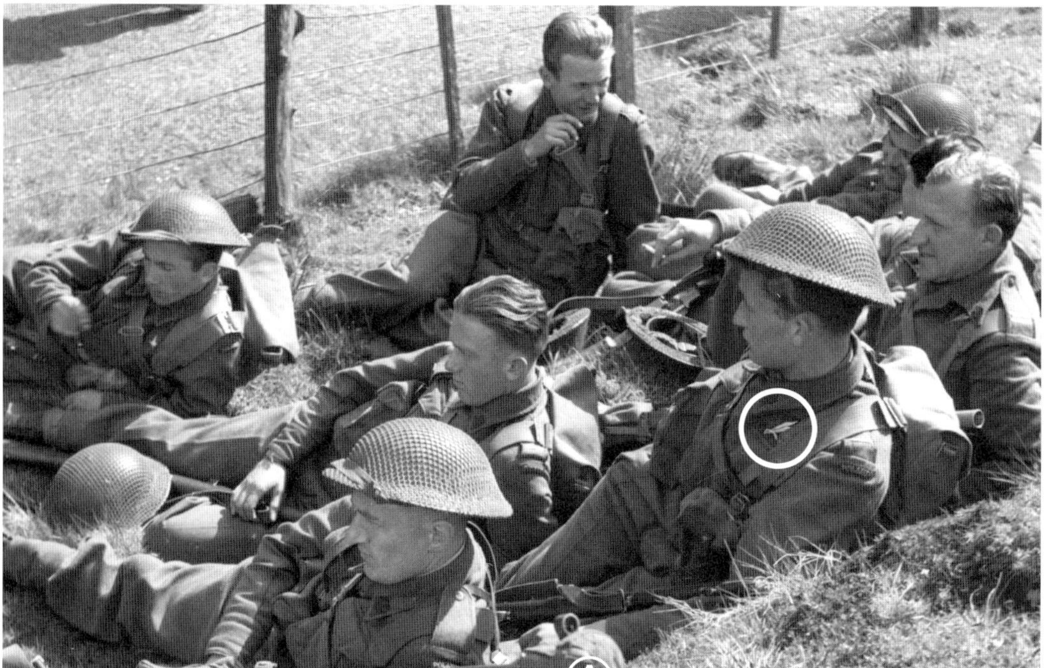
A

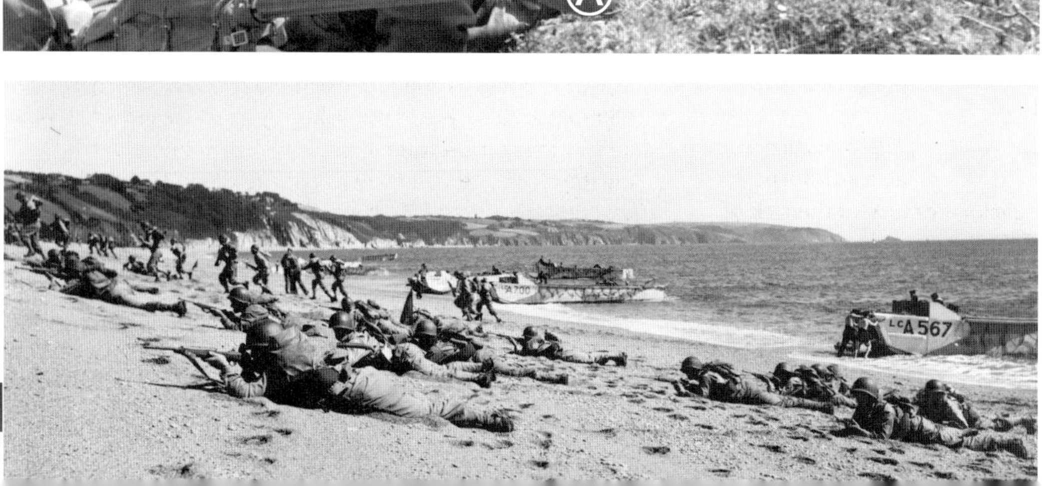
LCA 567

Opposite, Above and Above: Basic training at Camp Toccoa, Georgia by men of the 517th PIR. The physical training ensured not just an esprit de corps but a real physical edge over other troops.

Opposite, Centre: Paratroops had to fight as infantry when they hit the ground and received suitable training. These are from the 1st (Polish) Independent Parachute Brigade. The only surprise is that the Americans didn't train their glider pilots, who after landing, although with the best intentions, spent much of their time getting in the way. Note the Polish 'Diving Eagle' Para qualification badge (in circle) and the Boys anti-tank rifle (**A**).

Opposite, Below: Airborne units often had a sea-borne echelon because of the lack of sufficient aircraft or gliders. This is training at Slapton Sands.

1–3 Newbury, 10 March 1944 – 101st Airborne's Bty C, 377th PFA, practise putting their 75mm pack howitzer together. Other training included: recon selection and occupation of a position, exercises with stress placed on digging in, camouflage and concealment, speed in going into position and displacing rapidly both by day and night. Foot marches were also stressed, together with rocket launcher and small arms firing at a nearby range... Fire direction centers worked on crew duties during occupation and displacement, processing fire missions and training on all other aspects of gunnery that provided for accurate, predicted fires. Survey crews honed their skills in manual survey techniques, liaison parties refined their skills on radio operations and reporting procedures, and wire crews trained on every aspect of laying wire and ensuring internal and external battery communications would not fail...' Units made several company and battalion parachute jumps, as well as continue almost uninterrupted ground combat training. On D-Day the battalion was dropped east of Ste Mère-Église, supporting 502nd PIR. It lost 11 of its 12 howitzers and had to fight as infantrymen until the arrival of replacements on 14 June.

5 Personal Equipment

Fallschirmjäger wore jumpboots – *Stiefel* – high-sided to give support to the ankles on landing. The first model was of black leather, side-laced with 11–12 holes and a chevron-patterned rubber sole and heel. A later model wasn't as high and front-laced with a leather-studded sole. Their gloves were black, brown or grey elasticated leather gauntlets which were unlined or lined summer/winter.

The jump smock – *Knochensack* (bone sack) – came in various models: Model 1 (1936) was olive-green/grey gaberdine/waterproof cotton duck (canvas) step-in elasticated or drawstring tied short leg smock. Two slanted top and two horizontal pockets, double-zip fly front. Long sleeved.

Model 2 was olive-green/grey twill step-in with brass 'snaps' (button) fasteners to form the longer (mid-thigh) legs. There were four pockets, as above, a small equipment loop at the rear along with a flare-gun pocket, a single-zip fly front. Long sleeved.

Model 3 (late 1941) changed to a knee-length loose coat retaining the leg 'snaps' in gabardine/ waterproof cotton duck splinter pattern camouflage and later the tan 'water' pattern. Pockets as above. Hip openings allowed access to the trousers. Equipment loops and flare-gun pocket. As shortages cut in, waterproofing was not an option. These changes reflected the fact that Fallschirmjäger were now infantry so no longer needed a parachute.

Trousers – *Hosen* – were full length, made of field grey wool with two flapped side and rear pockets and ankle tapes. The outer leg seam pocket held a gravity knife and kneepads.

Lessons learnt in the field during Unternehmen Merkur led to improvements to Fallschirmjäger equipment. First, the paratroop's harness release was altered and improved – the old version required the soldier to stand and took more than a minute. The new version allowed the release while prone and took 10 seconds. Next, having to retrieve all their weapons from containers had left them unarmed for too long on Crete. Henceforth, they would carry automatic weapons and grenades during the jump. Finally, the jumpsuit would be improved so that it offered better protection on landing.

Opposite: Ready to get into the waiting Ju52 under the watchful eye of an Oberfeldwebel, these Fallschirmjäger are wearing early pattern grey-green smocks and have yet to exchange their Feldmütze for helmets. The smocks were worn over their equipment. They wear knee pads but not elbow pads.

Above: Unique among German equipment, the Fallschirmjäger's bandoleer allowed extra ammo to be carried. It hung around the neck and was secured by cloth loops. The 'snap' button pockets held an extra 100 rounds of small-arms ammo on top of the 60 already carried in the conventional waist pouches. Later, others were made to hold the magazines for the FG42. Initially they were in Luftwaffe blue canvas; later in splinter/other patterns and khaki tan.

Below: This Fallschirmjäger looks very happy to have acquired a British Bren gun *Beutewaffe* (booty weapon). However, his MP40 pouches won't hold the curved magazines used on the Bren.

1 The 1937 prototype Fallschirmjäger helmet, based on the Stahlhelm M35 shell had to meet a number of criteria: 1. Reduce the airflow from under the helmet whilst descending. 2. Give protection if a difficult landing and or under fire. 3. Prevent snagging the parachute or rigging. The flared brim and shroud of the M35 was removed, a shock-absorbing rubber inner was fitted between the zinc/aluminium helmet band and the leather 'cap' liner (not the 8–9 tongues of the M35). A 'Y' chinstrap was attached to the shell through the band with a friction buckle for adjustments. The slightly modified 1938 became the standard version. Like all German helmets it was painted to the surroundings or camouflaged using local vegetation attached via netting, wire or rubber/ leather bands. Specialist cammo covers were used as well.

2 German paratroopers guard captured weapons, Italy 1943. The man in front has an FG42 – Fallschirm-jägergewehr 42. Designed after Crete, it was made from stamped sheet metal and proved to be a good weapon with two major drawbacks: it was loud and produced a strong muzzle flash, which during night firing gave away the operator's position.

3 The German MGs were as good as any used in WW2. Here, an MG42 at Monte Cassino (note the padded winter jacket which was reversible (sage green on one side; white the other). Mass-produced, use of stamping, welding and riveting made the MG42 more cost-effective to make than the MG34.

4 This Fallschirmjäger is seen during the Norwegian campaign, 1940. Note his step-in overall/smock.

5 and 6 The Germans made extensive use of flamethrowers. The Flammenwerfer 35 (**5**) backpack system had a carrying harness, a cylindrical metal pressure tank and a smaller bottle on the left-hand side. The FmW35 was redesigned in 1941 as the FmW41 (**6**), a lighter and more easily carried version that was further modified in 1942 by the addition of a cartridge ignition system.

7 The MG34 was light enough to be carried by one man, and could be fired from the hip. Fed by belt or drum it had a rate of fire up to 800/900 rounds/min, something no other MG could do at that time. When mounted on the MG-Lafette 34 it was considered at that time to be a heavy MG for indirect fire.

8 The 8cm schwere Granatwerfer 34 was produced for Fallschirmjäger and Gebirgsjäger as a shorter, lighter tube version, the 8cm Granatwerfer 42.

9 The 7.5cm Leichtgeschütz 40 could be dropped by parachute in four pieces: barrel, breech assembly, carriage, and then wheel assembly. Ammunition made up the fifth element of the drop: a silk cloth bag containing the charge with a gunpowder igniter. The LG40 used dispersal of gas via a funnel-shaped Venturi tube to dissipate the recoil.

British Airlanding Troops

Carried in five Horsa gliders, a British airlanding platoon consisted of an officer and 25 men. Composed of an HQ and four platoons, their heaviest weapons were mortars, Bren guns and PIATs. Because they were carried by gliders without parachutes, they were able to carry more gear: haversacks, ammo pouches etc. The glidermen also wore regular army trousers.

Above left: The gliders also brought artillery – here *Gallipoli II*, a 6-pdr anti-tank gun of No 26 Anti-Tank Platoon, 1st Border Regt. It's in action knocking out a Flammpanzer at Oosterbeek.

Centre left: Normandy, 15 June, men from D/2nd Ox and Bucks LI – the unit involved in Operation Deadstick. Centre is Capt Brian Priday, 2IC to Maj John Howard, whose glider went astray. It reached the bridge over the Dives at Robehomme. They rejoined Howard and the rest of the unit on 7 June. The men wear para helmets, Denison smocks and two have toggle ropes around their waists. They are well-armed with (L–R) Bren gun; Sten Mk V with 'pigsticker' bayonet and .38 Smith & Wesson pistol in smock pocket; just visible, the handle of an Enfield pistol.

Left: 1st Canadian Parachute Bn during training. They are wearing Denison smocks, parachute helmets with plenty of camouflage in the scrim. Note the toggle ropes worn crossed around their body and the chest pouches worn with a yoke. They could contain various magazines or grenades – such as 2 Bren, 6 Thompson or 5 Sten (Mk III pouch only) magazines, 4 grenades, boxes of small arms ammo, rifle grenade blanks/bombs, etc.

British and Canadian Paratroop Equipment

Above and Above right: The British Para was seen, essentially, as an airborne infantryman but still required specialised equipment – the most iconic being the maroon beret. This group (heading off for some leave in August 1944) illustrates the basic equipment.

Helmet: The British parachute helmet was a modified copy of the 1938 German one. Initially, it had a rubber rim, soon removed, and was designated in typical Military Parlance, 'Helmet, Steel, Airborne Troops', or HSAT. Mk1. 1942. As with the German M35/38 there was rubber padding between the inner metal band and the leather inner rim with a three- or four-point attached leather chin-cup and strap, with double 'D' friction rings for adjustment. This was later replaced by an open chin-cup version. It had inner string adjustable support straps. Like the 1938 it would be camouflaged appropriate to the surroundings but not often painted other than in different climes. There was no special cover other than netting and scrim.

Boots: High side-laced crepe-soled Fallschirmjäger-type boots were trialled along with a higher version of the tried and tested 'ammo' boot. Neither was adopted, primarily because of the cost but also because the 'ammo' boot, laced the English way (ladder) to give better ankle support and with anklets –later putties – was more than adequate for the job. Additionally, the degree of control allowed by the X-type parachute and a proper landing-roll negated the need for a specialist boot – as well as the Fallschirmjäger knee and elbow pads.

Smock: At first this was a grey-green overall based on the Fallschirmjäger *Knockensack* (bone-sack) step-in zipped mid-thigh garment, big enough to wear over webbing to prevent snagging when exiting the aircraft and then discarded on landing, though this was not the case during the early days. However, this was surpassed by the Denison camouflaged smock that replaced it. The Denison was worn under the webbing but over the battledress blouse. It had a tail flap that buttoned under the crotch to prevent ballooning whilst descending, woollen knitted cuffs and four large patch pockets. Various different variations of camouflage were introduced and the Denison was a highly sought-after item.

Trousers: 'Trousers, parachutists' differed from the standard-issue 37 pattern by having a large press-studded thigh pocket, a pocket or looping for the Fairbairn-Sykes dagger and sometimes two shell dressing pockets at the back.

Toggle ropes: Unique to paras and commandos, this 6ft length of sisal rope had an eye-splice and wooden toggle at either end which could be joined to make one long rope. It was carried in the haversack, around the waist or around the back of the neck, under the arms and toggled at the back.

EQUIPMENT CARRIED BY THE INDIVIDUAL US PARACHUTIST
(from *FM31–30 Basic Field Manual*) in pounds

Items that may be carried, in addition to those shown, include demolition equipment, signal equipment, bayonet, extra ammunition, medical equipment, and the carbine. The amount of equipment carried is limited to that which allows a safe rate of descent. The type of equipment is limited by the fact that any protruding angular objects may foul the suspension lines of the canopy, and the possibility that such objects may cause serious injury to the parachutist, who may have to roll or tumble upon landing.

Helmet, steel, with liner	2.7
Parachute assembly, type T-5, complete (main pack on back, reserve pack on chest, static line, and static snap with safety pin)	33.5
Watch, wrist, 7-jewel	0.053
Ration (carried in pants leg)	.75
Clothing worn:	
• Suit, parachutist, jumping, summer (two piece)	3.7
• Boots, parachutist	4.4
• Gloves, horsehide, unlined	0.282
• Undershirt, cotton; drawers, cotton; socks, light wool; and identification tags	0.625
Articles carried in pockets:	
Center chest pocket:	
• Knife, pocket, M-2, with thong	0.3

Right chest pocket:	
• Maps, message book, and pencil	0.344
Left chest pocket:	
• Toilet tissue	0.125
• Compass, watch	0.125
• Whistle (when needed)	0.125
Right waist pocket:	
• Grenade, hand, fragmentatlon	1.25
Left waist pocket:	
• Grenade, hand, fragmentation	1.25
Right leg pocket:	
• Pistol, automatic, caliber .45, loaded with a clip of 7 rounds	2.762
• 2 extra clips, each 7 rounds	.0962
• Handkerchief	0.053
Left leg pocket:	
• Rope, parachutist, 2ft length	1.0
• Packet, first-aid	0.234

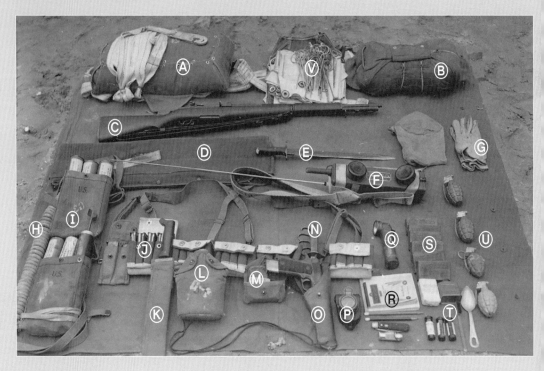

Right: Unlike the British and Germans, the American airborne didn't adopt the smock. The olive drab 1942 jacket was a bespoke item produced for them and first worn during Operation Torch. It had angled-flap press-stud large expandable pockets, two chest and two hip pockets (cargo) for ease of access whilst descending, a zipped knife pocket on upper chest to cut rigging/harness, full concealed zip front, buttoned cuffs and built-in belt. Prior to D-Day elbow patches were added and pocket seams reinforced. The 1943 version straightened the pockets and replaced the belt with a draw-string. Old hands kept their 1942 version. M1942 olive drab trousers (pants) had reinforced knees and two large reinforced cargo thigh pockets compressed by leg ties whilst descending. The 'Boots Parachute Jumper' M1942, 'Corcoran' – named after the company contracted to make them – were similar to the German, but brown instead of black, high topped to prevent snagging of the rigging lines, with leather or, later, composite heel and sole and tightly laced frontally to give maximum ankle support. In 1945 attempts to replace these 'cult' jump boots with the M43 Combat boots was met with major concerns because of the two buckles on the attached gaiters.

Opposite, Below: Layout of equipment of a US 503rd RCT signaller: **A** T5 chute; **B** reserve chute; **C** M1 Garand; **D** Griswold bag to hold the carbine (it breaks down into two or three pieces); **E** M1905 bayonet; **F** SCR-536 handie-talkie; **G** leather gloves; **H** coil of rope; **I** two packs of signal flares; **J** 25 x 8-round enbloc clips in five field-made pouches for the M1 Garand; **K** machete in canvas cover; **L** waterbottle and cover; **M** .45 ACP clips; **N** 1918 knuckle duster knife; **O** .45 M1911 Colt; **P** compass; **Q** TL-122 torch; **R** notepaper, pencils; **S** K ration packs; **T** medicine, soap, toothbrush and spoon; **U** Mk 2 fragmentation grenade; **V** signal panels and pegs.

Below: Australian paratroopers with their M42 Duperite helmets. They also used British steel helmets later in the war. Note, too, the Austen Mk 1 SMGs. The Australian 1st Parachute Battalion was formed in early 1943 but didn't see action during the war. It was disbanded in early 1946. Australian infantry units were largely equipped with British-designed but Australian-made small arms and support weapons.

6 Containers

Initially it was felt that larger weapons – rifles and MGs for example – were too bulky for paratroops to jump with and posed a snagging hazard whilst exiting the aircraft, descending and landing. Therefore, the parachutist would have a pistol and grenades to give him some form of protection after landing but the heavier/larger weapons would have to be retrieved from parachuted containers which had been dispatched at the same time. This worked splendidly provided (a) the paratroops could retrieve the containers easily and (b) there was little or no opposition – but proved costly for the Fallschirmjäger on Crete.

Experience, learned the hard way by both Allies and the Axis, led to the paratrooper carrying an SMG small enough to put under the smock, if worn, or tight against the body if not. The German MP38/40 had a folding stock and the British Sten a removable one. For the Americans the bulky and heavy Thompson was tightly strapped to the body. They also modified their existing M1 carbine by giving it a folding stock, thus making it the only personal weapon specifically changed for airborne troops.

Containers were still used for heavy weapons and the many other requirments of soldiers in the field behind enemy lines – food, water, ammunition and medical supplies being the most obvious. The British also developed the leg bag which was deployed as the paratrooper got close to the ground. It was attached to the man by a cord.

The images here show examples of the German supply container (*Abwurfbehälter für Nachschub*). There were various types: the *Mischlast Abwurfbehälter* 250 was the early bullet-shaped version (250 = 250kg); the wooden 700; and the most common steel versions. They were about 5ft (1.5m) long and 16 inches (0.45m) square and some had small wheels and a tow bar to allow them to be moved. One end had a crash cushion; the other the parachute attachment. Each contained weapons, ammo or supplies for four men and was colour and letter coded for identification of contents – eg red cross for medical; electric bolt for radio.

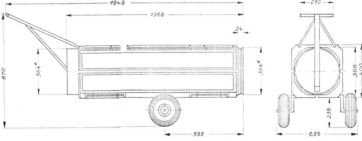

FM31–30 identifies that, 'Except for hand grenades and a small amount of ammunition for pistols or other light weapons, carried by descending parachutists, the initial ammunition supply for the squad is dropped in the delivery units that carry its other weapons. At least one day's supply for each weapon is dropped simultaneously with the squad. Delivery units for each group must be landed close to it. Delivery units are clearly marked to indicate their contents and the group to which they belong. Delivery unit parachutes may be marked by the use of colored canopies. However, the colors of canopies should be varied in different operations so that a canopy of a certain color will not always indicate the same piece of equipment. For deception, colored canopies may be used occasionally for personnel. Equipment containers are marked by colored coverings, smoke signals, colored streamers, or other readily recognized devices.' Various delivery bags were available this (**Below**) is the A-4 container, 30 x 24 x 12 inches, landed by a 24ft circular cotton canopy. It could carry 200lb of equipment. Other containers were the A-5 (**Opposite**), A-6 (12 x 12 x 30 inches) and A-7 for ammunition delivery.

Above and Below: Men of the 377th Parachute Field Artillery Bn train with parapacks – A4 aerial delivery containers. The containers were attached to the outside of the delivery aircraft, such as the C-47 or Curtiss C-46 Commando (**Opposite, Above**), this one on the way to Wesel during Operation Varsity. The artillerymen are working on the nine parapacks carrying an M1A1 75mm pack howitzer on an M8 carriage. Originally the weapon had been designed to be carried by mules, so it was light enough– it weighed 1,339lb – for airborne delivery and for the paratroopers to manhandle it once landed and assembled. Of course, finding nine undamaged parapacks, assembling the contents under fire and then pulling piece into action (chest harnesses were supplied) meant that a lot was left to chance, but the success of those guns that did, made the exercise worthwhile. The M1A1 could fire a 14lb shell to a max range of 9,610yd.

1

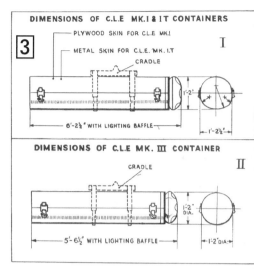

2

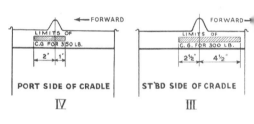

DIMENSIONS OF C.L.E MK.I & IT CONTAINERS

3 PLYWOOD SKIN FOR C.L.E MK.1
METAL SKIN FOR C.L.E. MK. I.T
CRADLE
I

6'-2½" WITH LIGHTING BAFFLE
1'-2½"

DIMENSIONS OF C.L.E. MK. III CONTAINER

CRADLE
II

5'-6½" WITH LIGHTING BAFFLE
1'-2" DIA.

←FORWARD
LIMITS OF
C.G FOR 3|50 LB.
2' 1'
PORT SIDE OF CRADLE
IV

FORWARD→
LIMITS OF
C. G. FOR 300 LB.
2½" 4½"
ST'BD SIDE OF CRADLE
III

1–3 The British Central Landing Establishment produced various containers, the later ones all-metal, with colour-coded parachutes – red for ammo; yellow medical; light blue food and water; green signals; white general. They also had a lighting system for use at night. Attached to the outside of aircraft, they could be dropped with paras or in resupply missions.

4 1st Polish Independent Parachute Brigade troops training with containers.

5 F type container – designed for use with radios (see example on page 213).

6 CLE containers could take many different loads. This one carries a Vickers .303 MG.

7 To move gear off the DZs, trolleys were supplied. This group is using one for kit after the Operation Varsity landings.

8 19 May 1944, 6th Airborne Division is being inspected by HM King George VI. The troops line up in full gear including leg bags. Developed in 1943 the bag was designed to carry a paratrooper's personal weapon, individual equipment and whatever was needed for his mission. While some bags were definitely heavy, weight had to be limited. The canvas bag was strapped to the right leg by two quick release friction-buckle canvas straps, just below the knee and above the ankle. Attached to a 15–20ft rope it would be released under control, just before landing – too quickly and it would be ripped off.

7 Communications

Edited excerpts from WSEG Staff Study No. 3 *Historical Study of Some World War II Airborne Operations:*

The character of an airborne operation dictates the requirements of the communication system by which its execution is controlled. Study of the records of World War II operations shows that:

a) Communications planning often left serious gaps in the overall system and in some instances the consequences to the operation as a whole were severe,

b) Equipment, operators and maintenance personnel, considered as an entity, produced a system deficient in reliability, mobility and range. This inevitably resulted in the necessity for a disproportionate reliance upon the initiative, aggressiveness and judgment of small unit commanders who, while extremely capable, were often in no position to make major battlefield decisions without information or some degree of guidance and control,

c) Loss and damage of communications equipment in landing accounted for a major share of the inadequacies experienced in drops and landings having poor geometry,

d) Available data on the World War II does not permit quantification of the communications problem. It can only be said that inadequacies sufficiently serious to jeopardize whole operations did occur.

Examples of problems:

• In NEPTUNE the forward headquarters of one airborne unit understood that they were to receive an *on-call* resupply mission on D+1 (119 C-47 loads, 442,000lb of equipment and supplies). Troop carrier HQ understood that the resupply mission was to be dispatched *automatically* unless cancelled by the airborne unit. ... No facilities had been planned for direct communication from the airborne unit on the ground to troop carrier aircraft in the air. The mission was flown. The result was the loss to the enemy of most of the supplies because the drop zone was not in the hands of the airborne forces. This caused difficulty and delay in the ground actions of the unit because of shortages in equipment.

Left: A signal crew boards a CG-4A for Holland. **A** and **C** Men carry DR-8 telephone wire spools – line was always fallback when positions were fixed. **B** Man carries a SCR-536; **C** Note wrist compass. 'The technical communication equipment carried by the communication platoon consists of light field wire with the means to lay and recover it; battery-operated telephones and telegraph instruments; sound-powered telephone sets; key and voice radio sets; and pyrotechnic and panel equipment. (FM7-20)

Above 82nd Airborne's Maj Jack Norton (L) and 1/Lt Hugo V. Olson waiting to leave for the Netherlands. Note the SCR-536 'handie-talkies'. With a range of at the most a mile, the SCR-536 was the first radio to allow men in action to communicate with their commanders – but only within short range. To talk to battalion or company HQ you needed a larger piece of equipment.

Above right: The SCR-300 was the next step up from the SCR-536 with a range of around 3 miles. It required a fungicide treatment for use in the Pacific Theatre. Radioman preparing for flight. The reserve chute will go over the top of the radio. Most of the container is battery – and batteries running out were a constant source of problems (see pp212–213).

Below right Men of the 506th PIR at the edge of Son woods. The second man carries an SCR-300 radio – a backpack 'walkie-talkie'.

• It has been shown that deficiencies both in communications planning and in equipment operation were apparent in NEPTUNE, MARKET and VARSITY, and that these deficiencies resulted in delays and casualties and general equipment and supply shortages. In NEPTUNE a more serious difficulty in communications arose from loss and damage to wire and radio equipment in the drops and landings. Records of the 82nd Airborne Division actions in NEPTUNE include estimates that as much as 95% of that unit's communication equipment was not available for use on D+1 through being either missing or damaged in drop or landings.

• At the Le Fière bridge across the Merderet river, three groups of troopers were actually operating in the area during D-Day, for much of the time completely unaware of each other. One force captured both ends of the bridge about noon of D-day before the enemy was deployed in strength in the area but, not knowing the whereabouts of any other force and thinking the group might be more useful elsewhere, the leader of the force took most of his men and departed. Several days of hard fighting and heavy casualties were experienced in regaining this vital crossing.

WSEG Staff Study No. 3 noted 'In MARKET, loss and damage to communications equipment did not occur to a serious extent except at Arnhem where it contributed to the isolation of the 1st British Airborne Division.' So often the communications equipment and signallers have been blamed for contributing to failure. at Arnhem. It's worth remembering that of the 348 men of the Divisional Signals Regiment, 28 died and 171 were missing – a casualty rate of nearly 60%. And the much-advertised 'incorrect crystals' story relates to the two sets brought to Arnhem by the US Air Support Signals Team from 306th Fighter Control Sqn. The impact of attrition on signals and signallers was significant, and few of the radio sets (6 × No 76, 17 × No 68P and 29 No 22) dropped by resupply were collected (less than 7.5% of a total of 106 tons despatched and dropped was). With all the sets requiring batteries, resupply of 110 batteries was needed every day but that didn't happen either.

There were three vital times when communications weren't there for the British paras: when the Airborne Recce Sqn was held back because it couldn't communicate with the divisional commander and thus didn't head for the bridge; the fact that Urquhart couldn't talk to Frost at the bridge for some days; and on D+1 and D+2 as the paras tried to reach Frost at the bridge, the attacks could not be effectively coordinated – the result was the severe mauling of 1st, 3rd and 11th Para Battalions and 2nd South Staffs, which were practically destroyed as fighting units.

The verdict of history has been that it was down to the equipment. Urquhart said, 'We were soon to learn that our radio sets were inadequate for the purpose, and their effectiveness was to be further limited by the sandy, heavily wooded terrain.' In 1943 the AORG had identified that 'the Army could benefit greatly by using VHF ….. regardless of the topography of the land or its electrical features' and that if the army persisted in using HF the result would be 'a particularly difficult problem for Army mobile sets. In some theatres of war the ranges are bound to dwindle to insignificance.'

Greenacre (2004) takes a more scientific approach and suggests (1) that the radio equipment wasn't the only reason for the problems; (2) that 'procedural errors and mishaps combined with poor timing and in some cases just bad luck were largely responsible for the breakdown of 1st British Airborne Division's internal radio communications during the early part of the Battle of Arnhem.' The risks had been pointed out before the mission and had been assessed as justified against the possible gains. In the event the 'risks and others combined to cause a catastrophic failure.'

Below: The Feldfernsprecher 33 was the standard Wehrmacht field telephone. Introduced in 1933, it could be connected to TornFu D2, BI, and F radio sets as a remote handset.

Below: Fallschirmjäger with a portable Torn Fu BI radio on Crete. The transceiver was introduced in 1936 and had a range of 15 miles (CW) and 7.5 miles voice.

Above: An improvement on the No 22 set, the WS62 was tested in 1944 and proved an excellent long-term replacement. It was particularly used as a vehicle-mounted transmitter and receiver – this one is in a Willys Jeep in the Royal Signals Museum, Blandford.

Right: The British CLE F-type container was designed to be able to drop radio equipment such as this WS76 set and R109 receiver. (Also in the Royal Signals Museum, Blandford.)

Below: If radio communication didn't work air recognition panels were worth trying. Allied personnel in 'Market Garden' used bright yellow unified recognition panels – trapezium-shaped with a loop at each corner to mark friendly positions for air drops. Quite commonly used as a neckerchief by the Brits, who also used anything they could to attract their aircraft when in the Oosterbeek Perimeter. (Note the Hartenstein Hotel, Urquhart's HQ, in the background.)

Below right: Polish paras with a Wireless Set No 18, an HF portable man-pack radio transceiver with a range of around 10 miles.

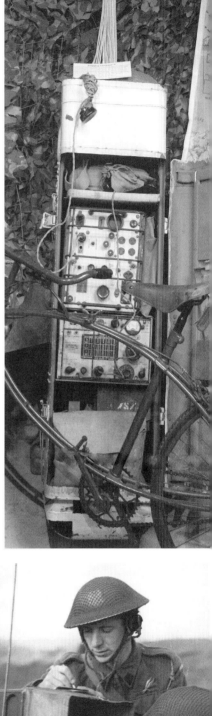

NAVIGATION AIDS

(Edited excerpts from WSEG Staff Study No. 3 and Warren: USAF Historical Studies No 97)

The value of dependable navigation aids became evident early in the development of the airborne weapons system. A critical lack of efficient aids was most apparent in the first US combat airborne operation in history, incident with the Allied invasion of North Africa (Torch). In conjunction with the Center Task Force at Oran, Algeria, on the morning of 8 November 1942, 2/503rd PIR was directed to make a parachute attack between TAFARAOUI and LA SENIA airfields, for the purpose of seizing and holding the airfields for Allied combat aircraft. To assist the pilots and navigators in locating their objective, a British naval vessel was to transmit a homing signal from a warship 17 miles and 300° from the initial point. In addition, Allied agents in the vicinity of the drop zone were to send a homing signal from a Eureka beacon (ground) to be picked up by the aircraft equipped with Rebecca receivers. Both aids at these initial points failed, and the pilots experienced much difficulty and delay in pinpointing their positions in the general area. The airborne force failed to achieve its planned mission, not having reached the original objective until 16:00 on D+1, and then with only 60 percent of their starting forces.

Subsequent airborne operations in Europe and in the Pacific improved proportionally in accuracy and concentration with the development and availability and improved reliability of navigational aids, pathfinder teams, and experience in their application. The highest accuracy and concentration achieved in European airborne operations was in the airborne invasion of Holland by the First Allied Airborne Army (MARKET). Presence of navigational aids for this next to the last airborne operation of the war in Europe is in sharp contrast to the first operation. Available by this time were the following navigation facilities:

a) Radio air
- MF beacons
- VHF/DF homing facilities
- MF/DF (for air/sea. rescue)

b) Radar and visual aids
- Eureka beacons – an air-to-ground radio location device for DZ/LZs, British but further developed in the US. Rebecca-equipped aircraft transmitted radio pulses to locate the ground-based Eureka beacon. By D-Day the system allowed speech transmission via SCR-563 'handie-talkie' radio able to take the hand-held BC-619 antenna
- Compass beacons (route checkpoints)
- Coded light beacons (on marker ships in the channel and on DZs)
- High-resolution AL-140 panels (DZs and LZs)
- Colored smoke (DZs and LZs)
- Occult lights (flashing) and searchlights (at check points in friendly territory)
- Photographs and maps for pilotage
- Trained pathfinder teams (air and ground)

The availability of adequate navigational facilities was far greater for MARKET than for TORCH. Such factors as weather, enemy action, human error, etc, at times subtracted from the ability of air crews to navigate even with adequate navigational aids. The fact is evident, however, that without a sound system of basic navigational aids, critical inaccuracies occurred even when these other influences were not present.

Problems

• Responsor beacons to mark points in hostile territory had to be set up by agents, partisans – at grave risk of discovery or betrayal – or pathfinders: but pathfinder flights reduced the chance of surprise for the main force. In addition, they might be shot down, as happened in Holland, or miss the zone by a wide margin, as some did in the invasion of southern France; and pathfinder troops might be neutralized by enemy action after reaching the ground, as many were in Normandy.

• Rebecca-Eureka beacon, in standard use by the troop carriers, had a range of less than 30 miles at the altitudes below 2,500 feet which were usually flown in airborne missions. More serious was the difficulty in making precise readings of the Rebecca scope when near the beacon. This made the normal margin of error with that equipment greater than a mile.

• Radar: airborne radars, including the SCR-717, produced a rough map of the terrain on a scope. Since only coastlines and large cities showed up well, such instruments were of limited value in airborne operations, although the SCR-717 did prove helpful in making an accurate landfall in NEPTUNE and in MARKET.

• The British Gee was used by all airborne missions in the ETO. Its effectiveness depended on the skill of the navigator, the aircraft's distance from the stations, and, especially, the plane's azimuth. Since Gee chains were bulky and complex installations, requiring months to establish, airborne operations which were small or were flown on short notice would seldom have a Gee chain ideally situated for their use. Thus, although in theory Gee could be accurate to within 100 yards, it was rarely precise to within a mile in operations. In AMHERST [a late war SAS operation in NE Netherlands and Germany] the average Gee error was over three miles.

Opposite: A Pathfinder team with their Eureka Mk IIIC beacon (US designation AN/PPN-2). Produced in 1944 it paired up with the Rebecca Mk IIA (SCR 729 or AN/APN-2). The Eureka had a folding antenna system that fed to the beacon. It was difficult to transport and use accurately.

Right: The Eureka/ Rebecca equipment was top secret and could have been used to mislead the Allies. It was, therefore, essential that it didn't fall into enemy hands. It was fitted with a self-destruct charge and these instructions.

DESTRUCTION NOTICE

WHY – To prevent the enemy from using or salvaging this equipment for his benefit.

WHEN – When ordered by your commander.

HOW – 1. Pull headset plug out of jack and pull antenna mast out of hole in beacon. Unscrew red dust cap from panel. It will remain attached by a wire. Jerk the cap away until the wire pulls out of the beacon. THIS IGNITES THE DETONATOR FUSE. Get at least 25 feet away within 3 seconds.

2. If possible, destroy and/or bury the antenna and antenna rods.

LEAVE NOTHING THAT CAN BE USED OR RECOGNIZED.

WHAT – 1. Detonate – The receiver transmitter.
2. Smash – the remaining parts.
3. Cut – The antenna and counterpoise rods and the antenna cable.
4. Burn – All instruction books.
5. Bury or scatter – all parts.

DESTROY EVERYTHING

Carrier pigeons sound old-fashioned but during World War II, the United Kingdom used about 250,000 homing pigeons for many purposes, including communicating with those behind enemy lines. During World War II, the US Army Pigeon Service consisted of 3,150 soldiers and 54,000 war pigeons, which were considered an undetectable method of communication. Over 90% of US Army messages sent by pigeons were received. The British Army Pigeon Service of the Royal Signals is represented in this reenactment photo (**Below**). The pigeon William of Orange was awarded a Dicken Medal for making the 400-mile flight back England with news of Frost's position at Arnhem.

8 Mobility

Making airborne troops more mobile was obviously a good idea and something that was solved in a number of ways: folding bicycles – such as the BSA airborne bicycle – and the miniature motorised Welbike that could be despatched in a container were both excellent for paratroops but larger gliders allowed jeeps and motorcycles better suited to rough terrain to be carried.

If they survived the drop they were used for such things as to facilitate command and control of troops, take wounded to aid stations and to tow artillery pieces – pack howitzers and anti-tank guns, although the larger British 17pdr guns needed a Morris C8. While much of the equipment was man-moveable, any distance required a tow vehicle.

Another useful piece of kit designed for airborne troops was the folding CLE container trolley that could itself be despatched in a container (see p209 photo 7). The US version was the M3A4 Utility Hand Cart, not made specifically for airborne use, but regularly used. These carts and trolleys had chest ropes so the pullers could use harnesses.

Once the airborne troops had been reached by their own forces, that would allow seaborne/land echelons to arrive with transport. However, towards the end of the war, especially as the Allies raced to the Baltic, airborne troops used every mode of transport – from civilian vehicles to the backs of Allied tanks (see p163).

Above: The Welbike was a super-lightweight motorcycle expressly designed to be folded down and air-dropped inside a standard parachute container – a CLE Canister. *Royal Signals Museum*

Below: Men of 1st Bn, Royal Ulster Rifles – part of 6th Airlanding Brigade, 6th Airborne Division, Normandy – leaving LZ-N, towing a 6pdr anti-tank gun. Note Bren gun by driver's side and C286 ammunition box on the front (where the spare tyre usually sits). It contained six rounds of anti-tank APCBC ammunition.

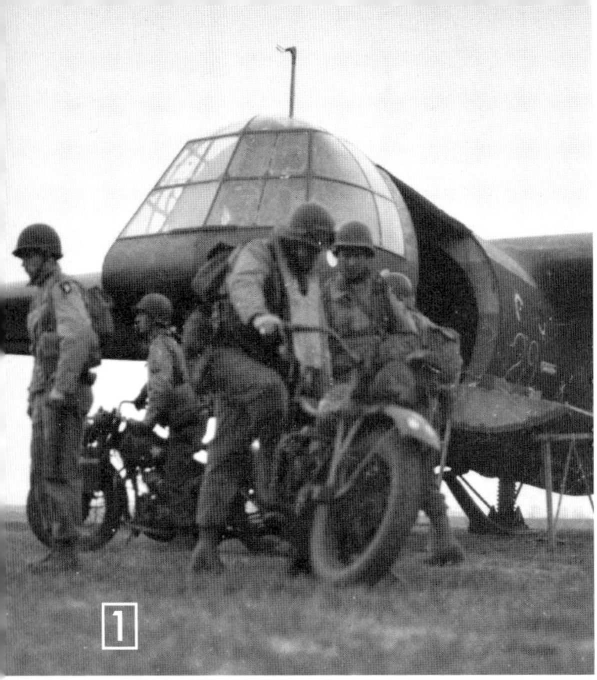

1

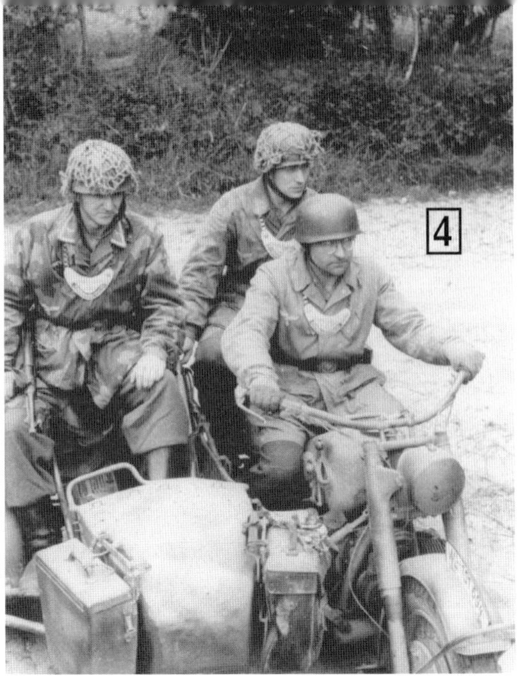

4

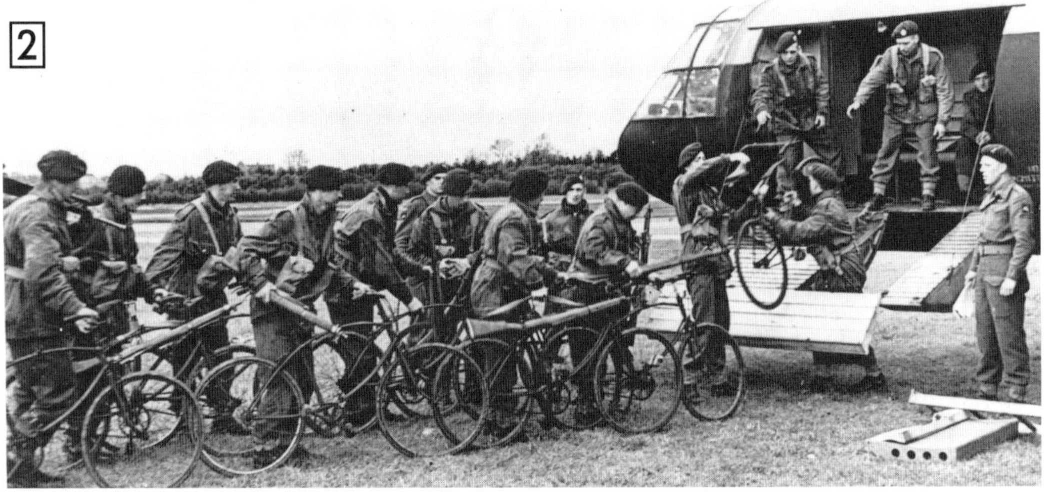

2

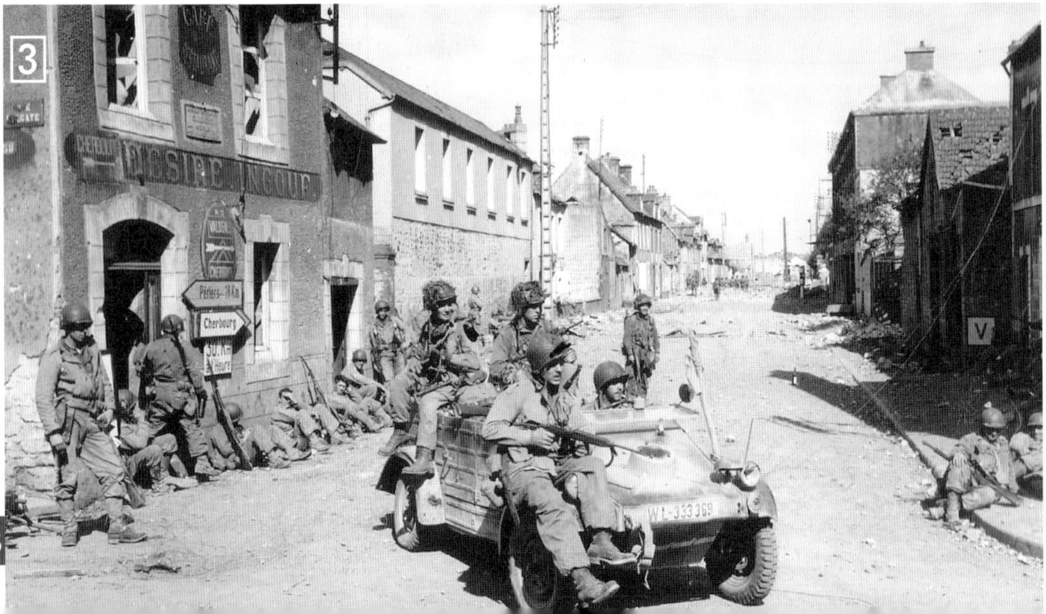
Périers—18 Km
Cherbourg

3

5

1 101st Airborne troops mount Harley Davidson WLA motorcycles during training at RAF Welford on 12 May 1944.

2 Loading folding bikes into a Horsa. Often quickly abandoned. The BSA folding bike, originally developed for use by Airborne troops, was the main type used.

3 101st Airborne enjoying a Kübelwagen in Carentan.

4 Fallschirmjäger Feldgendarmerie on a BMW R75 combo, Normandy 1944. Note that they are wearing the army pattern gorget.

5 and 6 CG-4As could take either a jeep or a trailer. The Horsa could load one of each along with a 75mm pack howitzer.

6

TETRARCH and LOCUST

The British Mk VII light tank Tetrarch weighed 7.5 tonnes and was airportable by the Hamilcar glider. About 150 were built. Armed with a 3-inch howitzer or a 'squeezed' 2-pounder gun. It had a crew of three who stayed in the tank during flight.

The alternative was the American, M22 light tank, the Locust which weighed 7.4 tonnes. About 800 built. Armed with a 37mm M6 gun (same as the M3 Stuart tank). It had a crew of 3 who stayed in tank during flight.

Neither tank was particularly successful and the Hamilcar also carried Universal carriers; 17-pounder anti-tank guns and towing vehicles. All vehicles were started up just prior to landing with exhaust fumes being expelled via special ducts – if the door was jammed the vehicles just drove through it.

The Hamilcar was used on three missions:

Operation Tonga	34
Operation Market	39
Operation Varsity	48

Tetrarch (**7**) was used in all three.
Locust (**8**) was used in Varsity.

7

8

Left: 11th Airborne casualty, Leyte. There are always casualties on every drop – even if unopposed. At Aparri, for example 2 men were killed and 70 injured. One of the main factors was dropping in bad conditions – at Aparri, a 20–25mph ground wind when 15mph was seen as the maximum safe velocity.

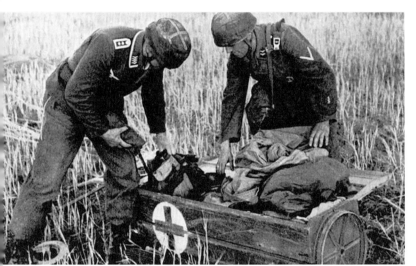

Centre left: Fallschirmjäger medics retrieve medical supplies from an early wooden container. Note external marking to help identify contents. The later version contained cases, with medical supplies such as bandages, dressings, slings,medical equipment – syringes, scalpels, forceps etc.

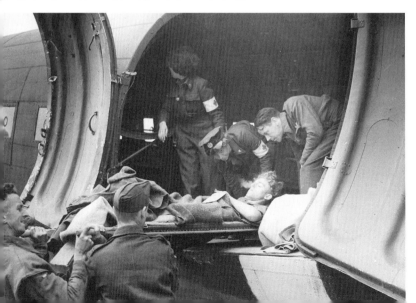

Below left: There was a significant increase in the number of casualties evacuated by air during the war. The US Medical Research Center puts US air-evac casualties during Operation Husky at 4.5% (between July 10 and August 10, 1943, a total of 5,967 patients) whereas the figure from Europe in 1944 was as high as 18%. One benefit of the C-47 was that it could be quickly unloaded and loaded under fire, a prime consideration in the medical evacuation mission.

9 Medical

All airborne forces made provision for medical treatment, although often the wounded had to await linkup with their attacking forces or air evacuation for continued care (see p91). This example of paratroop medical unit organisation is taken from the 82nd Airborne *Annual Report of Medical Department Activities* (edited excerpts) covering Operation Market.

'a. The organic medical detachments of the combat teams accompanied their units, taking first aid equipment which included blood plasma. Their function was to collect casualties and give essential first aid and prepare casualties for transportation.

'b. Collecting detachments of the medical company landed by glider D+1 and each consisted of 1 medical officer, 1 medical administrative corps officer and 30 enlisted men. 4 jeeps and 3 trailers of equipment, requiring 8 gliders for air transport. There were 4 such detachments. ... Evacuation has been extremely rapid. Casualties have been in the clearing station regularly 3–5 hours after being wounded.

'c. The clearing station has operated as a single unit, though capable of operating as two units if needed, the medical company and 50th Field Hospital each as independent units. The tactical situation has not made this necessary.

'The clearing element landed D+1 with 8 medical officers, 2 dental officers, 2 medical administrative corps officers and 133 enlisted men plus 6 medical officers and 6 enlisted men of two surgical teams. 11 jeeps, 22 trailers filled with equipment and 3,000lb of equipment loose in gliders. Air transport was 35 gliders.

'On D+8 a small X-ray unit which is organic equipment of the field hospital platoon was airlanded at Brussels and arrived overland.

'On D+9 the sea lift arrived and was composed of two medical officers, one dental officer and 25 enlisted men. 15 x 3/4ton ambulances, 6 x 21/2 ton trucks, 3 x 3/4 ton trucks, 2 x 250gal. water trailers, all the trucks loaded with equipment.

'In summary 67 gliders were used to airland the medical service units. There were 27 jeeps, 34 trailers, 18 medical officers, 2 dental officers, 6 medical administrative corps officers, 268 enlisted men and 10

tons of equipment airborne. 2 trailers and their equipment were not recovered. No personnel were lost in the airborne phase.'.

The Fallschirmjäger medical unit grew as the war progressed. Initially, in May 1939 *Fallschirm-Sanitäts-Zug.7* was 7. Flieger-Division's medical component. By May of that year it had grown to company size. In 1940, after the fighting in Holland, *Fallschirm-Sanitätsabteilung Flieger-Division 7* was created with four companies. CO was Oberstabsarzt Dr Heinrich Neumann, succeeded by Oberstabsarzt Dr Oskar von Berg in October 1940 when the unit was redesignated *Fallschirm-Sanitätsabteilung XI. Flieger-Korps.*

The *Abteilung* was fully involved in the battle of Crete and needed time to reorganise after losing a number of personnel. The unit's history becomes less homogeneous as the Fallschirmjäger were involved in different theatres and numbers grew. By the end of the war the establishment had included 20 *Sanitäts-Kompanien* and 10 *Fallschirm-Feld-Lazaretten* (field hospitals).

In many ways, the most extraordinary medical story of the airborne war was at Arnhem. 1st Airborne had taken 600 medical personnel with it – 16 and 133 Parachute and 181 Airlanding field ambulances – and they were desperately needed both during the battle and afterwards. Short of medical supplies and medical staff and with significant British – and German – casualties to look after, the Germans used British medics to set up a hospital at Apeldoorn. The fluent German spoken by Lt Col Martin Herford of XXX Corps' 163 Field Ambulance helped (he had crossed the river into Oosterbeek on 24 September), and the Willem III Kaserne Barracks became a hospital on 25 September. Barbed wire surrounded the hospital and it was guarded by elderly members of the Wehrmacht. Later, Divisional ADMS Col Graeme Warrack took command and most of the staff came from 181 Airlanding Field Ambulance. The hospital finally closed on 26 October, the senior staff having taken the opportunity to escape, Warrack crossing the Rhine in February 1945.

10 Organisation

Airborne forces require a great deal of organisation just to get them to their LZs and DZs. Other than the obvious training establishments, barracks and airfields, they need parachutes and parachute packers or riggers. They need specially trained aircrew to handle their aircraft – the tugs that pull one or more gliders, the crew that handle paratroop dropping and the glider pilots.

To enable them to reach their desired location they need navigational aids – at sea provided by specially tasked ships; on land provided by pathfinders who marked out the LZs and DZs with smoke, physical markings or by using communication aids such as Rebecca (see pp214–215).

Once on the ground, assuming they had been dropped close enough to make contact with each other, the airborne troops went about their missions. This was often an improvised force as paratroop delivery in World War II was a lottery – they often weren't able to assemble in their entirety. The Merville Battery action on D-Day is a case in point. Only 150 of the anticipated 600 paratroops undertook the action without their explosives or the Sappers who had been sent to do the job.

Having accomplished any immediate task, the troops would then fight as infantry until they were relieved by ground troops at which time they would be joined by other parts of their unit who had travelled overland (or in the case of 6 June 1944, by sea). While they were on their own they would be resupplied by air – another element that was less than successfully achieved: on 19 September at Arnhem, the RAF dropped 350 tons of supplies. 1st Airborne Division retrieved 28 tons. 10 aircraft were shot down.

The main building block of the military organisation of airborne forces was the company, a number of which would form a regiment (German, US) or battalion (British, Canadian), a number of which were then grouped together to make a division. In the case of the British there was an intermediate organisation, the brigade made of about three battalions. The regiments were either paratroop or glider, the latter being termed airlanding units by the British and Germans (*Luftlande*). The divisions would also include HQ, artillery (either para-dropped or glider-borne), AA, anti-tank, engineer, medical and signals units. British airborne divisions included a reconnaissance regiment of light tanks.

The constituent elements of the airborne divisions changed during World War II and often depended on how many aircraft were available to fly missions. It was rare for a division to be dropped in its entirety, in one location, at the same time.

Australian trainees get used to their parachutes.

Abbreviations

AB Airborne

AEC Airborne Engineer Company (US)

CG commanding general

CP command post

CW continuous wave – with radios, morse rather than using voice

DFS German Research Institute for Glider Flight

DZ drop zone – where paratroops land

EAM/ELAS Greek People's Liberation Army

ECB Engineer Combat Bn (US)

ECI *Esercito Cobelligerante Italiano* = Italian Co-belligerent Army – t fought with the Allies after the 1943 armistice

EDES National Republican Greek League

FFI Free French of the Interior

FJD/R Fallschirmjäger-Division/Regiment II./FJR6 = second battalion of 6th FJ Regt

GIR/B Glider Infantry Regt/Bn

IFF Identification Friend or Foe

KIA killed in action

le/sGrW *leichte/schwere Granatwerfer* = light/heavy mortar (Ger)

LZ landing zone – where gliders land

MIA missing in action

NKVD People's Commissariat for Internal Affairs – Russian secret police

Obfw *Oberfeldwebel* = sergeant (Ger)

Oblt *Oberleutnant* = lieutenant (Ger)

Oberstlt *Oberstleutnant* = lieutenant colonel (Ger)

PaK *Panzerabwehrkanone* = anti-tank gun (Ger)

PFAB Parachute Field Artillery Bn

PIAT Projector, Infantry Anti Tank

PIR/B Parachute Infantry Regt/Bn (US)

RCT Regimental Combat Team (US)

RK *Rückfallschirm, Zwangablösung* = backpack parachute, static line deployment (Ger)

RUR Royal Ulster Rifles

S/L/M/HMG sub-/light/medium/heavy machine gun

SNLF Special Naval Landing Forces (Jap)

2 South Staffs 2nd Bn, South Staffordshire Regt

(SS-)sPzAbt (SS-)*schwere* (heavy) *Panzer-Abteilung*

StuG *Sturmgeschütz* = assault gun (Ger)

T/O&E Tables of organisation and equipment (US)

TCG/W Transport Carrier Group/Wing

USMC US Marine Corps

VDV *Vozdushno-desantnye voyska* = airlanding forces (Rus)

WIA wounded in action

Photo Credits

The majority of photographs in this book – unless credited otherwise below – came from the US National Archives and Records Administration (NARA), in College Park, MD,. Thanks to Leo Marriott, Battlefield Historian and Richard Charlton Taylor for his help and valuable contributions. The individual photo credits are provided below if we have made mistakes here, please point them out to us via the publisher. **From official sources:** 44T, 47, 53, 54, 57, 58T, 60, 62, 80T (Airborne Missions in the Mediterranean); 80C (19 Field Survey Co, RE); 85 (all–First Allied Airborne Army Operations in Holland September–November 1944); 162B (XVIII Corps From the Elbe to the Baltic); 186(1), 188(2), 189(3) (CG-4A manual); 206 inset, 207 inset (FM 31–30); 44B, 69T, 88T and 89T, 95B, 125, 156T, 158inset, 159 inset. **albumwar2.com:** 22BL, 22BR (37191, 02788); 23TL (39065); 118T; 119B, 120, 122(both), 124(both), 01538 151B, 04869 152B, 07423 155T, 02805 155B, 164T??, 171???, 173(5&6), 04639 178(1), 180T, 16665 180B, 188(1&3), 189(4, 6, 7), 191(7), 05145 197T. **Argus Newspaper Collection of Photographs, State Library of Victoria:** 8–9, 127, 132(both), 168(1), 193(3), 203B, 216TR, 222. **Author's Collection:** 13BL, 31B, 65L, 70. **Battlefield Historian:** 4–5, 6, 40, 42(all), 51BL&BR, 55BL&BR, 61B, 64T&B, 65(all R), 66–67(all), 82(all), 86(1&3), 91BR, 92C, 100(both), 101(both), 106 (1&2), 107 (4&5), 108(1), 109(2–4), 160(all), 161B, 173(4), 176B, 177B, 183(9), 184(all), 191(6), 200T&C, 201(both), 208(1), 210, 213BL, 217B, 218(2&4), 219(5&7). **Bundesarchiv:** 15T (584-2154-06A), 19T (755-0161-25), 37(6), 38–39, 113T (567-1503B-17), 151C (585-2184-24), 153TL (585-2182-30A), 164B (146-1979-128-0), 170(7) (527-2348-21); 182(2) (569-1179-25); 182(4) (568-1531-32); 183(7) (568-1529-27A); 197B (576-1846-11A); 198(2) (304-0635-28); 198(3) (578-1939-20); 199(8) (577-1917-08); 205b (304-0634-07); 212L (585-2182-26A), 220C (141-0865). **Nik Cornish:** 136, 140, 141. **nationaalarchief.nl:** 26B, 94B, 163C. **Greene Media:** 63, 108T, 182(3), 183(6). **Library of Congress:** 2–3, 68, 69B, 71B, 128, 158–59, 172(1&2), 194B. **NARA:** 43T, 46, 47(all), 48(all), 49T, 49B, 50(both), 51T, 55T, 56(all), 58BL&BR, 59(both), 61A, 70T, 71T, 72T, 72BL **Narodowe Archiwum Cyfrowe (Polish National Archives):** 12, 13T, 14(both), 110, 112B, 117, 144, 147, 148(all), 149(all), 151T, 152T, 153TR&B, 170(6), 178–79, 178(2), 183(8), 190(1&2), 194C, 204TL, 209(4), 209(5–8), 213BR. **National Archives of Canada:** 64C, 162T, 168(3), 192(1), 200B PA206061. **Perry Castaneda map collection:** 25L, 107(3). **Via RCT:** 15B, 16, 17, 18, 19B, 20, 23TR, 23B, 24(all), 25(all R), 28, 30L, 32(all), 34(all), 35, 37(1–5), 38TL & CL, 39T, 113, 146(all), 154(all), 167, 169(4&5), 170(8&9), 178(4&5), 190(3), 196, 198(1, 4–6), 198(7,9), 204B, 205T, 212R. **Royal Signals Museum:** 213(TL&R) 217T. **Tom Timmermans:** 99 (via), 216B. **Martin Warren:** 191(5). **WikiCommons:** Cybinka (CC BY-SA 3.0) 10; 26T; Berthold Werner (CC BY-SA 3.0) 31T; 33 (US Military Academy); Guycarmeli (CC BY-SA 4.0), 43B, 114(all), Derevyagin Igor (CC BY-SA 3.0) 143BL, Николай Симагин (CC BY-SA 3.0), 143BR. **San Diego Air & Space Museum Archives:** 178(3). **US Navy Naval History and Heritage Command:** 182(1).

Bibliography

Documents

A Graphic History of the 82nd Airborne Division Operation Market Holland 1944.

Airborne Operations: A German Appraisal; Department of the Army Pamphlet No 20–232; 1951.

CSI Battlebook: Corregidor–February 1945; Fort Leavenworth, 1983.

CSI Battlebook: Operation Anvil/Dragoon; Fort Leavenworth, 1984.

CSI Battlebook: Rhine River Crossing; Fort Leavenworth, 1984.

FM31-30 Basic Field Manual Tactics and Technique of Air-Borne Troops; US War Dept, May 20, 1944.

German Report Series: Peculiarities of Russian Warfare; 1949.

German Tactical Doctrine; Military Intelligence Service, 1942.

HQ 1st US Infantry Division: *Selected Intelligence Reports vol II December 1944–May 1945.*

Infantry Tactical Manual of the Red Army, 1942.

Special Series No 30 Japanese Mortars and Grenade Dischargers; Military Intelligence Service, 1945.

Special Series No 32 Japanese Parachute Troops; Military Intelligence Service, 1945.

Tactical Employment in the U. S. Army of Transport Aircraft and Gliders in World War II, vol I and II; Department of the Army, 1946.

TME11-227A *Japanese Radio Comms Equipment,* WD, 1944.

TME30-410 *Handbook on the British Army;* WD, 1942.

TME30-480 *Handbook on Japanese Military Forces;* WD, 1944.

TME30-451 *Handbook on German Military Forces;* WD, 1945.

Training Memorandum No 50: Lessons from the Sicilian Campaign; 1943.

WSEG Staff Study No. 3 *Historical Study of Some World War II Airborne Operations:.*

Books and articles

Bowman, Martin W.: *Air War Varsity;* Pen & Sword, 2017.

Buffkin, Maj Ronald M.: 'Assault Gliders: A Reexamination'; Fort Leavenworth, 1991.

By Air To Battle; HMSO, 1945.

Campbell, David: *Elite 231 Soviet Airborne Forces 1930–91;* Osprey, 2020.

Charbonnier, Philippe: *6 June 1944 Soldiers in Normandy;* Histoire et Collections, 1994.

Crookenden, Napier: *Dropzone Normandy;* Ian Allan Ltd, 1976.

Davies, Howard P.: Key *Uniform Guides 2 British Parachute Forces 1940–45;* Arco, 1974.

Ellis, Chris: *Spearhead 3 7th Flieger Division;* Ian Allan Ltd, 2002.

Forty, George; *Battle of Crete;* Ian Allan Ltd, 2001.

Glantz, Lt Col David M.: *CSI Research Survey No 4: The Soviet Airborne Experience;* Fort Leavenworth, 1984.

Greenacre, Major John W.: 'Assessing the Reasons for Failure: 1st British Airborne Division Signal Communications during Operation "Market Garden"'; Defence Studies, 4:3, 283-308, 2004 (via DOI: 10.1080/14702430420000344777)

Greenacre, John W.: '"Flexible Enough to Adapt": British Airborne Forces' Experience during Post Conflict Operations 1944-1946'; 2017.

Griesser, Volker: *Les Lions de Carentan;* Heimdal, 2005.

Guard, Julie (ed): *Airborne;* Osprey, 2007.

Gukeisen, Maj Thomas B.: 'The Fall of Eben Emael'; Fort Leavenworth, 2004.

Gwinn, Maj John C.: 'Scratched: World War II Airborne Operations that Never Happened'; Fort Leavenworth, 2014.

Harclerode, Peter: *"Go To It!";* Caxton Editions, 2000.

Hoffman, Lt Col Jon T.: *Silk Chutes and Hard Fighting : U.S. Marine Corps Parachute Units in World War II;* USMC, 1999.

Horn, Bernd and Wyczynski, Michel: 'A Most Irrevocable Step: Canadian Paratroopers on D-Day, The first 24 hours, 5-6 June 1944'; Canadian Military History: Vol. 13: Iss. 3, Article 3, 2004. (Available at: http://scholars.wlu.ca/cmh/vol13/iss3/3.)

Horn, Bernd and Wyczynski, Michel: *Elite 143 Canadian Airborne Forces Since 1942;* Osprey, 2006.

Huston, Maj James A.: *Airborne Team;* Historical Division, CMH.

Jarkowsky, Maj J: 'German special Operations in the 1944 Ardennes Offensive'; Fort Leavenworth, 1981.

Kavanaugh, Maj Stephen W.: 'Comparison of the Invasion of Crete and the Proposed Invasion of Malta'; Fort Leavenworth, 2006.

Kuhn, Volkmar: *German Paratroops in World War II;* Ian Allan Ltd, 1978.

Lemna, Samantha: 'To Battle by Glider and Parachute: The Airborne Forces of the Second World War'; Lethbridge, 2004 (via https://hdl.handle.net/10133/4928).

Lowe, James Philip: 'Nadzab (1943): the first successful airborne operation' LSU Master's Theses, 2004. (via 3068.https://digitalcommons.lsu.edu/gradschool_theses/3068)

Lucas, James: *Kommando;* Arms & Armour Press, 1985.

Lucas, James: *Storming Eagles;* Arms & Armour Press, 1988.

Margry, Karl (ed): *Operation Market Garden Then and Now* vols 1 and 2; After the Battle, 2002.

Melzer, Jürgen Paul: 'Heavenly Soldiers and Industrial Warriors: Paratroopers and Japan's Wartime Silk Industry'; *The Asia-Pacific Journal* Japan Focus, vol18 iss17 no 2, 2020

Pierce, Robert M.: 'The Airborne field Artillery: From Inception to Combat Operations; Fort Leavenworth, 2004.

Ramsey, Winston (ed): *D-Day Then and Now* vols 1 and 2; After the Battle, 1995.

Reinhard, Generalmajor Hellmuth (et al): *Russian Airborne Operations;* US Historical Division, 1952.

Richardson, Maj Michael W.: 'Forcible Entry and the German Invasion of Norway'; Fort Leavenworth, 2001.

Smurthwaite, David: *The Pacific War Atlas 1941–1945;* HMSO, 1995.

Stahl, Peter: *Kreta: The German Invasion of Crete;* Military Arms Research Service, 1972.

Thompson, Leroy: *Combat Troops No 9 British Paratroops in Action;* Squadron Signal, 1989.

USAF Historical Studies No 74: *Airborne Missions in the Mediterranean 1942–1945;* USAF Historical Division, 1955.

Verier, Mike: *Spearhead 4 82nd Airborne Division;* Ian Allan Ltd, 2001.

Warren, Dr John C.: *Airborne Operations in World War II, European Theater;* USAF Historical Division, 1956.

Websites

https://www.med-dept.com/articles/ww2-air-evacuation/

http://ww2talk.com/index.php?threads/5th-scottish-parachute-bn-during-op-dragoon-and-op-manna.59636/